Do My Prophets No Harm

Do My Prophets No Harm

Revelation and Religious Liberty in the Bible

ROBERT KIMBALL SHINKOSKEY

RESOURCE *Publications* • Eugene, Oregon

DO MY PROPHETS NO HARM
Revelation and Religious Liberty in the Bible

Copyright © 2011 Robert Kimball Shinkoskey. All rights reserved. Except for brief quotations in critical publications or reviews, no part of this book may be reproduced in any manner without prior written permission from the publisher. Write: Permissions, Wipf and Stock Publishers, 199 W. 8th Ave., Suite 3, Eugene, OR 97401.

Resource Publications
An Imprint of Wipf and Stock Publishers
199 W. 8th Ave., Suite 3
Eugene, OR 97401
www.wipfandstock.com

ISBN 13: 978-1-60899-845-6

Manufactured in the U.S.A.

Scripture quotations marked NRSV are from the New Revised Standard Version of the Bible, copyright © 1989 national Council of the Churches of Christ in the U.S.A. Used by permission. All rights reserved.

Scripture quotations marked NEB are taken from the New English Bible, © The Delegates of the Oxford University Press and The Syndics of the Cambridge University Press, 1961, 1970. Used by permission.

Scripture quotations marked NIV are taken from The Holy Bible, New International Version ®, NIV ®, Copyright © 1973, 1978, 1984 by Biblia, Inc.™ Used by permission of Zondervan. All rights reserved worldwide. www.zondervan.com

Scripture quotations marked GNB are from Good News Bible/The Bible in Today's English Version. Copyright 1966, 1971, 1976 American Bible Society. Used by permission.

Scripture quotations marked NJPS are from Tanakh: The Holy Scriptures, The New JPS Translation. Copyright 1985 The Jewish Publication Society. Used by permission.

Scripture quotations marked NAB are taken from The New American Bible © 1970 Confraternity of Christian Doctrine, Washington, D.C. and are used by permission of the copyright owner. All rights reserved.

Contents

Abbreviations ix
Introduction xiii

1 Giving God a Contract Extension 1

2 Prophets Promote Prophecy 25

3 Universal Voice and Endless Canon 42

4 Cessation of Prophecy 60

5 A Thoroughly Modern Law was Found in the Mound 81

6 Jerusalem's Gang of Twelve 118

7 A Theology of Continuing Revelation 140

Epilogue 171
Bibliography 183
Subject/Name Index 187

Prophet Profiles

A Storm from the East (Job) 15

A Metaphor for the King's Son (Isaiah) 32

Snow on Solomon's Porch (Jesus) 68

A Command to Persevere (Hosea) 72

"Finalizing" the Canon (Ezra) 79

Matters of Sacrifice (Moses) 91

The King's Chapel (David) 97

The Egyptian Connection (Jeremiah) 110

On Free Expression (Solomon) 114

The Road to Bethel (Amos) 121

The Spirit Packs Its Bags (Ezekiel) 124

The Diviner's Cup (Joseph) 131

Hagar's Well (Muhammad) 156

Fortifying Babylon (Second Isaiah) 165

Abbreviations

ABD	*Anchor Bible Dictionary*. Edited by D.N. Freedman. 6 vols., New York. 1992
Abot	Avot
ANET	*Ancient Near Eastern Texts Relating to the Old Testament*, Edited by J. B. Pritchard. 3d ed. Princeton:Princeton University Press, 1969
b. Nid.	Babylonian Talmud Niddah
b. Yoma	Babylonian Talmud Yoma
BCE	Before the Common Era (i.e. BC)
CE	Common Era (i.e. AD)
E	Elohist source
Exod. Rab.	Exodus Rabbah
GNB	Good News Bible
J	Yahwist (Jahwist) source
JBL	Journal of Biblical Literature
KJV	King James Version
NAB	New American Bible
NEB	New English Bible
NIV	New International Version
NJPS	New Jewish Publication Society (Bible)
NRSV	New Revised Standard Version
OCB	*Oxford Companion to the Bible*. Edited by Bruce M. Metzger and Michael D. Coogan. New York: Oxford University Press, 1993

x *Abbreviations*

Quran	The Koran: Translated with Notes by N.J. Dawood. New York: Penguin Books, 1993
Sib. Or.	Sibilline Oracles
Sipre	Sifre
Sir	Sirach
t. Sota	Tosefta Sota

HEBREW BIBLE/OLD TESTAMENT BOOKS

Gen	Genesis
Exod	Exodus
Lev	Leviticus
Num	Numbers
Deut	Deuteronomy
Josh	Joshua
Judg	Judges
Ruth	Ruth
1–2 Sam	1–2 Samuel
1–2 Kgs	1–2 Kings
1–2 Chron	1–2 Chronicles
Ezra	Ezra
Neh	Nehemiah
Esth	Esther
Job	Job
Ps	Psalms
Prov	Proverbs
Eccl	Ecclesiastes
Song	Song of Solomon
Isa	Isaiah
Jer	Jeremiah

Lam	Lamentations
Ezek	Ezekiel
Dan	Daniel
Hos	Hosea
Joel	Joel
Amos	Amos
Obad	Obadiah
Jonah	Jonah
Mic	Micah
Nah	Nahum

NEW TESTAMENT BOOKS

Matt	Matthew
Mark	Mark
Luke	Luke
John	John
Acts	Acts
Rom	Romans
1–2 Cor	1–2 Corinthians
Gal	Galatians
Eph	Ephesians
Col	Colossians
Heb	Hebrews
Jas	James
1–2 Pet	1–2 Peter
1 John	1 John
Rev	Revelation

Introduction

THE TEN COMMANDMENTS HAVE fascinated and perplexed social reformers, legal theorists, academicians, church goers, agnostics and atheists the world over. This essay has been written to give voice to a nagging sense that interpreters of the great commandments have failed to apprehend the essence of these foundational statements of ancient Israel. This book draws from the fields of theology, history, and law. Its content is structured around the twin topics of religious liberty and prophecy in Bible times. Together these themes provide a vibrant interpretational key to the Bible and give it a structural unity.

Work on this volume began as an exploration of the idea that the Ten Commandments, in spite of several references to God contained in them, are entirely civic or secular law. It soon became apparent that the First Commandment ("Thou shalt have no other gods before me"[1]) was the key both to providing support for this thesis and to unlocking the content of the following nine.

The "first law" does not mandate orthodox religion, as some see it, or merely encourage the private honoring of God in homes and cult settings, as others see it. Instead, it enforces the political ethics of the land. Ancient Israel's human rights culture is constantly subjected to hostility from sources within and without her own borders. This foundational commandment encourages the citizenry of ancient Israel to seek after, find, and herald the liberating God of Moses and the Exodus, by exercising the prophetic gift. After all, what good is a law *promoting* love of God without a law *permitting* loyalty to this God?

---

1. We use the King James Version of the Bible in this essay, unless otherwise indicated. The glossary lists the other translations occasionally used. The KJV is particularly appropriate in a year the Christian world celebrates the 400 year anniversary of the KJV, first published in 1611. We also use the Protestant numbering system for the Ten Commandments, acknowledging that Catholics/Lutherans and Jews use a slightly different numbering.

Accordingly, I have undertaken to recast the roughly 1,300 year story which plays out from the time of the Exodus to the time of Jesus Christ in light of an understanding of the commandment as a right to political speech and religious conscience. In this piece I make only cursory mention of my interpretation of the other nine commandments (chapter 5), since I propose to develop them further in another work.

Both the Hebrew Bible (Christian Old Testament) and the Christian New Testament highlight prophet-based and popular dissent from one or another form of cultural or political oppression. The Bible tracks this theme across various locales in Mesopotamia, Canaan, and Egypt and across various eras of time from primeval to patriarchal, from wilderness to national settlement, and eventually from national exile to reconstruction and Roman occupation. Dissent is the story of the Bible from Adam to Abraham, Enoch to Ezekiel, Moses to Manoah, David to Daniel, Jeremiah to Jesus, and Peter to Paul. God himself encourages this very dissent by providing periodic oracular revelation through entirely new and contemporary voices. The need for a legal culture tolerant of religious diversity and new prophecy thus stems from the sensitivity of the Abrahamic people to regular and egregious periods of suppression of religious conscience.

Religious captivity is portrayed in a variety of forms in the Bible, as are solutions for circumventing or overturning it. Abraham lives in a culture in Ur and Harran noted for mandatory worship of the moon god Sin. He undertakes with his family a long migration into the hardship of permanent exile in Canaan.

Joseph is sold into slavery at the hands of his own brothers, jealous of his self-proclaimed religious ascendency. Moses undertakes the extraordinarily difficult task of confronting a Pharaoh who will not allow economic freedom or free worship to the children of Israel. He engineers a delicately conceived migration out of Egypt and forty years of nomadic preparation for the establishment of an autonomous tribal confederacy in Canaan. The new community, based on the covenant-making events at Sinai, is to be solidly based on God-given freedom for ethical monotheist religion.

The Judges engage in hot revolutionary activities against neighboring peoples who hold their rights and their properties hostage. David, Elijah and later prophets undertake dramatic action and literary-legal projects aimed at internal reform of nonsensical religious policies instigated by despotic kings. A few righteous monarchs, on the other hand, labor to correct popular cultural drift back to a culture of pagan nature worship. Nevertheless, the Bible story provides one with a sense that monotheism, ironically, almost necessitates religious pluralism. Even if there is only one God for Israel, this God is extremely hard to locate and apprehend. For long periods of time he remains "hidden." Thus, the nation must be hospitable to a variety of denominational/cultic seekers who wish to engage him and to prophets who claim a message from him.

The need for divine political reformers who bring messages from God, the Bible avers, will never subside or cease because nations and cultures refuse to desist from their noisome oppressions of one people or another. God sends prophets when he hears the cries of the people.

A GREAT LAW FOR RELIGION

If God's purpose is to protest oppression and protect rights for neighbors in the community, he is savvy enough to leave a record of his efforts aimed at assisting prophets and dissenting religionists. The Bible corpus provides indications that Israelites accorded God the right to speak and act and protected those eventualities as much as their own rights. The record they preserved is as much a record of his providential interventions into the lives of human beings as their own struggles in the diurnal world.

The Bible gives the Exodus/Sinai story a central place in its history. It recalls a regular renewal of focus on the protection of rights by means of its annual New Year celebrations in the fall at the festival of "booths." It revisits the need for such protections and renewals in its literary remembrances of life under political and religious domination at the hands not only of Egypt, but also Assyria, Babylon, Seleucid Greece, and Rome.

The twin topics of legal liberty and prophecy are inextricably entwined. During the course of my research I noticed the connection between the law enacting mandatory devotion to the God of the Exodus above all others (Exod 20:3; Deut 5:7), and the law in Deuteronomy defining authentic prophecy and affording protection to prophets (Deut 12–13, 16–18). What is mandatory about the First Commandment is not devotion to a specific form of sacrifice, creed or liturgy, but rather devotion to a specific free and democratic way of life which characterizes this God and reflects his "name." Prophets, who are critics both of backsliding politics and religion, are the primary beneficiaries of liberty.

They are citizens among the electorate who cherish their own God-given freedom and the God-given freedom of their neighbors to such a degree that they will speak out for it and fight for it. The experience of contact with the Almighty is apparently a highly motivating one in this regard.

Where there is a law protecting prophets and other dissenting citizens, there is a way for freedom. The Bible describes a variety of statutes and traditions related to religious liberty in addition to the laws protecting prophets specified in Deuteronomy. There are laws relating to the treatment of "strangers" (aliens), laws dealing with blasphemy, laws incorporating shrines and encouraging sacrifice, policies guaranteeing worship rights for foreign embassies on Israelite soil, and traditional policies demonstrating tolerance of the unorthodox "high places." The prophets of the Bible construct a theology that argues the need for a law of liberty. If the law supports, God then supplies a never-ending stream of new verses of his sacred tongue. Some inhabitants of early Israel understood this at least some of the time.

Especially noteworthy is the society's elevation of religious liberty to a first place in the constitutional law of the land—the First Commandment extolled by Moses at Sinai and by Jesus at Nazareth and at Jerusalem. This law is in turn re-iterated by a long string of historians, biographers, and literary prophets in terms only slightly nuanced from that which is found in the great commandment. It is this law that we focus on in this book.

This First Commandment is a constitutional legal precept much like the First Amendment of the United States Constitution—a law enacting religious liberty and the necessary supports to that liberty, such as freedom of speech, press, and assembly. This concept is intuitively attractive because it seems clear that ancient Israel could not have given support to so many distinctive religious views throughout her early, middle and later periods without some kind of legal encouragement given to them. For example, in the pre-exilic period, evidence of both biblical and extra-biblical devotion to a variety of gods survives, including Yahweh, Baal, Asherah, and literally dozens of others. During the exilic and post-exilic periods a wide variety of denominations of Yahwism appear to have proliferated, each with its own worship center or temple. We also see evidence of continuing tolerance afforded the worship of a variety of other apparently ethical gods. Reform movements during the time of

Gideon, Samuel, Hezekiah and Josiah narrowed the definition of legally acceptable religion somewhat, but still allowed for variety in religion.

Anyone who suggests the existence of a policy of religious tolerance in ancient Israel must be prepared to deal with scandalized protestations about religious violence in the pages of the Bible. I do not deal with this question in any particular detail in this treatise, except in a brief section at the end of chapter 5. However, I will say here that what the people in Israel and any other nation for that matter are capable of *doing* from time to time, is exactly the reason why the commandment is necessary in the first place. At root, the commandment is an attempt to diminish religion-inspired oppression and violence. While the great commandment countenances and encourages peaceful dissent, it contemplates violence only when a limited amount of force can be effective in overturning oppressive government or primitive religion.

CHAPTERS AND ARGUMENTS

This book explores evidence in the Hebrew Bible and Christian Testament that the sacred legacy of both ancient and modern civilizations cannot be finally written or dispensed with. It explores the idea that the Hebrew prophets and Christian apostles not only recognized the right of sentient mankind to believe, speak and publish prophecy freely, but also accorded God that same right.

The first chapter addresses the issue of closed canons and the death of prophecy, and finds in the story of Job a paen to the idea of new revelation and a starting point for the themes developed throughout this book. God is one who acts independent of the control of man. Job's entire understanding of religion changes when he experiences a surprising theophany which proves what he has always felt in his gut—that God's communications with man are not limited by parameters that conventional wisdom assigns to him. The chapter also poses and answers a question about Jesus. Why does Jesus show as much interest in an early historical Zechariah who does not have a prophetic book in the Hebrew Bible, as in a later historical Zechariah who does have such a book in the canon?

The second chapter explores commonalities in the experience of Bible prophets which tend to establish their legitimacy, and the legitimacy of their profession, in the eyes of the canon-makers. They each experience an epiphany, demonstrate an antipathy for heavy-handed monarchic government, and show a devotion to the study of history. The literatures of the prior prophets inform and inspire their own. The third chapter introduces the idea of biblical universalism, the notion that God finds prophets and elect peoples outside of Israel as well as within Israel. The position Israel's prophets take about the recurrence and importance of prophecy is apparently widely held throughout the ancient Near East. The fourth chapter reviews internal biblical evidence on the topic of the cessation of prophecy, and interpretive views arising out of modern academia on the topic.

The fifth chapter explores the legal structure of a prophet-based society, and shows how the law anticipates a mobile seat of government and periodic charismatic renewals of culture and cult. The sixth chapter examines an editorial by Amos on the topic of ongoing revelation, and looks at the use of highly idiomatic language throughout the Bible suggestive of God's expected future communications with sentient peoples. The seventh and final chapter notes that Bible writers are both theologians of the revelatory presence of God, and historians who notice and call attention to the accuracy of previous prophetic predictions. They expect continuous revelation based on the nature and providential character of God.

1

Giving God a Contract Extension

IT IS AN ARTICLE of faith in the major denominations of the Judaic and Christian traditions, or at least an unwritten one, that God no longer appears to man. God clearly revealed himself in olden times and gave special commission to prophets to speak in his behalf. For example, God revealed himself to Adam and Eve, Noah, Abraham, Isaac and Jacob, Moses, David, Elijah and the literary prophets of Israel. He later revealed himself in and through Jesus and the Apostles.

But God has not shown himself or given a spectacular new oracle to mankind at any place or time, in the Jewish view, since the last exilic and post-exilic prophets like Haggai and Zechariah, Malachi and Joel, or authorized an addition to the canon since the Book of Daniel, last modified in the second century BCE. For example, the Talmud reads, "The Spirit departed from Israel."[1] The "shekinah," or presence of God, which dwelled in the temple, departed as well.[2] There seemed to be practical justification for the idea of the absconding of God, because the temple housing God's presence was destroyed in 586 BCE. Horrific prophecies of national destruction were fulfilled in the Assyrian and Babylonian conquests of Israel and Judah, leading to a sense that God had abandoned Israel.

In addition, the Torah, or Pentateuch, was published in its final form in the time of Ezra in the late fifth century.[3] In this collection Moses was lionized in such a way as to cast doubt about the stature of subsequent prophets. The scope and depth of the law organized in its pages begged the question of whether there was need for any further divine commandment leading to salvation. For many, Moses and Torah

1. Barton, "Hebrew Prophecy," 495; see also t. Sota 13.2, b. Yoma 9b, 21b.
2. LaSor, "Temple," 733.
3. Neh 8; Ezra 7:10, 25; see also Sanders, "Exile and Canon," 58–59.

made the prophetic function obsolete. Some justification for the idea of closure seems to be expressed in Deuteronomy: "Ye shall not add unto the word which I command you, neither shall ye diminish aught from it." (Deut 4:2; see also Eccl 3:14; Sir 42:21)

On the other hand, God has not shown himself or given a spectacular new oracle to mankind at any place or time, in the Christian view, since the revelation to Jesus and the Apostles. The book of Revelation itself, positioned as the last chapter of the New Testament, warns, "For I testify unto every man that heareth the words of the prophecy of this book, If any man shall add unto these things, God shall add unto him the plagues that are written in this book . . . " (Rev 22:18) In the early medieval Christian church it was a common view, succinctly stated by Pope Stephen I, that: "Nothing is to be introduced except that which has [already] been received."[4] Such pronouncements had the effect of discouraging not only any dissident interpretations of Christian scripture, but also examination and acceptance of any new prophetic literature. Today the Catechism of the Roman Catholic Church reminds us that the prophetic era ended with Christ: "The Son is his Father's definitive word; so there will be no further Revelation after him."[5]

To underscore the shutting up of the heavens against any further speech from God, the Judaic tradition and the Christian tradition each, at separate times, officially designated the canons of their sacred literatures. After the textual traditions had been fixed slowly over time, the Jews placed a final, or near-final, exclamation point on their canon at Jamnia in 90 CE[6], and the Christians on theirs at Hippo in 393 CE and Carthage in 397 CE.[7] When the Christian tradition began to publish its own sacred literature in the first century CE, the mainstream Jewish tradition found no use for any of the new Christian literature. And when the Islamic tradition produced its own sacred literature around 650 CE[8], both the Judaic and Christian traditions declined to include any part of it in their own.

Only one type of oracular event is anticipated by caretakers of the ancient Judaic and Christian scriptures. Elements of both traditions

---

4. Quoted in Fogarty, "Scriptural Authority," 1024.
5. *Catechism of the Catholic Church*, 29.
6. Sanders, "Canon, Hebrew Bible," 841.
7. Gamble, "Canon, New Testament," 856.
8. Peters, *Voice*, 68.

cherish the notion of the return of a well known figure of the past, often seen as Elijah for the Jews, and clearly understood to be Jesus for the Christians. Jews, alternatively, look for a messianic king not previously known before, but in the lineage of David. Thus the prophetic enterprise is still open, but only to a figure coming at the absolute end of ordinary history. Until that time, both Jewish and Christian faiths assert that God's Spirit is available still on a secondary level, a level superintended by rabbis, priests, ministers, and individual believers.

Rabbinic literature speaks of "bat qol," or "daughter of the voice," which replaces "ruah elohim" or "Spirit of God."[9] Christians speak of "gifts of the spirit," which occupy a place of lower priority than the dormant or completed gift of the apostolic witness. (1 Cor 12:28) In the meanwhile, Jews and Christians live, for better or worse, in a kind of ongoing messenger-less world. From time to time Protestants lay claim to the idea of a return of inspiration[10], and the Roman Catholic popes have, since 1870, reclaimed the idea that some of their messages are divinely revealed.[11] Both traditions are comfortable with the idea that continuous revelation exists in the sense that the old scripture continues to reveal God's will to new individuals who read and grasp it.

The cessation of prophecy, if not always official policy in the churches, is a culturally enforced pattern of thinking for Jews and Christians despite numerous indications to the contrary in the Hebrew Bible and Christian New Testament. In both accounts, God is depicted as being by nature verbal and oracular. The very definition of faith is that of belief in a living and vocal God: "Our God shall come and shall not keep silence." (Ps 50:3) Joel, for example, predicts ongoing outpourings of Spirit: "I will pour out my Spirit upon all flesh . . . in those days will I pour out my Spirit." (Joel 2:28–29) Other prophets speak of the "pouring out" of the Spirit as well. (Isa 32:15; Ezek 39:29) Peter suggests at least one fulfillment of that prediction in his own day: "We also have a more sure word of prophecy." (2 Pet 1:19)

The idea of prohibition of additions to or deletions from the scripture is an argument without much substance as well. Entire books were periodically added or deleted in the scripture in the periods of time

---

9. Horn, "Spirit," 262–264.

10. Bromiley, "Doctrine of Inspiration," 139; see also Grudem, *Prophecy in the New Testament and Today*.

11. Coogan, *Old Testament*, 299.

before the final closing of those canons. This includes those books ultimately labeled lesser inspired "apochrypha," as well as controversial books like Ezekiel and Revelation which eventually were given permanent inclusion. Also, scholars believe several books were added to the New Testament after the date of the writing of the book of Revelation.[12] The prohibition of additions may be aimed by its authors more at minimizing interpretive modification (letting the original text stand as it was written), and maintaining fidelity to the foundational law. In this sense, it reflects customary admonitions of the same sort found in royal inscriptions, treaties, and law compilations of the ancient Near East.[13]

Each successive prophet in the 400-year long series of Old Testament literary prophets (roughly 840–440 BCE) effectively added to the scripture upon acceptance of the new work by the major traditions. Also, compilers of the Old Testament history sections added to and subtracted from earlier accounts when they published their own versions of things. Thus did the author of Chronicles, perhaps 150–200 years after the book of Kings had been penned. Each of the serially produced reminiscences of the New Testament disciples effectively added to the scripture upon its acceptance by the Christian traditions. For example, the works by Matthew and Luke came some decades after Mark and after the early source known as "Q" were written.

Some have argued that after a canon-making process is complete, it makes little sense to change it since the canon resulted from a high level of consensus and thus should be left alone.[14] To this we reply that such consensus turns out not to have been very widespread, and also that both the Hebrew Bible and Christian Testament were "finalized" numerous times over a very long period of time. Apparently, "final" is a term that applies only to a particular political situation at a particular moment in time. It is generally agreed that the Hebrew Bible, for example, was compiled in three phases. The law, or Torah, was given at Sinai roughly in 1,200 BCE, but was modified numerous times after that and not compiled into roughly final form until the time of Ezra in the late fifth century. Even then, the doctors of the Jewish law continued to tinker with its meaning for centuries. The literature of the prophets was not finalized until sometime after Joel and Malachi, who lived around

12. Robinson, *Are Mormons Christians?*, 46.
13. Levinson, "You Must Not Add Anything," 6–7.
14. Metzger, *Canon*, 275.

450–400 BCE. Lastly, the "Writings," such as Psalms, wisdom books like Proverbs, and historical reminiscences like Chronicles and Daniel were collected later and then officially added to the first two. The Christian testament was apparently not finalized even at the time of the great early councils in the fourth century CE, since a large segment of the Christian population deleted a number of books from the Bible of the Catholic Church more than a thousand years later at the time of the Protestant Reformation.

The God of the Bible clearly plans for and carries out an on-going series of authentic, high-level conversations with man. God is, from a time even before Moses and a time well after him, a communicative God, one who intends that his words be told or read to others by means of language, varied though that may be (Gen 11:1,7–9), in the same way it was first told or read to the messenger. (John 15:26–27)

God's message and literature is intended to be powerful and of lasting importance, written into stone as it were. (Deut 10:1–5; Josh 24:27) In a sense it is to be like the words of a covenant, never to be broken. But that literature and covenant are no more debarred from addition, modification, or renewal than is God's power to negotiate it or man's tendency to need rescue from new predicaments of history. In fact, God made covenants by revelation with new prophets and new peoples numerous times during Bible days, including: Adam and Eve (Gen 2: 16–17, 3:2–3); Noah (Gen 9:1–17); Abraham (Gen 15:6–11, 17:7–8); Moses (Exod 2:24, 3:4–10, 19:3–8), David (1 Chr 11:3; Ps 78:67–72; 2 Sam 7; Ps 89), and Jesus. (John 13:34, 14:31, 15:10) In each case he delivered a new message to a new prophet to underscore the importance of a new or renovated way of life.

Not only does God reveal himself to prophets at important times and various places throughout the story of early mankind, but he expresses his assurance that the phenomenon will not abate. Amos, for example, delivered God's promise that the Holy Spirit would not die (Amos 3:7), and Jesus promised the same as well. (John 14:26)

It is pertinent here to point out that the idea of God's continuing presence and revelation among mankind is supported by the very nature of religion and cult organization itself. Cult (church/synagogue/mosque) is an organized method of seeking contact with God.[15] One Hebrew word for prayer, "amad," means "to be in front of God." That is,

15. Vaux, *Ancient Israel*, 453.

the very object and purpose of prayer is to have an actual encounter with God. Another Hebrew word for prayer, "hithpallel," has a root meaning "to go between," suggesting the penitent's desire to exercise the gift of prophetic mediation.[16]

Those penitents who enter the professional priesthood are enjoined by the nature of that mediatory office to be "near to me [God]."[17] (Lev 10:3 JPS) In fact, even a prophet broadly skeptical of the activity of professional priests admits that it is the goal and challenge of each high priest to become an oracular prophet: "For the priests lips should keep knowledge, and they should seek the law at his mouth: for he is the messenger of the Lord of hosts." (Mal 2:7)

The root of the Hebrew word translated as "sacrifice" means to "draw near."[18] The purpose of both the outdoor and indoor temple sacrifices is to bring God very near to man. Thus the development of Old Testament sacrifice springs from a strong belief in the possibility and even probability of God's presence. It is not surprising, then, to learn that God speaks of the cereal and meat offerings in highly anthropomorphic and immanent/contiguous terms: "my bread," "my table," etc.[19] Old Testament "showbread" better translates "bread of the face"—the bread offering that brings God's face near to that of man.[20] The Eucharist shared in the synagogue and church in New Testament times is an adaptation of the same concept. The pouring out of oil to anoint a king or prophet signifies not only hope for the presence of the Spirit, but a belief in its advent. (1 Sam 16:13; Isa 61:1)

God is frequently portrayed in scripture as the "rock" of Israel. This name connotes not merely strength, but altitude. It refers in nature to the mountain places out of which streams of life-giving water flow to irrigate the fields of the land. (Ps 78:15–16) It refers also, both in the Hebrew Bible and New Testament, to the political and social policies, the "living waters," which stream forth from new prophets who receive those laws from on high. (Deut 32:4; 1 Sam 2:2; Ps 18:46, 61:2; Matt 16:18; 1 Cor 10:1–4)

---

16. Ibid., 459.
17. Milgrom, *Leviticus*, 220.
18. Ibid., 17.
19. Ibid., 18.
20. Vaux, *Ancient Israel*, 422.

The emotional heart of the Bible message is that a nation or a people who reject new and enlightened prophecy suffer infinitely for both the doctrinal and practical rejection of new wisdom from God. For example, when the northern kingdom of Israel rejected Isaiah's new word from God about the nation's Assyrian policy, the northern kingdom was summarily liquidated. When a hundred and fifty years later the southern kingdom of Judah rejected Jeremiah's new word from God about their foreign policy, the south went quickly into egregious captivity and was never able to get on its feet again.

REVELATION IN ANOTHER MAN'S BACKYARD

The general train of prophetic history in ancient Israel, or at least the Davidic court version of it, is similar to what other nearby nations such as Egypt, Mesopotamia, and Ugarit understood about the oracular process: a charismatic, Spirit-filled prince delivers a memorable hymn or prophecy which establishes him as a highly credible representative of a cherished god. For example, Pharaoh Amen-hotep IV (1352–1336 BCE), also known as Akhenaton, re-defined court worship in Egypt on the basis of a personal revelation from the god Aton.[21] Pharaoh Thut-mose IV (1400–1390 BCE) heard the voice of God, who told him "I am thy father . . . I shall give thee my kingdom upon earth at the head of the living."[22] In Mesopotamia's Uruk in Akkad, a rising new prophet about 1850 BCE declared the fulfillment of an earlier prophecy: "Dead Uruk has revived and the faithful shepherd concerning whom a command came from You has been established . . ." In return, God says " . . . pay attention to what I say . . . retain my words . . ."[23] In Ugarit before the time of Moses, a prophet opines, "Thy decree, O El, is wise: Wisdom with ever-life thy portion."[24]

Once the prophet dies, contact with and direction from the god is typically severely attenuated. In the case of Akhenaton, the "Amarna revolution" established by the prophet-prince quickly lost momentum, in much the same way the messianic movement of David lost force by the end of the reign of Solomon. (1 Kings 11) While the independent prophetic tradition (i.e., existing outside both government and priestly

---

21. "The Hymn to the Aton," ANET, 370.
22. "A Divine Oracle through a Dream," ANET, 449.
23. "An Old Babylonian Oracle From Uruk," ANET, 604.
24. "Poems about Baal and Anath," ANET, 133.

circles) is not as well documented outside Israel as inside it, we shall see in chapter 5 that there is reason to support the Psalmist's contention that the independent occurrence of oracular prophet-hood is a universal phenomenon, not a parochial or proprietary one.

On the other hand, a God tradition typically gains institutional momentum in the hands of younger associates of the prophet even as the presence of God, largely embodied in the messenger himself, disappears at his mortal death. In Israel, the school established by the prophet, while it is potentially capable of great things, often does not achieve much. In time, a new Spirit-filled prophet arises and accuses the temple priests and princes of the tradition of the former prophet of laboring in ignorance and iniquity. The interpretations of the backsliding tradition, compared to the actual doctrine of the original prophet, are likened to "chaff" next to "wheat." (Jer 23:28) Ultimately, a religious tradition born at the time of a prophet may either splinter into many related groups or disappear by absorption into larger, older traditions.

In Egypt, regular consultation with the god revealed by the prophet is solicited by aristocrats, military leaders, kings and peasants alike. These consultations are channeled through temple priests and non-controversial prophet-interpreters of the religion. For example, the petitioners ask for answers to questions about such things as potential military campaigns, legal and commercial matters, disease and recovery, and how to promote conception.[25]

The same sort of autonomic priestly service available to citizens of neighboring nations is provided by the priests of Yahweh in Israel after Moses, and later, David, are gone. Unfortunately, much about their answers to questions is speculative rather than reliable. Jeremiah judges that "both prophet and priest are profane." (Jer 23:11) In essence, the interpreters who proudly glorify the tradition know little of the authenticity of the original prophet and miss essential truths in his message: "From the prophet even unto the priest every one dealeth falsely." (Jer 6:13) It is to these pedestrian ecclesiastics and pundits who deliver merely their own opinions that Jeremiah's God directs such vitriol:

> When this people, or a prophet, or a priest asks you, 'What is the burden of the Lord?' you shall say to them, 'You are the burden, and I will cast you off,' says the Lord . . . 'The Burden of the Lord' you shall mention no more, for the burden is everyone's

25. Miosi, "Oracle in Ancient Egypt," 29.

own word, and so you pervert the words of the living God . . . I will bring upon you everlasting disgrace . . . which shall not be forgotten. (Jer 23:33–40 NRSV)

Some of the people, too, bypass even the professional prophets and resort to popular wizards and enchanters, seeking oracles not from God but from the dead: "But men will say to you, 'Seek guidance of ghosts and familiar spirits who squeak and gibber; a nation may surely seek guidance of its gods, of the dead on behalf of the living, for an oracle or a message?'" (Isa 8:19 NEB) But in fact the people would do better to discover God on their own rather than by consulting professionals or wizards. (Deut 4:29; Ps 14:2, 105:4; Prov 8:17)

The experience of theophany, or epiphany—here both roughly defined as an appearance of or communication from God—as attested both in Bible and ancient Near East literature, is a very rare one in terms of the short horizon of history, but a moderately plentiful one in the long term. In Israel, a nation periodically devoted to the concept, prophetic action or literature following divine appearance happens roughly on a 200 year cycle.

Often the high prophet stands head and shoulders above his contemporaries, and even his disciples. Moses alone "inquires" directly with God to obtain an extensive literary message (Exod 18:15), while the priests of the era continue to use speculative divinatory methods to obtain at best positive or negative answers to questions.[26] Subsequent prophets, such as Hosea, roundly condemn any media of heavenly communication, other than conversational oracular revelation, as infractions of the commandment against idolatry. (Hos 3:4)

While the authentic phenomenon is rare, there is still potential for any and all human beings to become messengers. Moses, for example, says "Would God that all the Lord's people were prophets, and that the Lord would put his Spirit upon them." (Num 11:29) The prophet Joel expects that the phenomenon has the potential to become widespread, and, as with Moses, not limited by gender: " . . . your sons and your daughters shall prophesy, your old men shall dream dreams, your young men shall see visions . . . in those days will I pour out my Spirit." (Joel 2:28–29) Peter, as well, outlines a similar challenge: " . . . ye also, as lively

---

26. Vaux, *Ancient Israel*, 349.

stones, are built up a spiritual house, a holy priesthood, to offer up spiritual sacrifices..." (1 Pet 2:5)

However, it is not necessary or even likely that prophecy will take place by means of the elect remnant of the prophet's followers. It may come, for example, in the form of a foreigner, one even who worships God by a different name. Cyrus, for example, spoke of Marduk of Mesopotamia, but Isaiah understood that this political liberator acted in the name, or the interests, of Yahweh of Israel. (Isa 45:1, 4)

In both the north and south of Israel during the divided monarchy, mainstream religion is associated with temple cities—Bethel and Dan in the north, and Jerusalem in the south. While these mainstream cults are founded by regionally esteemed leaders—Amaziah/Jeroboam in the north, David/Zadok/Nathan in the south—the priestly schools associated with them quickly become pedestrian. Interpreters of the original prophet proliferate and join professional ranks. The world knows a great deal of these stand-ins but sees little recurrence of the moments of the originals. There are long periods of time during which there is no great, proactive, unsolicited message from God which condemns the existing political and religious establishment and is delivered by a non-professional prophet of the same ilk as the originator of the movement. Or at least there is no such message that is tolerated by the now mainstream tradition.

In fact, there is often a reactionary political process that works against such a critical voice when it is finally aroused in Israel. Elijah and his political-military designee Jehu worked against great odds to bring about ethical reforms in the kingdoms of both the north and the south. These reforms, as in the days of Akenaton in Egypt, and David in Israel, did not last long. For example, in Jerusalem, the evil Athaliah was overthrown and replaced by a malleable boy-king by the name of Joash, who initially ruled benevolently in the spirit of the times. (2 Chr 24:4–14) But later in his term Joash distained the admonitions of a number of ethical prophets and turned to idolatry. (2 Chr 24:17–19) A prophet by the name of Zechariah, the son of the respected southern priest Jehoiada, challenged Joash's policies:

> And the Spirit of God came upon Zechariah the son of Jehoiada the priest, which stood above the people, and said unto them, Thus saith God, Why transgress ye the commandments of the Lord, that ye cannot prosper? Because ye have forsaken the Lord, he hath also forsaken you." (2 Chr 24:20)

The people of Judah, encouraged by King Joash, stoned the prophet Zechariah to death. (21)

Jesus of Nazareth recalled this episode on more than one occasion. (Luke 11:51, 13:34) He sensed that it was a turning point after which Israel became increasingly hostile to recurring or "new light" prophecy. The historical fact of the death of Zechariah at the hands of institutional power helped the young rabbi understand that the people of Roman Palestine would not embrace his ministry and message until they accepted once again the doctrine that God is never finished speaking to his people: "Ye shall not see me, until the time come when ye shall say, Blessed is he that cometh in the name of the Lord." (Luke 13:35; Ps 118:26) The people "see" or "get" Jesus only when they "bless" or accept the significance of the name of God. (John 12:45) That name is revealed to Moses as one which describes a living, vocal God who supports the cause of human freedom (see chapter 5). It is exactly this blessing that the new Christian community then pronounced upon the Judaic tradition, testifying that the pages of its scripture should not be closed, and upon the Judaic God, that he was capable of a new election of people to be his own. (Jer 31:31–34; Heb 8:8–12) Joel, as well, associates the outpouring of Spirit with belief in "the name of the Lord." (Joel 2.28–32)

Joel suggests that the God whose name and character was clarified at Sinai is still capable of raising up a new people: "And it shall come to pass, that whosoever shall call on the name of the Lord shall be delivered." (Joel 2:32) Unfortunately, Stephen understands that religious people in New Testament times are as resistant to acceptance of the Spirit's re-newed voice as those in Josiah's day: "Ye do always resist the Holy Ghost . . . as your fathers did, so do ye . . . " (Acts 7:51)

In the ancient Near East, coming "in the name" is an expression associated with the sending of a high level ambassador from one king to another. Until the people accept the actual concept that the king of heaven can send another ambassador when he wants, they will surely ignore that messenger. When they reject the messenger, they effectively reject the one who sent him. They choose a mute god in favor of one who exercises a personal right and power to speak.

On the other hand, if they are intellectually prepared to accept new prophecy, they are more likely to examine the claims of a prophet, no matter what some say of him. When Peter recognized Jesus as "messiah" or "Christ"—one anointed to mediate the presence of God—he let Jesus know he understood prophecy had not come to an end, in spite of what the Sadducees and Pharisees taught. (Matt 16:16; Mark 8:29; Luke 9:20) When Jesus asked the people to "believe" (John 16:27, 17:8) he asked them to give the doctrine and message of new prophecy a hearing.

It happens that much of God's message to mankind, like the messages and stories of Elijah and Zechariah, is published broadly enough throughout the culture that it is preserved through time. But apparently some is not well preserved and slips into invisibility. There is much to suggest that archeology has yet to uncover many early records of revelations of God to man. At Qumran, for example, several previously unknown psalms were recovered.[27]

The Bible itself contains records of discovery of long-lost ancient manuscripts, buried in libraries accessible to curious readers, and not yet covered over by the rubble of war or the shifting riverbeds of time. In the days of King Josiah, 600 years after Moses, an old writing from the hand or a scribe of Moses himself was discovered and brought to light by Hilkiah the high priest. (2 Kings 22:8) That original source was incorporated into the book of Deuteronomy and was influential in Josiah's social reforms of the day. In the time of Zechariah, a number of other judgmental prophecies were directed against King Joash, but these "accounts . . . of the many oracles against him" must be numbered among the lost oracles, since the book in which they were recorded, "Commentary on the Book of the Kings," has not as yet been recovered. (2 Chr 24: 27 NRSV) A number of Paul's letters, mentioned in the existing Epistles, have been lost. (1 Cor 5:9; Eph 3:3) The Gospel of John suggests there were many remembrances of Jesus not widely reported by the time of his own book. (John 21:25) The sayings of Jesus found in the Gospel of Thomas may be one of them. Conversely, some written accounts well known early on apparently are now missing, such as the Q source (German "quelle"), a document from which both Matthew and Luke apparently draw for accounts they report in common.

BLIND FOR A MOMENT: JOB'S EXPERIENCE OF GOD

Spiritual seekers, together with archivists and archeologists, however, must have the courage to believe that certain passages of the ancient record mean what historians of the language indicate they mean, and not what the ideological priests of the day say they mean. If God and the

---

27. Sanders, "Canon, Hebrew Bible, Dead Sea Scrolls," 842.

people are willing to bless one who comes with a message "in the name of the Lord," and if the name of Jehovah, or more properly Yahweh, means "God lives," then the student confronts the notion that God does indeed speak again to man, even after a canon of scripture has been closed by a particular worshipping tradition. (1 John 5:13) The Jesus followers who were Jewish had to believe and accept that Jesus opened the heavens once again, even though the Sadducees long before, and Pharisees, more recently, had declared them closed.

In the Bible, Job expresses frustration that there is no go-between available in his day—one to relay messages back and forth between God and man: "Neither is there any dayman [umpire[28]] betwixt us, that might lay his hand upon us both." (Job 9:33, 16:21) Abraham exercised this function, for example, between God and the people of Sodom, when he reasoned with God about the level of acceptable collateral casualty pending the destruction of the city. (Gen 18:22–33) Job does not, at this moment, recognize he is capable of stepping into those shoes himself, but in time begins to explore the idea. (Job 19:23–27)

The book of Job, in fact, presents a story of a man whose suffering ultimately provides an opportunity to accept and experience the notion of ongoing oracular revelation. This includes the possibility that God might draw extraordinarily close to him and buoy him up, the possibility that God himself might serve as witness, rescuer, redeemer. (Job 8:6–7, 16:19, 13:7–12, 22:30, 42:10)

In fact, after a long and discouraging period of conversation on the subject of theology with his friends, Job, who accepted with them the conventional wisdom concerning the completion of prophecy by his day (Job 11:5–7), experiences a manifestation of its continuity in his own life. The chronicler of the debate and the larger story used language common in the larger Near East milieu to describe this experience. This was the language of the oracular storm—wind, cloud, and heavenly fire. The cloud and the fire had accompanied Moses' vocal God in the wilderness, and was closely associated with Canaanite oracles in the coastal society of Ugarit even before the time of Moses. Job finally meets his maker while still alive. God speaks to him "out of the whirlwind." (Job 38:1, 40:6) He reports: "Now, my eyes have seen thee." (Job 42:5) God sets his life right again, and gives him a sacred message to deliver to mankind. Job then left an extended oracle as a witness of his own per-

---

28. J.A. Crenshaw translates the Hebrew word thusly, in "Book of Job," 867.

sonal connection with heaven and the viability of new prophecy in his own day. (Job 38:1—41:34) Job also obtained converts to the idea of a present God among the very friends who had previously frustrated his growing interest in the notion of prophecy. (Job 42:7–9)

The idea of "belief" in the New Testament is intimately tied up with the same concept in the Old Testament—trust in God's power and capacity to send new messengers at new times in history in order to achieve old purposes. In exercising this belief, the people reciprocate God's trust that some, perhaps many, of the people will have the intellectual and spiritual capacity to receive such a messenger. In Isaiah, the prophet complains that few can countenance the idea of a new prophet: "Who hath believed out report and to whom is the arm of the Lord revealed?" (Isa 53:1) Paul cites this same verse and relates it to the dim view taken of divine revelation in his own day. He suggests that the very definition of faith is acceptance of the reality of an ongoing conversation between God and humanity: "Faith cometh by hearing, and hearing by the word of God." (Rom 10:16–17) In John, the idea of new prophecy is of such decisive importance that belief in God is defined as belief in the prophetic messenger. (John 14:1) Disbelief in new prophecy, conversely, is the very definition of sin. (John 16:9)

In fact, Jesus made it clear that belief in the Christ was ultimately belief in the sovereign power of the Father to anoint a prophet and send him to the people once again: "He that believeth on me, believeth not on me, but on him that sent me. And he that seeth me seeth him that sent me." (John 12:44-45) Jesus himself does not judge those who reject him, but rather "the word" which Jesus brings judges them instead. (John 12:47–48) In fact, not only Jesus' word, but all the words of the scripture judge them, for the scripture speaks of others to come. (John 5:46–47)

As Jesus stood in front of the council that would judge him and take away his life, he evidenced a pronounced cynicism as to the efficacy of announcing his messiahship and about persuading the Sadducees as to the reality of new prophecy. They asked, "Are thou the Christ? ... And he said unto them, If I tell you, ye will not believe." (Luke 22:67) In fact, he was like the prophets of old whom the aristocratic predecessors of the Sadducees never accepted or respected, a clamoring, God-appointed agent of the interests of the poor. Such prophets were summarily rebuffed at the hands of the priestly institutional interests of those earlier days. The priestly Sadducee aristocrats, even hundreds of years after the prophecies of the literary prophets were fulfilled, still pointedly refused, according to Josephus, to include the extraordinary sages like Isaiah and Jeremiah in their canonical book of scripture.[29]

Profile—A Storm From the East (Job)

A prominent citizen by the name of Job sat on a stone outcropping overlooking his home and fields in the territory of Edom. He stared vacantly out across the space of day, not taking any real note of his extensive properties, nor the ashes of a building on an adjoining parcel. Instead, he worked a potsherd across his left arm, scratching away at several of the boils that had begun to erupt on his skin not long after a series of calamities struck his flocks, his servants, and his sons.

"I cannot countenance such a God," Job thought, as he grimaced in pain. "I am a fish out of its element, flopping for life on an embankment. God is the very fisherman who has brought me this exhaustion."

Job, previously enamored of the idea that Qos[30] could be counted on to be watchfully protective over the faithful, reflected now that for weeks after the events which destroyed his dearest possessions, he could not trust any intimation in response to an inquiry he might make of God in prayer.

"The priests say that God long ago absented himself from the vocal service of high prophets, but the priests also assure us that God, in compensation, will still work from a distance to warm and heal the suffering heart and body of a devotee. Where is the answer to my prayer?"

Job's thoughts turned to the interloper Elihu, an itinerant divine from Judea, who had recently confronted the community with his excitements. Elihu plied Edom's leading landholders with the notion that a new day had come upon Edom, a day of God's looking upon the poor and marginalized, a time of God's drawing near to mankind again and speaking his will.

Now, desperate for confirmation or refutation of such a theology, Job mused, "Oh that I knew where I might find him! That I might come even to his seat! . . . I would know the words that he would answer me and understand what he would say unto me." (Job 23:3, 5)

As he agonized over this conundrum, a gust of wind deposited grainy dust in his eyes and temporarily blinded him. And then he heard a voice.

29. Porton, "Sadducees," 892.
30. The name of the national god in Edom; see Pritchard, *Atlas*, 68.

SLATHERING ON THE SUBLIMINAL: ORACLE PROMOTION IN BIBLE BOOKS

The Hebrew Bible is organized into three large divisions in the Judaic tradition: the Torah or Pentateuch; the Prophets, which combines the history of prophet-judges and kings with the literature of the prophets; and the Writings, accessory materials like Psalms and Proverbs. The Christian testament is divided into gospels, letters and certain other writings like Revelation. Each of these six general sub-divisions of the Bible, as well as each of the books contained in each of the divisions, present positive statements about the prognosis for ongoing oracular utterance in the civilizations of man.

The Book of Genesis, after summarizing the primeval revelatory experiences of Adam, Eve, and Noah, makes the oracular experiences of four successive generations of prophets from Abraham to Joseph the substance of the remainder of its pages. (Gen 12:6–7, 26:2, 28:10–22, 37:5–11, 45:7–8, 50:19) The Book of Exodus presents the revelation experience of Moses, the founder of the nation of Israel, as the centerpiece of the entire Old Testament. It also provides such anchors to prophecy as the First Commandment and the law of altars. (Exod 20:3, 24) The First Commandment, as we shall see in chapter 5, is a civil law providing protection for prophets, who, like Moses, proclaim freedom and human rights for their peoples. The book of Leviticus frames the concept of God's presence among the Israelites in terms of the temple rituals, and in particular the Day of Atonement, or Yom Kippur, on which day the temple is cleansed of the impurities of the nation so that God's spirit can continue to appear in the inner sanctum.

The book of Numbers develops a number of themes related to divine revelation, including God's accompaniment of Israel in her travels in a dark cloud over the tabernacle (Num 9:15–23), the story of the Syrian prophet Balaam and his oracle with respect to Israel (Num 22–24), the sharing of the spirit of prophecy with the seventy elders (Num 11:16–25), and the story of tolerance extended to the dissident prophets Eldad and Medad. (Num 11:26–30)

The book of Deuteronomy, as we mentioned above and will expand upon in chapter 5, legislates a full-fledged law promoting legitimate prophecy. (Deut 12–13, 17–18) It also provides not only second and third versions of the prophecy commandment, (Deut 5:7–8; 6:4–5) but also Moses' promise of others like himself who will benefit from that law and that heavenly propensity in the future. (Deut 18:15)

Indeed, each of the major sources of the Pentateuch, as well, makes special mention of this theology of continuing revelation. The earliest source used in the so-called five books of Moses is the southern "J", or "Jahwist" source. Its narrative in Exodus 19–24 makes the revelation at Sinai the centerpiece of its version of the history. "J's" story of Abraham and Lot depends heavily upon oracular revelation.[31]

The northern "E' or "Elohist" source is characterized by its insistence, in Joseph's speeches to his brothers and Moses' address to Israel, that history is best told by a bidden prophet of God. (Gen 45:7–14, 50:15–26; Exod 20:18–20) Destruction of the nation, furthermore, can only be forestalled by the intercession of a prophet like Moses. (Exod 33:11)

The "P" or "Priestly" source is characterized by its humanizing of God, so that closeness to him is easier than it usually is in the ancient Near East. No longer is contact with holy objects or nearness to a holy God so dangerous that one's life is put into jeopardy.[32] (Lev 7; Isa 55:3) The fatal power typical of the sanctuaries of other nations was no longer operative in a democratic nation like Israel, where any citizen, and not merely a prince or a high priest, might entertain an appearance of God.

The book of Joshua develops the theme of a law, written in stone on Mt. Ebal, which welcomes the oracular presence in Israel. (Josh 8:30–35) The book opens with an epiphany experienced by Joshua whereby God indicates "As I was with Moses, so I will be with thee . . ." (Josh 1:5) Its middle pages summarize the efforts of the prophet anointed by Moses to continue the oracular work on the west side of Jordan. Its last pages constitute Joshua's entire farewell address as an oracle from God. (Josh 24)

The book of Judges pursues the theme by citing oracles delivered to a series of individuals: an unnamed prophet at Bochim (Judg 2), Deborah (Judg 5), Gideon (Judg 6), and the parents of Sampson. (Judg 13) Samuel relates how God's revelatory presence returned to Shiloh after a long absence (1 Sam 3:21), and how Samuel's oracles directed him to anoint first Saul, and later David. (1 Sam 9, 16) It also summarizes David's "Last Words," in which the shepherd king indicates "The spirit of the Lord spake by me, and his word was in my tongue." (2 Sam 23:2)

The books of Kings present the stories of the theophany of Elijah (1 Kgs 19), and the activities of such oracles as Isaiah (2 Kgs 19:5), Huldah

---

31. The reader can review various theories about authorship of the Pentateuch by consulting a Bible dictionary like the Anchor Bible Dictionary.

32. Milgrom, *Leviticus*, 11, 16.

(2 Kgs 22:14), Ahijah (1 Kgs 14), and "a prophet of Judah." (1 Kgs 13) It also relates the story of Solomon's communication with God in the matter of his quest for "wisdom." (1 Kgs 3) We will see in chapter 7 that the receipt of knowledge of the natural world is a variety of more general scientific revelation,[33] subsequently authenticated as a legitimate form of prophecy by the inclusion of several wisdom-oriented books of the Bible, such as Job, Ecclesiastes, and Proverbs.

The books of 1 and 2 Chronicles provide a long list of "minor" prophets which we list and examine in chapter 2. It summarizes David's re-establishment of a mainstream church on the basis of prophetic prerogative. (1 Chr 13, 16:4; Ps 78:70) It also records Solomon's protestation about whether God's revelatory presence can actually ever be safely ensconced within physical or proprietary confines made for him by man: "Will God indeed dwell with men on the earth?" (2 Chr 6:18)

The books of Ezra and Nehemiah record the story of the rebuilding of the temple to allow for ministration of ancient sacrificial ordinances designed to mediate God's presence (Ezra 5), and of restoration of the law relating to the oracle-producing commandments. (Neh 8) It also presents an able statement of the goal of verbal inspiration from God: "Thou gavest also thy good Spirit to instruct them." (Neh 9:20) The books of Ruth and Esther speak to the heart of prophetic religion— public policies relating to redemption of land, the destitute and alien, and religious liberty.

Psalms is a veritable library of oracular utterances penned by David, Asaph and others, using the motifs associated with revelation that we will review in chapter 6. These include the terms "face," "cloud," "glory," "voice," "servant," "angel," "spirit," "son of man," "firstborn," "image," and "name." The Book of Proverbs elaborates the notion that wisdom about creation "uttereth her voice in the streets . . ." (Prov 1:20) and "pour(s) out my spirit unto you." (Prov 1:23) Furthermore, when man desires revelation, general or special[34], God has the means to give it: "The spirit of man is the candle of the Lord, searching every inmost part." (Prov 20:27 NRSV) Ecclesiastes adds its witness to the revelatory tradition with the notion that the temple is a place of general and spiritual learning which one ought to be receptive to: "When thou goest to the house of God . . . be more ready to hear . . . let thy words be few . . ." (Eccl 5:1–2)

---

33. Monk, *Religious Meaning*, 108–110.

34. By "general" we refer to that which an individual can discern by study, and "special" that which the individual needs God's assistance to discern.

The books of Isaiah, Jeremiah, Ezekiel and the "minor" prophets relate personal theophanies and other encounters with the divine. They include also special oracles against surrounding nations (see Amos 1–2), and intimations or predictions about "days" of the Lord's return to vocal presence, might, and prominence amongst both the good and the evildoers of the region. (see Zeph 1:14, 17) The book of Daniel relates a series of events around oracular dreams given to political leaders and interpreted by the wisdom scientist Daniel (Dan 2:28, 4:24, 5:24–28), and the oracular dreams attributed to Daniel himself. (Dan 7–8, 10–12)

Finally, each of the New Testament's four gospels emphasizes continuing revelation. Matthew's book stresses Jesus' continuity within and fulfillment of the Old Testament Jewish tradition of Messiah. Here Jesus has a strong interest in details of Judaic law and the habits of its champions, as did all Old Testament prophets. Mark's gospel stresses the New Testament's continuity with the "Son of God" tradition in Israel, as exemplified by the inspired Davidic kings of Judah, and others in Judaic history who exercised the gift of healing, teaching, and spiritual beneficence.[35] Luke and Acts emphasize the continuity of Jesus and Paul within the ancient prophetic tradition. (Luke 7:16) John positions Jesus as revealer of the "word" or intelligence of God in Jesus' own personality (John 1:1–5), not unlike prophets such as Moses, who served with respect to Aaron "instead of God" and with respect to Pharaoh as a "god." (Exod 4:16, 7:1) The letters attributed to Paul emphasize his stature as an independent prophet/apostle. (Acts 9, Gal 1–2; 1 Cor 13:1–3) The book of Revelation is, as its name suggests, an example and a testament to the notion of continuing revelation. Revelation discloses that "the testimony of Jesus is the spirit of prophecy." (Rev 19:10)

A PATENT ON ONE PROPHET AND A CURSE ON ANOTHER (OR, THE CASE OF THE BAD SAMARITAN)

The institution of prophecy, both its legitimate and illegitimate varieties, is not limited to Israel. It starts with Adam and Enoch and fans out over the known earth and waxes and wanes where it does. There are prophets in Mesopotamia, Egypt, Palestine, Assyria, and Phoenicia. The Bible speaks of one Syro-Mesopotamian prophet by the name of Balaam, who demonstrates both legitimate and illegitimate uses of prophecy in

---

35. Ehrman, *New Testament*, 68–70.

an interesting historical incident involving Israel while he serves in the employ of Moab. (Num 22–24) Balaam's existence is independently attested outside the Bible as well, from the archeological site of Deir Alla east of Jordan. Balaam's story is instructive because it demonstrates how prophetic traditions, confronting one another from the vantage point of neighboring nations, can be used to criticize and defame rather than support religious diversity, which we argue is the foundation of the Israelite tradition.

Some sacred teaching, known by one tradition within a single nation, is not well known to another people of that same nation. Even within the confines of the small nation of Israel, many insulated themselves and refused to acknowledge or read the testaments of closely-related cult traditions of neighboring cities or regions within the nation. The Samaritans of post-exile Israel, for example, refused to admit all the great prophets after Moses, and accepted only the five books of Moses as scripture. They left David, Elijah, Isaiah, Jeremiah and Ezekiel out of their own sacred history, although they knew about active traditions associated with those great civic and priestly defenders of the ancient faith.

One can imagine that the sensibility of the Samaritans must have been much like that of Christians today who fear to go near a piece of non-canonical literature from their own tradition, like the Gospel of Thomas, or a newer literature outside the Christian tradition altogether, like the Quran of Islam. On the other hand, Jews shied away from any association with the Samaritans because they did not accept the additional prophets that the Pharisees did.

This long-standing mutual disdain prompted an astonished Samaritan woman to remind the friendly, ecumenical-minded physician from Nazareth that "The Jews have no dealings with the Samaritans." (John 4:9) This, however, was not news to Jesus, for, coming from Lower Galilee as he did, he had lived geographically further away from Jerusalem than even the Samaritans. He had long observed the tug of war between the two local monotheistic traditions, Judaism and Samaritanism, and now felt deeply the refusal of the mainstream Judaic tradition, once champions of new light, to honor any more new light in their own tradition. They were now like the Samaritans whom they had always thought were beneath them. Moved to compassion, he taught the woman from Samaria that one had now come whose work was poised to overturn the short-sighted traditions of both.

There were times, too, when traditional loyalties and allegiances were not the only hurdles to surmount in cross-cultural understanding, times when the gentle tug-of-doctrinal-war was more like the hot fire of hatred and persecution. For example, new light literature was subjected to book burning in the time of King Jehoiakim, who wanted to purge Jeremiah's prophecy from the land. (Jer 36:20–32)

The problem with horizontal sharing of and vertical succession in prophetic leadership, as we have suggested above and as many of the prophets note, is that it can come to be treated as an unalterable organizational patent on access to the mind and heart of God. Men and their churches do not want to give up rights to what is in the beginning a proprietary and place-located relationship with God. But God has made clear the patent has an expiration date and is not everlasting. The patent effectively expires upon the death of the prophet. This is perhaps most clearly chronicled in the case of the death of Joshua, who apparently was the only one of the seventy elders of Israel after Moses to retain a good measure of the prophetic gift. The people quickly lost touch with God and the commandments after his demise. (Judg 2:10–15)

The return of prophecy, after a precipitous decline, is likely to happen in a different locale than the original, and the newly elect people there may even speak a different language or live in a different nation entirely. If it was God who confounded the one universal language and distributed variety in tongues to the nations (Gen 11:1–9), presumably, then, God is able to speak in each one of them.

When the prophet blesses others with a promise of reception of the gift, many of those people assume they that automatically become inheritors of the authentic version of the gift. The blessing of prophecy, like the promise of posterity given to Abraham, is sincere and inevitable, but it may well not play out immediately. Within a period of time after a prophet speaks in a particular culture, his words are pirated to institutional interests. Mistaken interpretations of his essential views are either innocently or consciously promoted.

In fact, the scripture makes it clear that there are way too many illegitimate prophets, and far too few legitimate ones. This is a great frustration to God and an impediment to the progress of humanity. God stands ready to reveal his will and fulfill his earlier pronouncements. He has placed no ceiling between the earth and the heavenly realms, but mankind clearly has. "The Lord saw it, and it displeased him that there was . . . no man, and wondered, that there was no intercessor." (Isa 59:15–16) "The Lord looked down from heaven upon the children of men to see if there were any that did understand, and seek God." (Ps 14:2) Here the Lord is looking for "any," anywhere. Also, "God looked down from heaven upon the children of men, to see if there were any that did understand, that did seek God. Every one of them is gone back: they are altogether become filthy; there is none that doeth good, no, not one." (Ps 53:2–3)

But God does not sulk away to a far off place and abandon the earth: "For the eyes of the Lord run to and fro throughout the whole earth to show himself strong in the behalf of them whose heart is perfect toward him." (2 Chr 16:9) Here the Lord goes traveling abroad to all the nations of the earth in search of a gracious and studious heart. God hangs out at those places where people pass by: "Doth not wisdom cry . . . she crieth at the gates . . . unto you, O men, I call." (Prov 8:1–4) Here is the pathetic image of a progressive God, expressed in a soft and sensitive female voice, positioning himself/herself at the place where people congregate, where they come and go, and crying out for someone to listen to sense, to science, to history, to humanity, to observation and truth, in short, to sacred wisdom. The word and will and wisdom of God is offered not just in the wilderness and in the fields, but in the city. But even when God finds an intercessor, the outcome is not often good: "When I called, ye did not answer; when I spake, ye did not hear." (Isa 65:12)

The problem is both a vacancy of effort by the people and zealous but short-sighted actions by the priestly interpreters of the tradition. The people do not take time to read their own literature carefully, or to read it in a language they understand. They rely on interpreters who themselves may not have read the literature carefully, or whose interests seem to require a specific interpretation that may not be supported by the sacred writ itself. The great prophets rue the fact that the people focus so much attention on authorized spin doctors of the mainstream churches. This leads to excruciating reversals of emphasis in theology. For example, "The prophets prophesy falsely, and the priests bear rule by their means; and my people love to have it so . . ." (Jer 5:31)

One item of conventional theological wisdom, protested by all the literary prophets, is expressed in two words: "Prophesy not." (Amos 2:12) The doctrine of continuous revelation is replaced by a doctrine which is its polar opposite. The God who "keeps not silence" (Ps 50.3) becomes the God who "speaks no more." In order for this elegant flip-flop to take place, the entire focus and interpretation of the scripture must be masterfully manipulated so the people cannot easily see the original meaning of the passages of scripture.

Isaiah reminds us that this fashionable demeaning or neglect of the words of an earlier prophet effectively lulls a people into a deep sleep, to the point that they cannot understand what the manuscript says or intends:

> For the Lord hath poured out upon you the spirit of deep sleep, and hath closed your eyes: the prophets and your rulers, the seers hath he covered. And the vision of all has become unto you as the words of a book that is sealed, which men deliver to one that is learned, saying, Read this, I pray thee: and he saith, I cannot; for it is sealed: and the book is delivered to him that is not learned, saying, Read this, I pray thee: and he saith, I am not learned. (Isa 29:10–12)

Here Isaiah is speaking about books of ancient provenance subject to considerable variation in interpretation in his own day. These books are sealed to the learned because the meanings of words have changed, and the contexts of history and culture have also changed radically. For example, the classical Hebrew used in the earliest days of Israel differs considerably from the Hebrew of the rabbinical tradition. Without more anthropological and archeological and linguistic information, how can even the learned make an educated guess? The unlearned, for their part, don't have a prayer, since they don't know the language of the original manuscript, or don't understand even the words rendered in translation into their own language. Here Isaiah seems to argue for a scientific approach to biblical study rather than merely a confessional or liturgical-based one.

In the meanwhile, for periods of time that seem excruciating in Israel, individuals complain that God's presence no longer seems accessible: "Why hidest thyself in times of trouble?" (Ps 10:1) "How long wilt thou hide thy face from me?" (Ps 13:1) "Wilt thou hide thyself forever?" (Ps 89:46) Others, unlike Job, do not actually attain to high prophethood, but steadfastly believe such a one is to come. Such are Simeon and Anna (Luke 2:25–38) and John the Baptist (Luke 3:15–17), who seek to bless whomever comes "in the name of the Lord."

In sum, there are rare times when God's vocal spirit is readily available—spoken and heard. But there are many more days when God lies in wait at the city gates and finds all are too busy with other understandings to hear that voice. But there are also times, too, when God's spirit effectively withdraws from a city and even a nation, when the society is so fully given over to licentiousness and book burning that no progress can be made with them. God warns about such a time: "Seek ye the Lord while he may be found ... call ... while he is near." (Isa 55:6)

2

Prophets Promote Prophecy

IN ANCIENT NEAR EAST countries a political leader often assumed a semi-divine status, typically at the time of coronation. This ecclesiastic elevation is recalled in its Israelite variation in the so-called Zion theology,[1] and given specific voice in Psalm 2, where the leader is "born again" in a sense, as he assumes the role of specially protected "son" of God. A new Davidic king in the southern kingdom is anointed by God through the priest, who proclaims "I have set my king on Zion, my holy hill." At this point the king answers, "I will tell of the decree of the Lord: He said to me, 'You are my son; today I have begotten you.'"[2] (Ps 2:6 NRSV) In the northern kingdom the practice of hereditary or dynastic kingship was less ardently revered.

Much later, the followers of Jesus broke from the notion of the theorists of the southern kingdom which posited that God's blessing for civic governance falls only on one individual or one lineage in the nation. They taught that each human being can be priest and king, (1 Pet 2:9; Rev 1:6) if only reborn by receipt of the actual Spirit, not merely the bureaucratically conferred spirit of God. (John 3:3) Davidic kings had each nominally received the Spirit, but only a couple, according to Deuteronomistic historians who pronounced each one either "right" or "evil,"[3] actually seemed to be somewhat acquainted with that spirit.

While kingly prophetism is rare in Israel, we find a relative abundance of citizen prophets, those who spring from the mundane socio-economic strata of society. We review aspects of their stories below. Kings

1. The theology of Jerusalem-based Davidic lineage kingship.
2. Coogan, *Old Testament*, 277; It is possible Israel believed that the act of acclamation by the people conferred this special status on the leader, as much the anointing itself. This idea will be explored in another essay.
3. Gottwald, *Politics*, 80.

themselves often spawned yet a third variety of prophets—professional prophet-pundits. These "prophets" are given employment in the administration of the monarchy, or at least are given access to the king. Such divines have an interest in spiritual and political matters. Their job is to lend an aura of sanctity or sagacity to the administration of the king or to serve as conduits to determine divine favor or disfavor on matters of state. They are usually careful to support the interests of the king while still nominally claiming independence from him. Sometimes an authentic high prophet has an association with the monarchic court, as Isaiah and perhaps Jeremiah seem to have had.

Unlike kings and court pundits, the major independent prophets of the Bible report an experience of theophany, an extraordinary opening of the heavens during which God communicates personally with them. The detail surrounding a theophanic calling is often tucked away somewhere in the early chapters of the prophet's literary corpus, almost as if to say there is a difference between what the nation has been hearing from the court pundits, and what they will be hearing now.

Such a calling serves an extremely important place in Israel's history for several reasons. First, it positions the prophet in the authentic prophetic tradition. This alerts the instant audience to the prospect that large events are on the verge of happening, much as they were in the days of the earlier prophets. God is now once again placing a providential hand into the affairs of men. We will see that the prophet uses other devices to identify with former divines as well, such as quoting frequently from those earlier messages, and interpreting those messages in surprising new ways.

Secondly, the close relation to God which the calling suggests provides a rationale, which the prophet seems to need as much as the constituents, for what comes to be a persistent criticism leveled at institutions in society. Whether the prophet likes it or not, he has been asked by God to do this work. As we will see below, the invitation is so powerful that the prophet feels almost kidnapped into a type of work which does very little for him in terms of personal economic or social success. Thirdly, and of inestimable importance, the calling demonstrates that God cares about people in the present day as much as he did in former days. It demonstrates that God is, after all, just. He does not favor the ancients over the moderns.

Fourthly, the call, the activities performed pursuant to the call, and the predictions made about the future, serve as a standard against which court personnel and others called "prophets" can be judged. The work of true prophets is substantiated not only by the fact they claim a personal encounter with God, but also by the fact that the work they do seems truly inspired, and by the fact that the outfall of subsequent history will demonstrate that the prophet was working with a full deck of cards. The work of the false prophets, on the other hand, is fairly easily discredited by those who take time to notice.

Finally, the calling serves as a direct challenge to political and ecclesiastic leaders who themselves claim a pre-eminently close relationship to God, yet who act in ways which suggest otherwise. This challenge was perhaps most pointedly put by the Nazarene, when he excoriated the priestly political leaders of his day: "Ye have neither heard his voice at any time, nor seen his shape." (John 5:37) The events of Jesus' baptism, temptation, Sermon on the Mount, and teaching of the Lord's Prayer, aside from pronouncements such as this, each convey a sense of continuation of thematic elements relating to oracular revelation from the Hebrew Bible/Old Testament.

For example, the baptism is the setting for theophany and calling. (Matt 3:16–17) The wilderness temptation suggests the importance of the oracular word—every word that proceeds forth from the mouth of God—as against the worldly calling to wealth, or "bread alone." (Matt 4:3–4) The Sermon indicates that the poor "in spirit" are to be blessed with a welcoming into "the kingdom of heaven," presumably at the hand of an oracular prophet who mediates the Spirit rulings of heaven in their favor. (Matt 5:3) The Lord's Prayer teaches its proponents to ask that God's plenary "will" be known for today and be "done" on earth. (Matt 6:10)

The message that the prophet is asked to pass along to the people and their leaders deals primarily with the weightier commandments of Jewish law (Matt 23:23), and especially the Ten Commandments, known as "the covenant." (Isa 24:5; Matt 22:40; Luke 1:72) These commandments constitute the broad socio-political-ethical law of the land. The prophet's thinking and actions are based on the original intent of these foundational laws. The prophet is forced to speak out because this constitutive law has been neglected or re-interpreted in ways that cause the both individuals and the nation to fail.

Therefore, the prophet is called to agitate for reform, challenge institutions and agencies, encourage specific public policies and actions, and organize followers—so called schools or "sons" of the prophets. What follows the calling, then, are adventures like Moses' confrontation with the king of Egypt and Elijah's confrontation with the regent of the northern kingdom, Amos' face-to-face criticism spoken to the high priest at Bethel, Isaiah's pep-talk against surrender to Assyria, Jeremiah's opposite message encouraging submission to Babylon, and Jesus' confrontation with the high priest Caiaphas and Roman authorities in Jerusalem.[4]

TUG OF A TIDAL WAVE: THE HIGH PROPHET CALLING

The authentic prophet experiences this very specific moment of calling usually in the young adult years, and in a couple of notable cases (Ezekiel and Jesus) at around 30 years old. The calling is roughly equivalent to the storied Christian "born again" experience. For the citizen-prophet, however, it is not merely a change of heart and a change of course. When the prophet meets God, he/she is invited to a very high leadership position. If the prophet is not always called to be governor or judge or king like Joshua or Deborah or David, nevertheless he is called, like Elijah and Hosea, to shadow such leaders and to publically evaluate their political policies. He is called to be God's supreme voice and messenger for the period of his remaining life, and forevermore by means of his preserved sayings, his specific example, and his overall story. He is called to be servant, son, watchman, shepherd, and sign, as we will see in chapter 6. He is called to be despised or ignored by those whom he loves, and to serve the best interests even of those who hate him.

The compilers/editors of those books of the prophets for whom a portion of their literature is available to us today, often use purely formulaic language to describe the experience of calling, since the prophet's own words are not available to them. For example, they preface the literature with: "The word of the Lord that came to _____"; "The vision of _____"; "The burden which _____ saw." Alternatively, they recall that the prophet says, "Thus saith the Lord." The pattern of encounter with the divine experienced by Moses comes to be a template for other callings. God identifies himself (Exod 3:6), gives assurance that the prophet need not fear (Gen 15:1; 21:17), and promises an ongoing rela-

---

4. I intend to review the activities of the prophets in more detail in another essay.

tionship. (Gen 26:24) This ongoing relationship, for example, is promised to Joshua, Gideon and Jeremiah.

A few prophets stress the nature of the calling as a process of speech, writing, or communication, rather than a calling to use forceful politics or militarism. One uses the metaphor of purification of the mouth (Isaiah), and others the insertion of a message into the mouth (Jeremiah, Ezekiel). Many are informed that they will experience rejection. Several use the metaphor of God speaking to Israel both as parent and as spouse, stressing both the didactic function of the heavenly king and the co-operative and co-important function of political equals.[5]

Ezekiel's calling is of the vision type, a scene of heavenly creatures giving glory to God. (Ezek 1–2) Once having established his credentials as distinctly other-worldly, God gets down to practical business, the business of this life and this earth. Ezekiel remembers: "I heard a voice . . . And he said unto me . . . stand upon your feet . . . and he said unto me . . . I send thee . . . to a rebellious nation." (Ezek 1:28—2.3) The overall message of the prophet to the nation is this—to re-establish the institution of prophethood: "Whether they will hear, or whether they will forbear . . . yet shall (they) know that there hath been a prophet among them." (Ezek 2:5) Ezekiel is to exercise this office by interpreting the ancient scripture correctly, and to apply that interpretation to the day at hand. (Ezek 2:8–10)

Jonah, too, is given a civic calling: "Go to Nineveh." (Jonah 1:1–2) Jesus identifies closely enough with this characterization of the prophet's calling that when certain of the people ask him for a sign, he refers them to the successful preaching activity of Jonah, and reminds us that the preaching of repentance, and the receiving of it by the people, is the most portentous event or "sign" that can be orchestrated by God. The implication of this, of course, is that each one of the people whom Jesus addresses holds in their hands the power to actualize that miraculous sign.

The prophet wishes to tie his calling to a definitive point in history so that later generations can have a context in which to study and learn from his message. Isaiah, for example, states "In the year that King Uzziah died, I also saw the Lord." (Isa 6:1) Isaiah's disciple, writing during the Babylonian exile 200 years after his namesake, characterizes God's voice as shrill, pain-wracked: "A voice cries out, proclaim a message ...." (Isa 40:6–8 GNB)

5. Coogan, *Old Testament*, 321–322.

Several prophets provide their audiences with autobiographical accounts of the enormity of the experience of theophany. It is a kind of "swept off your feet" experience which stems from the otherworldliness of the meeting, and also from the scope of the assignment. That assignment, like the one given to Jonah, is to warn one or more nations of the hazard of destruction, and beyond that, to activate a reform or a revolution to try to derail the coming horror.

In the ancient world, God's vocal or spiritual presence inspires shaking, not merely of the knees of the prophet, but also the environment about the prophet. For example: "The posts of the door moved at the voice of him that cried . . ." (Isa 6:4) The passing by of God's presence in New Testament times was recalled by one who attended the crucifixion of Christ: "The earth did quake, and the rocks rent." (Matt 27:51) Also, "The veil of the temple was rent in the midst." (Luke 23:45)

The earthquake-like physical enormity of the theophany is memorable also in a different way. Jeremiah says it is not unlike the social force used in seduction, something subtle, yet something that cannot be averted: "Oh Lord, you have enticed me . . . you have overpowered me." (Jer 20:7 NRSV) Amos describes his theophany in terms that travelers in Egypt and Palestine can understand. His experience was a shaking of one's being of the type one gets when hearing the sound of a nearby lion: "The lion hath roared, who will not fear?" (Amos 3:8) Amos also remembers the calling as a kidnapping: "The Lord took me." (Amos 7:15) Ezekiel felt a pressure to perform in a similar way: "The hand of the Lord was strong upon me." (Ezek 3:14) Second Isaiah gives the sense almost of a soldier asked to repeat the command of a superior officer: "I have put my words in thy mouth." (Isa 51:16) The first Isaiah indeed echoes the same sense: "For the Lord spake thus to me with a strong hand." (Isa 8:11)

Jesus gives almost the sense of one taking dictation: "My doctrine is not mine." (John 7:16) He had not planned for his life to be this way: "I am not come of myself." (John 7:28) It is almost as if God has declared a state of emergency and resorted to extraordinary police powers. Even his disciples have come under the strong hold of God: "No man is able to pluck them out of my Father's hand." (John 10:29)

The prophetic calling is of such a breathtaking scope and requires such ambition that the prophet often expresses his inability to handle it. Moses, for example, protests his disability (Exod 3:11, 4:1, 10), as does Jeremiah, who believes he is too immature. (Jer 1:6) Samuel is not sure that God speaks to man and needs the encouragement of the old high priest to embrace the call. (1 Sam 3:1-10) Others wrestle with the fact they have no professional training in the priesthood or in court politics, no certification for the work, as Amos: "I was no prophet, neither was I a prophet's son; but I was a herdman and a gatherer of sycamore fruit." (Amos 7:14) Could there be a preparation more bereft of reasonable professional liturgical or political training than an orchardist? Jesus questions his own suitability for the full measure of the calling as well: "If it be possible, let this cup pass from me." (Matt 26:39)

Habakkuk confesses, "O Lord, I have heard thy speech, and was afraid . . . " (Hab 3:2) But God encourages Habakkuk that the message, though ridiculed at the present time, will eventually be fruitful: "Write the vision . . . that he may run that readeth it. For the vision is yet for an appointed time, but at the end it shall speak, and not lie: though it tarry wait for it; because it will surely come . . . " (Hab 2:2-3)

The responsibility imposed upon the prophet to speak up is one that weighs heavily upon him. In the first place, God's encouragement to do so is of a high and persuasive order of magnitude: "The Lord shall cause his glorious voice to be heard." (Isa 30:30) God's specific urging is that a normally unnoticed man should become very noisy: "Cry aloud, spare not, lift up thy voice like a trumpet." (Isa 58:1) "The mouth of the Lord hath spoken it . . . The voice said, Cry." (Isa 40:5-6)

But God chooses one who is primed and ready for the task. God has confidence the prophet will be serviceable like a good worker: "Behold my servant . . . I have put my spirit upon him . . . he shall not fail nor be discouraged til he have set judgment in the earth: and the isles shall wait for his law." (Isa 42:1) Here, the purpose of prophecy is to restore good judgment and good laws in all societies of the earth. This is done through the spiritual admonitions of a living God who has delivered a message to a mortal prophet in the present day. The message has a focal point in a prophet and in the nation's capitol, as Zechariah suggests: "Living waters shall go out from Jerusalem." (Zech 14:8) The most important component of the new revelation is to define God as one whose name means he will have a continuing vocal presence among his people: "Therefore my people shall know my name . . . they shall know . . . I am he that doth speak." (Isa 52:6)

Indeed, God's precise message seems to vary according to the righteousness of the people. At one time it may be a prophecy of doom, while at another time a prophecy of great hope and imminent greatness. Thus God can inspire Nahum to rail indefatigably against Assyria for her sins at one point, and at another time inspire Jonah to deliver a message of confidence in and great hope for Nineveh of Assyria. There always seems to be a battle between justice and mercy raging on within him.

In fact, some distancing from professional ranks like that protested by Amos perhaps serves God well, since men of professional and political stature are quick to embrace conventional wisdom of the sort that springs from learning and tradition: "They speak visions of their own minds, not from the mouth of the Lord." (Jer 23:16 NRSV)

Hosea's calling requires of him something perhaps even more terrifying than the society-wide task given Jeremiah and Amos: "When the Lord first spoke . . . he said . . . 'Go and get married.'" (Hos 1:2 GNB) Hosea's call was to position himself in the midst of the social mainstream of the community and to personally experience its difficulties and the rapid decline of its institutions. He was led to believe that as marital faithfulness declines, so does the nation. (Hos 2) He was called to live the drama of family life at a time when there was not much chance of success in it. A hundred years after Hosea, success in marriage and family life had so little chance in Israel that Jeremiah was advised by God to forego the institution altogether. (Jer 16:1–9) The horrific events about to engulf Judea, not to mention the dwindling social supports for the institution, made it too feeble a prospect to merit Jeremiah's serious attention.

Profile—A Metaphor for the King's Son (Isaiah)

The professor sat at the writing table in his Jerusalem library after the devastating siege of Judah by Israel and Syria in 734 BCE. Having some years before heard the voice of God asking him to attend to political and religious polemic against the authorities of the day, he now sensed it was time to chronicle the political events he had just witnessed, but from the point of view of the heavenly king who called him into prophetic ministry. Some years before he had tried to calm Ahaz, the King of Judah, with the prospect that Judah would be safe from destruction without resorting to a league with Assyria and incurring all the cultural and financial indebtedness that brought with it. (Isa 7:3–9; 2 Kgs 16:5–9)

The king and prominent court and religious figures had turned a deaf ear to his contention that God was speaking through him, and that the advice given was solid, based as it was on divine initiative and diligent searching of the history of the Near East. Now the teacher heard an intimation of God's will that it was time to instruct potential disciples rather than the court, and to do so by committing his prophecies in written form for their safekeeping. (Isa 8:16–18)

His order of papyrus from Lake Huleh near Dan had arrived only days before. The quality of the plant leaves, he mused, was not as high as the expensive paper from Egypt, but it would do. He had trained his oldest son She'ar in the process of pressing the leaves together at right angles, gluing the sheets and then copying his father's manuscripts. This task the young man shared with other students in the school.

Now, his younger son Maher interrupted his thought. "Father, can I take the ball outdoors and play in the street?" Isaiah put aside a bowl of lentil and leek pottage he had been sipping at while deep in thought, and with a nod of his head gave permission. The youngster reached for some newly dried raisins mixed with roasted pistachios, gathered from the terebinths in the provinces, and ran outdoors with the ball, made of stuffed and stitched leather. "He is more interested in sport than in politics," smiled the prophet, "but he is young."

Today he would review one more time the lines he earlier had drafted onto several wax-coated writing boards. He would make final changes to the manuscript and then begin to copy the material onto the papyrus sheets. He would use a reed as a pen, a bamboo-like cane with a woody, jointed stem, dipping it in an ink mixed from carbon soot and animal fat. His mind already raced ahead to the ultimate goal. He would provide several copies for his students and set up a course of study concerning the content of the oracles. But he could not refrain from thinking he must also send copies to court officials, select elders and merchants as well. He would then erase the wood tablets by heating and smoothing over the wax, so that they would be ready for a new work.

The lynchpin of his new written prophecy would recall the prediction he had made to Ahaz in a second meeting. If Judah followed the prophet's advice, within a decade the land would revert to the kind of political independence and economic productivity it enjoyed during the period of the Judges. (Isa 7:10–17)

Once again he contemplated the metaphor he had chosen to convey to the King the rejuvenating power the people might exercise in order to return to political independence. He had decided to use a metaphor of infant maturation—the brief, yet substantive period of time from birth to the time of legal accountability for sin and crime. This is a time during which a child takes amazingly rapid steps toward understanding the requirements of society. Israel was effectively such a child once again, since she had lost the social and political maturity she had had during the time of Judges. However, she now had access to a political prophet who had the ability to teach her and model for her the difference between right and wrong, as a father would a child. (Isa 6:10–17)

So now he wrote the sad words for posterity to read, the words of a divine offer shunned: "Behold, a virgin shall conceive, and bear a son, and shall call his name Immanuel . . . For before the child shall know to refuse the evil, and choose the good . . . The Lord shall bring upon thee . . . days . . ."—days, he thought, both ripe and abundant and at the same time full of "briars and thorns." (Isa 7:14–17) He knew that both the king and his own disciples would understand the reference to the current pregnancy of Ahaz's wife. Isaiah himself would have charge of the upbringing of the child and would assure his familiarity with the law of Moses, and with reform policies urgently needed in the kingdom. There was thus still a prospect for a brief period of enlightened independence, but Ahaz's decision for confederacy with Assyria, Isaiah knew, meant that Judah's time as a nation was now severely limited. In any event, he felt certain there would come others after him willing to risk estate and life to call Israel back from dependence upon despots to dependence upon humane law instead.

LOOKING OVER THE SHOULDER: PROPHETS GLORIFY THEIR PREDECESSORS

Once convinced of a duty to serve as messenger for God, a prophet takes great care both to link himself with earlier prophets and to make connections with any other divine who might be prophesying at about the same time in other parts of the realm. He also takes care to predict the coming of others after himself.[6] Virtually all prophets, for example, mention Moses and refer to the foundational story of Israel. Amos recalls or uses parts of David's psalms. Micah, Hosea, and Isaiah prophesy in a contemporaneous cluster of voices and each uses the metaphor of the covenant lawsuit, which portrays God as prosecutor of those who have

---

6. This section is indebted to Coogan, *Old Testament*, particularly chapters 14–21.

neglected the responsibilities incumbent upon them as stipulated in the constitution of the nation.

Joel quotes Micah (Mic 4:3; Joel 3:10), Zechariah quotes Micah. (Zech 3:10; Mic 4:3) Second Zechariah frequently quotes earlier prophets, and especially Amos. Second Isaiah builds upon Isaiah, and Third Isaiah (Isa 56–66) uses Second Isaiah. (Isa 60:3–4, 49:22) Jeremiah uses Hosea's dual metaphor of God as parent and as spouse, (Jer 3:19–20; Hos 2) and Jeremiah also quotes Micah. (Jer 26:18; Mic 3:12) Obadiah and Jeremiah appear to refer to each other, or perhaps both use a common source. (Obad 1–14; Jer 49:7–22)

Ezekiel and Jeremiah refer to one another's sayings and metaphors: the northern and southern kingdoms are like sisters (Ezek 23; Jer 3:8); the prophet is like a watchman (Jer 6:17; Ezek 3:17, 33:7); the prophetic calling has to do with purification and communication. (Jer 1:9, 15:16; Ezek 1:1–3, 12–14, 2:10) Both quote and attack the same popular proverb about victimization by the previous generation.[7] (Jer 31:29; Ezek 18:2) Prophets after Amos adopt the format he first introduces in the Bible—the oracle to the nations.

Jesus makes common cause not only with the most storied prophets before him—Moses and Elijah—but with many others as well. He speaks about and thus honors Jonah (Matt 12:38–41), Isaiah (Matt 8:17, 13:14), and David. (Matt 12:3–4) He quotes or paraphrases Hosea (Hos 8:2; Matt 7:21), Micah (Mic 7:6; Matt 10:35, Mark 13:12), Malachi (Mal 3:1, 4:5, Matt 11:10; Hos 6:6–8, Matt 12:7), Habakkuk (Hab 2:11; Luke 19:40), Daniel (Dan 2:44, Matt 12:28; Dan 7:13, Matt 26:64; Dan 9:27, 11:31, 12:11, Matt 24:15), Joel (Joel 2:2, Matt 24:21), Zechariah (Zech 12:12, Matt 24:30; Zech 13:7, Mark 14:27; Zech 11:16–17, John 10:12), Ezekiel (Ezek 18:7, Matt 25:35), Jeremiah (Jer 7:11, Matt 21:13; Jer 1:7, Matt 10:19; Jer 32:17, Mark 10:27), Quoeleth/Ecclesiastes (Eccl 11:9, Luke 12:19), Isaiah (Isa 29:18, Matt 11:5; Isa 29:13, Matt 15:9; Isa 61:1, Luke 4:18), and Job (Job 31:1, Matt 5:28; Job 1:7, Matt 12:43; Job 22:29, Luke 18:14). He also draws from Psalms. (Ps 82:6, John 10:34; Ps 22:1, Matt 27:46)

Most prophets experience murmurings against their leadership like that against Moses in the wilderness, and in fact most are rejected by large sectors of the population. We have discussed, for example, that the Samaritans rejected the literature of both the major and minor literary prophets in their entirety. Many prophets have confrontations

---

7. Levinson, "You Must Not Add Anything," 31–32.

with mainstream priests or court prophets—for example Amos versus Amaziah (Amos 7:10–17), Micaiah versus Zedekiah (1 Kgs 22), Jeremiah versus Hananiah (Jer 28), and Jesus versus Caiaphas (Matt 26:57–68). This recalls Moses' struggle with Pharaoh and his priests.

The Bible demonstrates clearly the importance of on-going meetings between God and the prophet, even during an individual prophet's lifetime. One epiphany is not enough. The patriarchs each have multiple direct encounters with God. After the "burning bush" encounter with God (Exod 3:1—4.17), Moses returns to Sinai and meets with God a second time. (Exod. 19:1—24:18) Later yet, he has a third major revelation. (Exod 33) The literary prophets each recall a first manifestation with special warmth, but also outline subsequent revelatory prophesies at later times in their ministries. For example, the people ask Jeremiah for a revelation on a specific topic. After preparation and effort, Jeremiah asks and obtains a word from God on the subject. (Jer 42)

Indeed, the Psalmist believes it is possible to have the regular companionship of the spirit of prophecy and experience something like the omnipresence of God:

> Whither shall I go from thy Spirit? Or whither shall I flee from thy presence? If I ascend up into heaven, thou art there: if I make my bed in hell, behold, thou art there. If I take the wings of the morning, and dwell in the uttermost parts of the sea; even there shall thy hand lead me, and thy right hand shall hold me. If I say, Surely the darkness shall cover me, even the night shall be light about me. (Ps. 139:7–11)

It is in these regular visitations and subsequent spiritual reflections that the prophet comes to understand his path and the objectives he must pursue for the remainder of his life.

SUCCESSION AMONG THE SONS

Legitimate prophets like Moses, David and the literary prophets not only announce their own credentials but confidently predict others like themselves to come after their own days are completed. The prototypical reference to such an occurrence is Moses' farewell address prediction: "The Lord thy God will raise up unto thee a Prophet from the midst of thee, of thy brethren, like unto me: unto him ye shall hearken." (Deut 18:15) Aside from Joshua, the first clear stamping from the Mosaic mold, Elijah is also presented as an able successor to Moses.[8] Often a forerunner-type prophetic voice announces the imminent advent of the prophet in question. For example, a "man of God" approaches Eli and announces on behalf of God: "I will raise me up a faithful priest that shall do according to that which is in mine heart and in my mind." (1 Sam 2:35) This presumably refers to the prophetic accession of Samuel himself.[9] David, at the urging of Nathan, revels in a potentially unending line of prophets coming out of his own princely loins. (2 Sam 7:16, 25) John the Baptist announces the advent of one greater than himself. (Matt 3)

Isaiah promises: "There shall come forth a rod out of the stem of Jesse . . . and the Spirit of the Lord shall rest upon him . . ." (Isa 11:1–2) Also, Isaiah predicts another advent of the storm cloud-type "glory" that accompanied Moses and the ark in the wilderness by day, and the "fire" of his presence that accompanied them by night: "Thou shalt be visited of the Lord of Hosts with thunder, . . . with storm and tempest, and the flame of devouring fire." (Isa 29:6) Isaiah foresees the day when "the Spirit be poured upon us from on high . . ." (Isa 32:15) The later Isaiah writes, "My Spirit that is upon thee, and my words which I have put in thy mouth, shall not depart out of thy mouth, nor out of the mouth of thy seed, nor out of the mouth of thy seed's seed, saith the Lord, from henceforth and for ever." (Isa 59:21)

Amos goes so far as to say God will not act at all in the future without announcing his intention through prophets. (Amos 3:7–8) Hosea mentions God's modus operandi is to "multiply visions . . . by the ministry of the prophets." (Hosea 12:10)

Jeremiah, acknowledging the corruption of much of the Davidic lineage of kings, writes: "I will raise unto David a righteous branch . . ." (Jer 23:5) Ezekiel predicts another coming like David: "I will set up one shepherd over them, and he shall feed them, even my servant David." (Ezek 34:23) Zechariah stresses, "In that day . . . living waters shall go out from Jerusalem . . ." (Zech 14:8) Obadiah opines, "Saviors shall come . . ." (Obad 21)

Malachi uses a similar literary convention, and speaks of the return of a powerful voice like one from the past: "I will send you Elijah the prophet." (Mal 4:5) He also suggests God does not operate among the

---

8. Walsh, "Elijah," 463–465.
9. Hildebrandt, "Cessation of Prophecy," 174.

people without using a human leader: "Behold, I will send my messenger, and he shall prepare the way before me." (Mal 3:1)

Joel predicts a time when the voice of prophecy will be like days of yore, when there will be several contemporaneous prophets: "I will pour out my spirit on all flesh . . . Your sons and your daughters shall prophesy." (Joel 2:28) Jeremiah, Ezekiel, Hosea, Malachi, and Joel understand this will be essentially a time of great learning and faith, and thus of the democratization of the Spirit of prophecy. (Jer 31:34, 32:41; Ezek 11:19, 18:31, 34:25–27, 36:26–27, 37:14, 26, 39:29; Hosea 2:18; Joel 2:32)

Daniel speaks of the coming of a powerful prophet, the "son of man," the same term used by God to apply to Ezekiel, and meaning, generally, human being. (Dan 7:13; Ezek 2:1) Jesus uses the "son of man" term for himself as he lives and breathes in mortal life (Matt 26:24), and also apparently to apply to the rising of his power and reputation after his death. (Matt 26:64) He also speaks of a future visitation by a "son of man" much in the same way other prophets predicted the advent of new messiah figures. This will take place in the distant future after "wars, . . . famines, and pestilences, and earthquakes . . ." (Matt 24:3, 6–7, 11) However, many in the meantime will take on the name of "Christ" (Matt 24:5)—that is, the semblance of having been anointed by God—but they will be "false prophets." (Matt 24:11)

Jesus criticizes those who search the scriptures because "in them ye think ye have eternal life," yet they deny his coming as messiah, anointed of God. It is nevertheless those very scriptures which prove that there is to be a revelator like Jesus: "They testify of me." (John 5:39) Biblical prophecy is of little use unless its prognostications come to pass. When people deny Jesus, they deny the predictive capacity and the value of their own scripture. To underscore this point, at the beginning of his ministry he reads from the scroll of Isaiah and announces that what he has just read is fulfilled on the very day of its reading. (Luke 4:21) In a post-Easter appearance, Jesus teaches two of his followers that the scripture from the time of Moses through the time of the last prophets speak of one such as himself to come.[10] (Luke 24:27) By such means and reports, we can assume that the doctrine of ongoing prophecy obtained an even greater currency and credibility after than before Jesus' death.

The existing prophet often blesses others about him with encouragement toward the prophetic gift, which is to be used either in pursuance

---

10. Peters, *Voice*, 155–56.

of the priestly profession or the princely profession. Moses, for example, provides for the sharing of the prophetic spirit with seventy community leaders/elders: "I will take of the spirit which is upon thee, and will put it upon them ...." (Num 11:17) Indeed, a people properly enlightened will not cease in giving prophecy: "When the spirit rested upon them, they prophesied, and did not cease." (Num 11:25) Elijah, as well, establishes a type of prophetic succession by investing Elisha to succeed him (2 Kgs 2:1–15), as David does with Solomon, Samuel with David, and Isaiah, Jeremiah, and Hosea likely with their own followers.

Biographers of the earlier prophets see later prophets as fulfilling the sacred predictions of their forefathers. The Deuteronomistic historian of Israel (the writer or at least the editor of Deuteronomy, Joshua, Judges, Samuel and Kings), for example, took pains to describe Elijah activities in tones which recalled the founder Moses. Each of these two early prophets undertakes a journey eastward to escape a king's wrath. Each lodges with another family. Each returns to challenge the political ruler.[11]

The prophets themselves see that their own lives, or the lives of contemporaries, are anticipated by earlier prophets. The Psalmist believes that "In the volume of the book it is written of me." (Ps 40:7) Zechariah believes the priest Jeshua of his own day is the "branch" spoken of by Isaiah. (Zech 3:1–10) Jesus, for his part, believes he is the one spoken of not only by Moses (John 5:46) but by Isaiah. (Matt 12:15–21; Isa 42:1–4) The gospels demonstrate that Jesus receives semi-public affirmation at the hand of Elijah as well as Moses at the time of the transfiguration. (Matt 17:1–7)

The concept of the coming of a future prophet is invariably associated with the arrival of God's own rule of ethical law, which essentially means God's kingship over Israel. God's resurgence is predicated on the prophet's rising. The prophet's rising is predicated upon God's own action. This paired advent is summarized in a number of places. "Behold the days come . . . that I will raise unto David a righteous Branch, and a King shall reign . . . The Lord Our Righteousness." (Jer 23:5–6) Similarly we find, "And I will set up one shepherd over them . . . even my servant David . . . and I the Lord will be their God, and my servant David a prince among them; I the Lord have spoken it." (Ezek 34:23–24) Again, "Behold I will send my messenger, and he shall prepare the way before

---

11. Walsh, "Elijah," 464–65.

me . . ." (Mal 3:1) Jesus voices a similar sentiment, "I am in the Father, and the Father in me . . ." (John 14:11)

Indeed, while most prophets speak either explicitly or in only slightly veiled fashion about others to come after themselves, none speaks of any conclusion to prophetic revelation. It is a clear concern of the prophets to try to forestall the slipping back of the religious and political culture into the comfortable ideology that God no longer speaks to man. Each one knows it may be some time before another authentic voice surfaces, but each also publishes word that society ought to expect this to happen again.

Predictions about future prophets are linked to instances of the Day of the Lord, when God comes in power and intervenes in history once again. When vivid pronouncements about the future actually do come to pass, a new prophet living in that future judges them fulfilled in the present day. This pronouncement, however, is only half of his job. He has a responsibility to look ever more future-ward to new eras of time, new international and national circumstances which require God's assistance. New prophecy is needed each dawning era in order to demonstrate God's ongoing ability to foretell tectonic events that the old prophets did not have any hint of, about nations and peoples that were not even formed when the earlier prophet wrote. Second Isaiah passes along God's concern about this: "New things do I declare, before they spring forth I tell you of them. (Isa 42:9) Thus, Second Isaiah does not accept the conventional idea of mainstream religion that the old scripture describes in detail all future events. He believes that there is too much history and too much future for one book to contain all of legitimate prophecy. More books are needed, and more prophets to take dictation from God in order to fill them up.

In sum, prophets and historians take care to detail ongoing meetings with God, live model lives, impart some of the same spirit to others about them, and predict yet others who will come in the future. But they also review the long and fruitful history of the prophetic tradition leading up to their own prophesies. The book of Jeremiah records God's reminder: "From the day that your ancestors came out of Egypt I have until this very day kept on sending to you my servants, the prophets." (Jer 7:25 GNB)

Jeremiah underscores the reality and necessity of continuing prophetic leadership by stressing that it is God's primary occupation. For example, he writes: The Lord hath sent unto you all his servants the prophets, rising early and sending them." (Jer 25:4) Here and elsewhere "rising early" suggests that sending prophets is the meat of God's vocation as God. (Jer 26:5, 35:15, 44:4; compare 26:18)

Hosea summarizes the history of Israel's oracular communication with God in similar terms: "And by a prophet the Lord brought Israel out of Egypt, and by a prophet was he preserved." (Hos 12:13) The implication of Hosea's comment is that if Israel is to remain great as a nation, she needs the periodic services of a prophet. In the book of Kings, the historian frequently assumes the prophet-based history of the nation.[12] (2 Kgs 9:7, 17:13, 23; 21:10, 24:2)

Jeremiah goes so far as to say that the goal of a nation such as Israel is not to restrict prophets to a few heroes of the past, but to build the institution and the people to a point where all citizens acknowledge and allow for free prophecy: "I will put my law in their inward parts, and write it in their hearts . . . they shall all know me . . ." (Jer 31:33–34)

The book of Second Chronicles, as well, is particularly notable for its long list of memorable prophets, for most of whom no prophetic literature survives: Ahijah (10:15); Shemiah (11:2); Shemaiah (12:5, 7); Iddo (12:15, 13:22), Azariah (15:1–7); Hanani (16:7–9); Micaiah (18:7); Eliezer (20:37); Jahaziel (20:14, 17); a "man of God" (25:7), "a prophet" (25:15); Oded (28:9–11); Hozai (33:19 NRSV); Huldah (34:22–28); and Jeduthun (35:15). The Chronicler thus gives credibility to the notion of the importance of updated messages from a communicative God to a well favored people. Chronicles, as a book of history, also gives credence to the concept of ongoing revelation by quoting from the literature of the prophets such as Amos, Isaiah, Jeremiah, Zephaniah, Ezekiel and Zechariah.[13]

---

12. Zimmerli, and Jeremias, *Servant*, 22.
13. Albertz, *Israelite Religion*, 550, 657.

3

Universal Voice and Endless Canon

ADAM IN YOUR DNA:
REVELATION IN THE BARBARIAN KINGDOMS

THE TITLE OF THIS chapter, "Universal Voice and Endless Canon," follows the idea suggested by the Chronicalist (2 Chr 16:9) to which we introduced the reader in chapter 1. The Hebrew God goes through the entire earth looking for a suitable vessel through which to proclaim a new message for a society or societies with which the prophet is familiar. God, for example, found Cyrus in Persia and called him his "anointed" messiah. (Isa 45:8) We have established above that God, according to Bible authors, editors, and compilers, is capable of so doing because he is the sovereign creator and ruler of the entire world. (Isa 46:1) We also endeavored to show in chapter 1 that it is the goal of human beings to achieve contact with God through religious organization and worship activities. Therefore, both parties have a solid interest in the oracular revelation that results from God finding a trustworthy messenger.

We have also shown that a prophet initiates a tradition of discipleship while he/she is alive, which then typically thrives once the prophet is gone. Such a community is referred to as the "sons of the prophet" or "a remnant." The prophet hopes the followers will leaven reform in the broader nation or in many nations. We also mentioned there is evidence of prophecy of the Hebraic type in other nations and cultures with which Israel is familiar, such as Egypt. This is often of the type that David's lineage provided for Israel—a race of (hopefully) ethical kings inspired by God to govern a people in independence and prosperity. We also demonstrate in chapter 5 that Israel and other nations make room for prophecy by enacting freedom of worship for a wide variety of sacred traditions.

In this section we will look at evidence in the biblical story and in biblical theology showing that Yahweh found and spoke to aspiring prophets long before the Israelite national tradition was established. We will see that he also found and spoke to prophets in nations surrounding Israel during the time of settlement in Canaan.

We will also review evidence God found and spoke to prophets outside the mainstream Judaic tradition after the Torah was finalized during the Babylonian exile. That manual of spiritual-legal history was intended to serve as the ultimate and final scripture of Judaism for the post-exile community. Clearly, however, the oracular literature of the sixth, seventh, and eighth century prophets was later added to the Torah, as were the historical works produced by the Deuteronomists and Chroniclasts, and the writings of the Psalms and other books of our modern Hebrew and Christian bibles. This begs the question why the Judaic and Christian traditions, or any other religious tradition for that matter, should feel comfortable about their own modern promotions of a doctrine that God's canonical voice has been stilled.

Much sacred literature is generated within nations surrounding Israel, which resembles Israel's canon in elevated style and enduring content. This literature, on the other hand, is available to us in fragmented form. This suggests that while there are ongoing prophetic traditions in these other areas, adherents of those traditions may not have taken as much care to gather the literature of prophets into a recognizable collection as the Jews did with their own prophets.

In sum, in order to establish the existence of God's work in traditions other than Israel, we will look both before the time of Moses, and after the time of Joel and Malachi, when Israel believed its own oracular tradition had ceased, to see what is happening with God's vocal spirit in other cultures of the Levant and of the known earth. We will also look at the period of time of the heyday of Judaic prophecy to see what is going on in both Semitic and non-Semitic cultures of the ancient Near East world then.

Ancient Israel remembered the primordial days of humankind in Mesopotamia. The Bible suggests that, in the beginning, God asserted himself as sovereign of all his created peoples, specifically by playing a providential role in founding the Eurasian and African nations: "When the most high divided to the nations their inheritance . . . when he separated the sons of Adam, he set the bounds of the people." (Deut 32:8)

Also, from the beginning God looked about among his nations, seeking any who would look to him as he looked to them (for conversation). At the time of Enos, Adam's grandson, mankind began in earnest to do such a thing, for "then began men to call upon the name of the Lord." (Gen. 4:26) Another of Adam's early offspring, Enoch, "walked with God" (Gen 5:22), presumably obtaining direct revelation to guide his people. The book of Enoch, likely written during the Hellenic period, is an attempt to honor, and perhaps attempt to intuit the teachings of, this early patriarchal prophet.[1]

Generations later, God spoke to the Mesopotamian prophet Noah and established Noah's lineage as his chosen people throughout the eastern Mediterannean, as the Bible's "Table of Nations" demonstrates. (Gen 10) The descendants of Noah's son Japheth settled to the north of Palestine in Anatolia, or Asia Minor (modern Turkey). The descendents of Noah's son Shem established the Semitic people in Syria, Arabia, and Mesopotamia. The descendants of Noah's son Ham settled in Egypt and elsewhere in Africa. Our discussion below will establish that there is independent, that is extra-biblical, corroboration of a historical prophetic tradition in all three of these sectors of the ancient world.

The story of Noah (Gen 6–9) describes Noah's devotion to oracle-based lifestyle, which devotion then plays out again in the Abrahamic cycle of events and the Mosaic story as well. There are two fundamental themes in the Noachic story of the lineages. There is first a promise of progeny to re-populate the nations of all the earth (Gen 9:1, 7, 19), which is fulfilled in the nations derived from the sons and grandsons of Noah. (Gen 10:1–32) But there is also a commandment or law, given as a standard to be met, in order to effectuate the promise. (Gen 9:8–17)

What results from this early beginning is the long-term outplaying of the promise in a history of alternate blessing and cursing (consequence) depending upon adherence to the law. The first episode of cursing is described in the case of Ham's son Canaan. (Gen 9:25–27) The next is the incident of the tower of Babel, which produces the hardship of exile—"scattering"—but also the opportunity for a new development of free culture in the nations resulting from the scattering. (Gen 11:1–9) The expectation is that God can and will rein in these far-flung nations, if offered the ear of the people: "Say among the heathen that the Lord reigneth; the world also shall be established that it shall not be moved:

---

1. Albertz, *Israelite Religion*, 575.

he shall judge the people righteously." (Ps 96:10) If the nations allow an ethical God to govern, they will not have to scatter ("move") again.

One other important theological statement about God's work in non-Israelite nations can be discerned from the early history in Genesis. The Hebrew word for the first political being, "adam," actually translates "human being" or "humanity" as a whole, rather than to a single individual.[2] Thus the experience of Adam is meant to be generalizable to human beings all throughout the earth, just as the later experience of Noah was meant to be. In deed, rabbinic literature indicates that God intended to have a relationship with all people,[3] since he created all in his image.[4] Adam's pre-fall body was said to have contained the seed of all subsequent descendants of the earth.[5]

God's affinity for all the nations is enhanced theologically by the fact he is one God. Israel eschews the notion of a plurality of gods[6] and holds instead to the high god tradition of those nations who place faith in a single national or tutelary god, whose powers either transcend those other gods who are worshipped as ancillary to the one high god (monolatry), or whose program replaces them altogether (monotheism). Israel's high God, like creator gods in Mesopotamia and Egypt, and like the oracular storm gods in Syria, Phoenicia, and Philistia, is thus defined by his creative affinity with human beings and by his willingness to communicate with them. Having created all the earth and all of human kind, this God takes more than a little interest in all the phases of the earth's history. All of history is attributable to him, for better or for worse: "I form the light, and create darkness: I make peace, and create evil: I the Lord do all these things." (Isa 45:7) As we will see in chapter 7, God has the same kind of interest in the fate of nations that a good prince has in the success of his kingdom, and a good father has in the happiness and prosperity of his family.

The fact that ancient Near East history warrants that communities in various places worshiped a high or favored god, and used a bewildering variety of different names to identify such a God, certainly adds credibility to the Bible assertion of the universality of oracular revelation in the

2. Taylor, "Unity," 747; Sib Or 3:24–26; 2 Enoch 30:13–15.
3. Sipre Deut Art 31.
4. Abot 3.18; b. Nid 31a.
5. Exod Rab 40:3.
6. It is often held that true monotheism did not pervade Israel's consciousness fully until the writings of Second Isaiah, but we do not enter that debate here.

known world at the time. Definition of a particular god's character, after all, came by means of a founder's claim of communication with such a one. The Bible itself adds credence to the idea that humankind accepted god-names from other cultures as reflecting the one high God of all the earth. Balaam, a Bible-recognized prophet from Syria, divined presumably either by Haddad or Rimmon, the gods of Syria, by Chemosh, the god of Moab, or by a generic name for God, such as El.[7] Jonah, too, presented his Yahwistic message utilizing a generic name for God, so as to emphasize God's universal domain. (Jonah 1:9) King Mesha of Moab believes the God Chemosh of Moab is angry with his people and that they suffer oppression as a result. This echoes the Israelite idea that God accepts involvement in, or responsibility for, all that happens to a free-willed people.[8] Joseph received revelation for the nation of Egypt (Gen 41:25) and Daniel for Babylon. (Dan 2:47) The One God is properly the God of both those nations, though the people of Egypt know him as Amun and the people of Babylon know him as Marduk.

It is clear from the Old Testament itself that similar social, economic, and political programs coming from gods with different names can be equated with the same God. For example, Moses' God was known as Yahweh, but the God of the ancestors in Canaan some 600 years before was El-Shaddai, and God told Moses these were one and the same God. (Gen 17:1; Exod 6:2–4) Also, about the time the Jews had fully forgotten the details of the heritage which Yahweh bestowed upon them 600 years before, and went into abject captivity in Babylon in 587 BCE, that heritage was encouraged by virtue of the high god traditions of Marduk and Ahura Mazda, born in the Babylonian plain and the Iranian hinterlands respectively. God spoke inside and outside Israel, and both Israel and the entire world benefited. The doctrine of Second Isaiah is very explicit about the existence of only one high ethical God in the world. All of political history is appropriately attributable to this god, no matter what his name.

It is true that the Bible considers Israel to be a particularly favored nation, one chosen or elected by God to serve in a sort of missionary capacity to the other nations of the earth, at least for periods of time in its history. (Gen 12:3; Deut 4:5–6; 1 Kgs 8:41–44; Isa 2:2–4, 42:6–7; 49:6) At other times, nations outside Israel set an example for Israel to follow and tutor the children of light in the ways of civic and spiritual rectitude. (Isa 56:1–8)

7. Zevit, *Religions*, 684.
8. Coogan, *Old Testament*, 293.

The Bible focuses on just one of the many offspring of Shem (Gen 11:10–30), as we will see in the following subsection. Abram and his wife Sarai have an important story, and their lives become an example of the prophetic story presumably unfolding elsewhere as well. We will see below that some of that story actually is available in the literature of Egypt and Mesopotamia, among others.

Prophetic pronouncements of the harsh judgment type, mirroring those of prophets like Jeremiah, can be found in Egypt during a period earlier than that of Abraham. One example is "The Admonitions of Ipu-wer."[9] The Prophecy of Neferti, also, speaks of a prophet who foretold the downfall of the Old Egyptian Kingdom.[10] The so-called "Uruk prophecy" from about 1850 BCE in Akkadia (Northern Mesopotamia) presents a message from the goddess Ishtar predicting the rising of a great political leader. The prophecy reads:

> A king will rise in Uruk who will judge the judgment of the land, give the right decisions for the land … he will rebuild the temples of Uruk and restore the sanctuaries of the gods. He will renew Uruk . . . . After him his son will arise and become master over the world. He will exercise rule and kingship in Uruk and his dynasty will be established forever. The kings of Uruk will exercise sovereignty like the gods."[11]

Here the greatness of a king derives from his ability to restore religious plurality in the land.

MELCHIZEDEK ON THE MANTLE: PROPHECY ON THE BORDERS OF ISRAEL

It can be observed that the Bible places Abraham in an oracular milieu, from his beginnings in Mesopotamia, through his wanderings in Canaan and Egypt, and in his own right as progenitor of several generations of oracular prophets. The Sumeria of Abraham's upbringing is notable for a famous early Mesopotamian prophet-prince by the name of Gilgamesh, who joins the gods after his death.[12] The Gilgamesh epic was written

---

9. "The Admonitions of Ipu-wer," ANET, 441.
10. "The Prophecy of Neferti," ANET, 444.
11. Quoted in Weinfeld, *Social Justice*, 58.
12. Bauer, *History*, 64.

down for the first time at or not long before the time of Abraham, though other parts of the story were likely added much later.[13]

Also, two Mesopotamian creation stories, dealing with sacred matters of early interactions between God and man similar to that presented in Genesis—Enuma Elish and Atrahasis—were available to Abraham before his migration to Haran and Canaan.[14] These two accounts of primordial mankind speak of a heavenly council of a type referred to in Job, Psalms, and Jeremiah. (Job 1:6; Ps 82:1; Jer 23:18) One of the functions of this council, in both biblical and extra-biblical tradition, is to send representatives to earth to accomplish providential goals, or to deliver messages to tempt or to educate human beings.

Abraham also is exposed to the Sumerian and Chaldean reform traditions which subject kings to the rule of law and a tradition of proclamations of freedom at the time of coronation, which we review in chapter 5.

Once Abraham settles in Canaan, he has encounters with ethical kings who recognize and respect the institution of prophecy. Abraham finds safe haven in the Canaanite cultural tradition of Melchizedek, under whose priestly and perhaps political jurisdiction he and his retinue apparently fall. (Gen 14:17–20) Melchizedek resides at Salem, whose politico-cultural tradition is hospitable not only to Abraham but also to David many hundreds of years later. Abimelech, the Canaanite King of Gerar, recognizes the institution of prophecy. The Bible recalls his statement: "For he [Abraham] is a prophet." (Gen 20:7) Abimelech knew prophecy because his native Canaan had a contemporaneous prophetic tradition itself, likely the savior-king variety, which Melchizedek seems to have represented at that time.

During the time Abraham's offspring settled in Egypt, having left Canaan due to famine, prophecy showed up back home in the fifteenth century along the northern coast of Canaan at Taanach, by Megiddo.[15] Some time later, after the Israelites have left Egypt and entered Canaan, prophecy is in evidence in Byblos of Phoenicia as well.[16] Ezekiel speaks of Tyre of Phoenicia as God's elect nation in an (undated) earlier period of time: "Thou (Tyre) has been in Eden the garden of God . . . and I have

13. Ibid., 71–72.
14. Hamilton, *Pentateuch*, 34–39.
15. "Akkadian Letters," ANET, 490.
16. Albertz, *Israelite Religion*, 315.

set thee so: thou wast upon the holy mountain of God . . . Thou was perfect in thy ways from the day that thou wast created, till iniquity was found in thee." (Ezek 28:13–15)

In the time of Moses, we see another dispensation of humane law, and a story of liberation, promise, land and prosperity much like that associated with Abraham, only now connected to the oracular event at Sinai. Jethro serves as a prophet-level adviser to Moses. In fact, although Jethro is a priest from a foreign land, he conducts Israel's first sacrificial worship after becoming a new nation. (Exod 18:12) He is comfortable with a God of prophecy and the new nation is comfortable with his credentials as well. There is no indication he is a convert to Yahweh, and he does not travel on with the wandering nation.

The phenomenon of prophecy is known outside Israel at this time as well. During the time that the tribes are living in the wilderness on the lam, they run into another branch of the Semitic prophet tradition. The text of the book of Numbers recalls an incident involving a Syro-Mesopotamian prophet by the name of Balaam. Balaam sees positive connections between traditions he is familiar with and the new tradition formed by Moses in the wilderness, which desires to function "alone" among the nations. (Num 23:9) He does not contest either their right or their ability to obtain divine revelation for their own nation. Interestingly, independent attestation of the existence of an early Iron Age prophet named Balaam has been found at the site of Deir Alla (Succoth), east of Jordan.[17]

Once Israel crosses Jordan, they enter a land which archeological digs demonstrate had active temple traditions through which local belief communities solicited the presence and voice of God. Temple or cult complex sites are found before the time of the first Jerusalem Temple at Ai, Megiddo, Hazor, Ebal, and Lacish. These sites may reflect ongoing pre-national religious traditions or syncretistic worship, perhaps involving both Israelite and non-Israelite groups or traditions.[18]

MANY EXODUSES

The Bible statements we have relied upon above, together with the testimonies of certain of the literary prophets following below, establish a doctrine of national election somewhat different from that which is

---

17. Zevit, *Religions*, 371.
18. Ibid., 652–53.

usually touted. If the old people and the old religion are too flaccid or too diseased to tone up to God's requirements, or if the old religion, the old rituals, the old prophecies, and the old covenant with the old chosen people somehow lose their meaning and the people no longer wish to live the way of local ethical self-determination, God will establish a new covenant with a new people using new rituals and new prophecies. God will look for other nations, perhaps ones far away from the old chosen people and of a far different culture. He will look for a new prophet, a new body of believers, a new testament. When he finds a willing one, he adds yet another voice, another vote, to the book of those who would elect God as their exemplar, as their king, as their leader.

Amos points to two other Exodus-type experiences Israelites are familiar with, which seemed in his day to overshadow even that of Israel's own deliverance from Egypt: the exodus of the Philistines from Caphtor (Crete), and the exodus of the Syrians from Kir. Amos writes, "Did I not bring Israel up from the land of Egypt, and the Philistines from Caphtor and the Syrians from Kir?" (Amos 9:7 NRSV) At times the Bible argues the theory of Israel's special election among the nations. (Exod 19:4–5; Deut 12:5–7, 14; Deut 4:5–8; 2 Sam 7:10–16) On the other hand, Amos here argues that Israel does not have an exclusive claim on the God of freedom, that there are, and always have been, many people and nations favored by Yahweh.

Amos' understanding of the prophetic tradition in Syria is corroborated by the discovery of a prophetic text at Hamath, from around the same time he is writing in the eighth century.[19] Amos apparently understood from his own contemporary sources what moderns have learned about the Philistine migration from the island of Crete.[20] Thucydides and Herodotus speak of the massive Dorian push into Mycenaea in the twelfth century. This apparently violent in-migration from the north, coupled with famine and pestilence, precipitated a migration of Mycenaeans from the Greek peninsula and from Crete southward by sea toward Egypt and Canaan in the twelfth century.[21] Amos uses the salvific verb "bring up" to argue that this migration was motivated by oppression and was assisted by Yahweh.[22]

19. Albertz, *Israelite Religion*, 315.
20. Hess, "Caphtor," 870; other students believe the island of Cyprus is a reasonable choice as well.
21. Bauer, *History*, 281–284.
22. Brueggemann, *Texts*, 94.

Amos also mentions the Ethiopians as highly favored by God: "Are ye not as children of the Ethiopians unto me, O children of Israel?" (Amos 9:7) Isaiah, as well, predicts a day of coming oracular connection between the Ethiopians and the God of the Hebrews: "A time is coming when the Lord Almighty will receive offerings from this land . . . this strong and powerful nation . . . who are feared all over the world." (Isa 18:7 GNB)

It is apparent then, that at moments of vulnerability, Israel felt very small and her history very short in comparison with that of the nations roundabout. It did not help that Israel was constantly reminded that God would be forced to abandon her if she neglected the covenant of freedom and grace accepted by her ancestors. Jeremiah, for example, speaks of the coming day of a "new covenant" between God and the people of Israel, though in a different day and perhaps place than in Jerusalem. (Jer 31:31–34)

Ezekiel mentions three heroes of fabled righteousness, true prophet-heroes known throughout all of Israel, none of which, however, are actually Israelite: "The word of the Lord came again to me, saying . . . when the land sinneth against me . . . though these three men, Noah, Daniel, and Job, were in it, they should deliver but their own souls by their righteousness . . . " (Ezek 14:12–14) The Daniel mentioned here is not the Daniel in Nebuchanezzar's court, but another ancient Daniel (or Danel), who is a Phoenician ethical hero pre-dating Moses and mentioned in the annals of Ugarit. Job is from Edom, and Noah from Mesopotamia.[23] These prophets clearly are proto-typical for Israel, and all three demonstrate God's independent prophetic work in other nations.

But many, or most, nations in and around Canaan clearly have slipped into in-hospitability with respect to the God of civic freedom. When Israel enters Canaan after forty years in the wilderness, it is with the understanding that she must vanquish, or pacify by civic conversion, the seven evil peoples resident there whose cultures would quickly and easily subvert the new civic values of Israel if subsumed into the confederacy of ethical tribes. (Deut 7:1–5)

Also, during the time of Kings, Yahweh is clearly displeased with the high god traditions of six nations ringing Israel, nations whose connection to the oracular God of Noah and Abraham ought to have positioned their contemporary cultures a good deal better than it apparently has.

---

23. Coogan, *Old Testament*, 537.

Amos' oracles against these six nations—Damascus, Gaza, Tyre, Edom, Ammon, and Moab—indicates they treated neighboring communities with haughty disdain and ignorant violence. (Amos 1-2)

The major and minor prophets contribute to the Bible theology of universalism by pronouncing such "oracles against the nations." These oracles, common from Amos onward, indicate that surrounding nations have a sufficient foundation of knowledge of God and commandments to warrant judgments against them when they slide into licentiousness and political ignorance. The prophets are cognizant of international ethics and politics, and assume that the struggles of other peoples are the same as their own.

The standard for relations between God and other nations is recalled in Psalm 96: "The world also shall be established that it shall not be moved; he (God and rulers) shall judge the people righteously." (Ps 96:10) Also: "O let the nations be glad and sing for joy: for thou shalt judge the people righteously, and govern the nations upon earth." (Ps 67:4) But the great powers to the east and north of Israel—Assyria, Babylon, and Persia—ultimately make a colonial client out of her, the first two falling far short of God's expectation for them. Assyria and Babylon are positioned by the literary prophets of Israel as instruments of God's sovereign power to humble Israel. (Isa 10:5; Jer 25:9, 27:6, 40:9, 42:11-12) Unfortunately, they go well beyond his calling to them and commit unnecessary cruelties and atrocities, which result from their own swelled national egos. (Isa 10:5-15; Isaiah 36-37; Jer 6:23, Jer 50-51) Only Persia, whose King is explicitly called by Yahweh, carries out its responsibilities in a reasonable manner. (Isa 45:1-7; Ezra; Neh)

But even evil Egypt and outrageously cruel Assyria will one day take up the banner of the God of gentle freedom: "In that day shall Israel be the third with Egypt and with Assyria, even a blessing in the midst of the land: whom the Lord of hosts shall bless, saying, Blessed be Egypt my people, and Assyria the work of my hands, and Israel mine inheritance." (Isa 19:24-25) Even beyond this, "He shall judge among the nations, and shall rebuke many people (by means of prophets) . . . and . . . nations shall not lift up sword against nation . . . " (Isa 2:4) The Psalms celebrate a similar expectation: "All the nations you have made shall come and bow down before you, O Lord, and shall glorify your name." (Ps 86:9) The psalmist prays on behalf of all nations who know Yahweh. In the following, the poet lumps Israel with all the nations and uses the universal "us" to situate God in an autonomous relationship with all nations: "God be merciful unto us, and bless us . . . that thy way may be known upon earth, thy saving health among all nations." (Ps 67:1)

If many of the nations still lack politico-spiritual sophistication, God is capable of remedying that by removing the distance between himself and the people: "He will destroy in this mountain the face of the covering cast over all people, and the veil that is spread over all nations . . . And the Lord God will wipe away tears from off all faces . . . " (Isa 25:7–8) God, having created the world, feels a responsibility to bring it to full fruition by means of prophetic leadership: "For thus saith the Lord that created the heavens . . . he created it not in vain, he formed it to be inhabited . . . I have not spoken in secret . . . I the Lord speak righteousness, I declare things that are right." (Isa 45:18–19) The prophet indicates God calls strange nations to him and would speak to them: "Incline your ear, and come unto me: hear, and your soul shall live . . . Behold, thou shalt call a nation that thou knowest not, and nations that knew not thee shall run unto thee . . . " (Isa 55:3–5) Zechariah summarizes, "Many nations shall be joined to the Lord in that day, and shall be my people . . . " (Zech 2:11)

That man should be afforded religious liberty, the main message and purpose of prophecy, is touted outside of Israel as we will see in chapter 5 ("Knock on the King's Door"). One sure means by which God will rule the nations is through the type of covenant made first with Adam, and then with Noah, Abraham, Moses, and David: a covenant for the rule of humane law that is summarized by the Decalogue. Laws approximating those of the Decalogue can be seen in the codes of republican Greece, in ancient Sumeria and Akkad, in the ancient Laws of Manu in India and in the writings of later Indian reformers such as Mahavira and Buddha, and as far away as China, where Confucius promoted them and noted that they characterized the ethics of Chinese prophet-rulers long before his own time. Rome's Cicero spoke of the existence of an international law of humane conduct between and among the peoples of nations. Israel's own tradition indicates that the readers of the Bible should not be surprised to find the freedom-oriented Decalogue tradition broadly distributed across the ancient world: "For this commandment which I command thee this day, it is not hidden from thee, neither is it far off . . . But the word is very nigh unto thee, in thy mouth, and in thy heart, that thou mayest do it." (Deut 30:11)

To assure its readers that God has exalted foreign nations and individuals in Israel's own time, the book of Ruth explains how the gentle and humane spirit of a foreigner is an example to all of Israel, and how the seed of a Moabitess generates the life and lineage of one of Israel's greatest prophets, King David. Also, while Jonah's mission to Assyria demonstrates that at least one of its cities, Nineveh, is capable of real repentance, Jerusalem herself is not capable of so great a return to God and she is ultimately destroyed.

The Bible itself suggests confluence with the broader ancient Near East history by setting many important stories in nations outside of the Promised Land. Indeed, Israelite prophets can function as well in courts of foreign kings as in their own, as the stories of Joseph in Egypt and Daniel in Babylon indicate. In both those nations God speaks to the leaders of foreign people in dreams, and the Israelite prophets serve merely to interpret the dreams. Both kings have little difficulty understanding the genuineness of the prophetic dissertations. (Gen 41, Dan 2)

Joseph is intimately involved in the culture, government, and religion of Egypt. He serves as a prophet not of Israel, but in fact of Egypt, as is suggested by the mention of his divining cup. (Gen 44:1–5) The prophet Isaiah predicts that a great "savior" will come to Egypt and turn Egypt to the god of Israel. (Isa 19:19–22) It is this prophesy that Onias IV referred to when building his new temple in Egypt. (see chapter 4)

We have advanced the argument that God speaks to man well beyond the closing of the canon of a particular denominational tradition. In summary terms, we point out that after the early canons of the south and north (J and E) were published, still other versions of the Hebrew ancestral story were formulated, and eventually four or more of them were incorporated into the Pentateuch we know today, just as four versions of the gospel were later incorporated into the New Testament. The Judaic canon was enlarged with the addition of the literature and history of the prophets later on, and still later by the addition of the "writings" such as Psalms and other books. This scripture was closed at about the time the Christian story was being written. After the Christian canon was closed, the Islamic canon came into being. Indeed, fresh prophetic voices have come inside each of these monotheist traditions well after each of the canons were closed, claiming to re-establish original principles and disputing the notion that God's voice is stilled. So we see, then, that western monotheist revelation has a vertical history within its own foundational and interpretive culture, as well as a horizontal history across a number of nations and denominations contemporaneous in time.

While churchly denominations and political factions foreign to one another shun each other's national revelations, there is every indication throughout the Bible text, on the other hand, that God glories in nations who compile their own sacred literature apart from Israelite scripture, particularly when they are better ethically than Israel in her regular periods of decline. Malachi contrasts lurid sacrifices Israel makes to him with those made by other nations: "I have no pleasure in you . . . neither will I accept an offering at your hand. For from the rising of the sun to its setting my name is great among the nations, and in every place incense is offered to my name, and a pure offering; for my name is great among nations, says the Lord of hosts." (Mal 1:10–11)

Finally, God certainly spoke to Israel in Babylon, well outside the traditional temple dwelling place of Yahweh in Jerusalem, and that new revelation soundly rejected the Zion theology notion that God only speaks through priests in Jerusalem. Ezekiel and Second Isaiah published profound meditations that have convinced many of the sophistication of the revelations they received from God there.

Ezekiel, known to have been influenced by Jeremiah's prophesies, seems to have self-consciously endeavored to fulfill Jeremiah's prediction of a new elect people by authoring a new covenant—a new political constitution for Israel—during his stay in Babylon. (Ezek 40–48) Ezekiel also added his voice to that of the universalism expressed in Deuteronomy 32 by publishing a parable of the history of God's workings in the nations. He likens God to a lioness who periodically sends out her young whelps to obtain food. (see also Amos 3:8 and Hos 11:1) She raises her first cub and teaches him to hunt, but in time he becomes a man-eater and is caught in a pit and is carried off to Egypt. She then raises another of her cubs to be a fierce hunter—independent, able to take care of himself. Once grown, he prowls with other adult lions but then terrifies the inhabitants of the surrounding areas. The people catch him and carry him off to Babylon. (Ezek 19:1–9) The reference to rogue lions is an unmistakable judgment on prophet-led democratic nations like Israel which turn violent and imperialistic, and inevitably end up in captivity and in chains. Ezekiel's judgment on Israelite history is that the prophet-initiated generations of Abraham and of Moses eventually lose their civility and suffer for it by exile in Egypt and in Babylon.

The parable can be interpreted as applying either broadly or narrowly, anciently or recently (in Old Testament terms). In the narrow and contemporary reading, the first whelp sent out is King Josiah's son Jehoahaz II, who replaces him after his death.[24] This son was quickly exiled to Egypt. (2 Kgs 23–24) Josiah's next son, Jehoiakim, replaces Jehoahaz II, but is ultimately exiled to Babylon. The broad reading allows that the prophet Jacob, whose sons terrorized Canaan, ultimately is re-settled in Egypt, where the outfall of the experience is not good. The second whelp is prophet-inspired Israel re-constituted by Moses in Canaan—ultimately carried off into captivity in Babylon, "so that his voice should no more be heard upon the mountains of Israel." (Ezek 19:9)

Ezekiel interprets his own parable as a lament for the "princes of Israel" (Ezek 19:1) and the desolation of God's chosen people. The implication of the parable is that after each prophet is sent to build an ethical kingdom, the people go astray and begin to terrorize their neighbors rather than act civilly toward them. The moral of the story is that young lions (princes who are prophet prospects) will be captured and carried away if they are not ethical. The good news is that the mother lion (God) seems to be capable of generating more whelps to send out of her den in her effort to feed her children. She may, however, need to relocate her den before this happens, just as God may need to seek out a new place of security for his message. The implication of the parable also is that once a people give up their prophetic moorings, they seem unable to fully recover. When Israel returns from captivity to Judea, the people must settle for Ezra's Persian-blessed re-coloration of the laws of Moses, suitable for private culture and worship, rather than Ezekiel's broad-based civic constitution for an enlightened new independent nation.

Ezekiel justifies the need for an entirely new civic and priestly dispensation in a nation in the far distant future (under the leadership of a new prophet) by likening the existing situation in Israel to an old vine.

> And the word of the Lord came unto me, saying, Son of man, what is the vine tree more than any tree, or than a branch which is among the trees of the forest? . . . Behold, it is cast into the fire for fuel . . . Behold, when it was whole, it was meet for no work: how much less shall it be meet yet for any work, when the fire hath devoured it, and it is burned? Therefore thus saith the

---

24. Anderson, *Old Testament*, 604.

Lord God: As the vine tree among the trees of the forest, which I have given to the fire for fuel, so will I give the inhabitants of Jerusalem. And I will set my face against them . . . and I will make the land desolate. (Ezek 15:1–8)

For Ezekiel, the vine (Israel) is not inherently greater than any other tree (nation) in the forest. No genetic constitutive factor assures it a greater glory, beauty, and fruitfulness than any other. In fact, Ezekiel disgustedly says of the vine: "Shall wood be taken thereof to do any work? Or will men take a pin of it to hang any vessel thereon?" (Ezek 15:3) Its utility as wood is actually less than that of other trees. Nevertheless, God is capable of renewing the forest of Israel once again: "A new Spirit will I put in you." (Ezek 36:26)

APOSTASY BEGS FOR A WORD (OF EXPLANATION)

The Lord blesses all the nations of the earth where freedom and independence is established according to his laws: "Bless the Lord in all places of his dominion." (Ps 103:22) Isaiah stresses that God will find other prophets in nations other than Israel, who will remove ignorance and re-institute the commandments: "He will destroy . . . the veil that is spread over all nations." (Isa 25:7)

Israel was chosen in the same way that God selected his chosen people from the time of Enoch and Noah. Hosea earlier used the same metaphor that Ezekiel used concerning the grape vine. He relates, "I found Israel like grapes in the wilderness; I saw your fathers as the first ripe in the fig tree at her first time." (Hos 9:10) Of all the descendants of Noah, the patriarch Jacob, whose name was changed to Israel, ripened to a point of sweetness in God's mouth before any other. Therefore, Isaac gave him a blessing above that of his brother Esau, a blessing that predicted ascendency among nations. (Gen 27:27–30) Later, then, God stated: "Israel is my son, even my firstborn." (Exod 4:22) Egypt, previously firstborn in terms of her cultural greatness, passed the torch to Israel at the time of the great democratic revolution led by Moses.

The purpose of the firstborn is to establish a fruitful, lasting legacy in terms of the peace, independence and happiness of his people: "But the Lord hath taken you, and brought you forth out of the iron furnace, even out of Egypt, to be unto him a people of inheritance, as ye are this day." (Deut 4:20) God, like human fathers, gives a double portion of his blessing, his inheritance, to the firstborn, the one who is oldest and wisest, the most experienced, the one who provides the most significant labor on the father's enterprises.

But the Bible narrators indicate that God can and will withdraw his blessing from his firstborn if and when another child is found to be worthier. Thus he took away the firstborn portion from the older Manasseh and gave it to the younger Ephraim, foreseeing that Ephraim's descendants would be a greater nation than Manasseh's. (Gen 48:19)

During the time in Egypt, the people neglected the Abrahamic covenant commandments and embraced the gods of Egypt. (Exod 32:4) God wondered if he could maintain a presence among the people of Israel. Moses' willingness to be God's messenger answered that question in the affirmative. Moses happily was able to establish a nation under God as a result.

Writers in the Israelite tradition establish that apostasy in Israel begins long before the time of the Babylonian captivity. It begins, in fact, even at Mt. Horeb at the time the nation is first established, by means of the golden calf incident. That initial apostasy forestalls Israel's entry into Canaan by forty years. Once in Canaan, after the death of Joshua, the people immediately turn to idolatry. (Judg 2:11–13) During the period of Judges, religion-inspired cultural renewals help Israel regain some lost ground. In time, God looks to David to be an intercessor. "David thy servant" (2 Chr 6:42) defended the commandments, the notion of continuing revelation, and the idea that God can establish an entirely new political and ecclesiastic order outside the stale, traditional, institutional order.

But such a new order is not guaranteed perpetuity by any means. God does not dwell exclusively with one chosen people and one chosen prophet: "I the Lord thy God am a jealous God, visiting the iniquity of the fathers upon . . . them . . . that hate me, and showing mercy unto the thousands of them that love me and keep my commandments." (Deut 5:9–10) God becomes "jealous" when his chosen people look toward any other ethical system than the one set up in God's commandments: "They have moved me to jealousy with that which is not God . . . They have provoked me to anger with their vanities: and I will move them to jealousy with those which are not a people . . . I will spend mine arrows upon them. They shall be burnt with hunger, and devoured with burning heat, and with bitter destruction." (Deut 32:21, 23–24)

In other words, God will return the jealousy they caused him by throwing his support to a culture which is deemed not to be "a [chosen] people." When God reaches a point of no return, when the final warning of his watchmen goes unheeded, he will leave his faithless people and look for another, perhaps poor and unfortunate and not nearly so prosperous and proud as his fallen people. Hannah, mother of Samuel, praised God for this quality: "He raiseth up the poor out of the dust, and lifteth up the beggar from the dunghill, to set them among princes, and to make them inherit the throne of glory: for the pillars of the earth are the Lord's, and he hath set the world upon them." (1 Sam 2:8)

When a prophet prophesies, he does so for the instruction of all the people of the earth, not just for those who happen to be God's favored people at the moment. Thus David can write, "This shall be written for the generations to come, and the people which shall be created." (Ps 102:18) Here, generations seems to refer to new chosen peoples, those in the spiritual lineage of God and prophet, though not necessarily the physical or cultural lineage of the Judaic people, or even the Christian. In the future, new peoples of God will be created when the old are tired of God and forsake his ways. David's temple minister Asap compared Israel to "a vine out of Egypt; thou has . . . planted it . . . didst cause it to take deep root, and it filled the land." (Ps 80:8–9) God's work through David and his retinue caused the vine to flourish again. A psalm attributed to David also saw that God would eventually leave the vine unprotected if they left the covenant neglected: "Why hast thou then broken down her hedges, so that all they which pass by the way do pluck her?" (Ps 80:12) In time, the Lord's servants will no longer be from the house of Israel; but instead, "The Lord God shall call his servants by another name." (Isa 65:15)

4

Cessation of Prophecy

IT IS STRANGE INDEED that the cultural tradition which perhaps, more than any other, remembers and extols spirit- and wisdom-based oracular revelation in its sacred literature, should ultimately forbid the recurrence of any further such revelation and literature. But that is exactly what the scions of the Judaic and Christian religions have done. That old light religion should be forever opposed to new light religion explains better than anything else the politicized nature of religion as an institution. It demonstrates the place that mainstream religion occupies as one of the fundamental institutions of power of any society.

Both those great traditions certainly developed sophisticated end-of-prophecy doctrines after they canonized their books of scripture. Indeed, there are indications of similar, earlier reactionary processes and persecutions against new voices before the final canon nails were driven into the coffins of Judaism and Christianity. These early "no new voices" movements were excoriated by some of the same prophets whose works were ultimately included in the sacred books. This chapter examines the rationales that were used, then and now, to justify exclusion from the scripture and marginalization of new messengers.

DESTROY HIM BEFORE HE AFFECTS THE REVENUE STREAM: THE AWFUL TALE OF BIBLICAL CESSATIONISM

It should not be forgotten that jealousies arose between primordial/patriarchal figures understood to be prophets and political rivals inside or outside their families or retinues. Abel was newly accepted of God (Gen 4:4) and then killed by his brother Cain.[1] Noah alone heard and respected God's voice in his day (Gen 7:1), while others at that time rebelled

---

1. Jesus considered Abel a prophet. See Luke 11:49–41.

"before God," repudiating his essential character. (Gen 6:11) Abraham, known in Canaan as a prophet (Gen 20:7), experienced economic and, likely, religious strife between his retinue and that of Lot, his kinsman, such that the parties had to separate. (Gen 13) Ishmael "mocked" (Gen 21:9), or persecuted, the enlightened young Isaac, who was "born after the Spirit." (Gal 4:28–29) Esau "hated Jacob" when their father Isaac announced that Jacob would receive from God "the dew of heaven" (Gen 27:28)—that is, the utterance of God to a prophet. (Deut 32:1–2) Jacob's son Joseph, touting his own new revelation (Gen 37:5), was disparaged and eventually deported by his own brothers. (Gen 37:25–28)

Later, Moses' claim of providential leadership by the "mighty hand" of God was disputed by Pharaoh (Exod 3:18–19)[2] and denigrated by Miriam and Aaron (Num 12), Korah (Num 16:1–3), and Dathan and Abiram. (Num 16:12–14) Amos, Isaiah, Micah, and Jeremiah each worked in environments adverse to new revelation. (Amos 2:12; Isa 30:10; Mic 2:6; Jer 11:21) Shemaiah called on the high priest to prosecute new light prophets like Jeremiah: "It is your duty to see that every madman who pretends to be a prophet is placed in chains with an iron collar around his neck. Why haven't you done this to Jeremiah of Anathoth? . . . (Jer 29:26–27 GNB) The Spirit told Ezekiel: "They shall put bands upon thee." (Ezek 3:25) After all, an early "epic tradition" of Israel, a precursor of the unified Pentateuch, had already been passed along in variant written form in the north and south, and the people, edified by that astonishing revelation, had no need for further intelligence from God.[3] The later unified tradition came to be viewed as the Five Books of Moses, and, for some groupings of Israelites, all revelation coming after it was classed as mere interpretational venture aimed at clarifying the immutable law. Moses, in this view, was a super-prophet, one who operated on a plane above all others. If there ever was "one like Moses," it perhaps was Elijah, viewed by some segments of the population as the last true prophet of Israel. He had ascended bodily to heaven without dying, thus removing from earth the last human vehicle

---

2. Ramses II, the best candidate for the Pharaoh who was Moses' historical adversary, discriminated heartily among the native denominations of his country, and thus could be expected to provide even less quarter for the imported and disruptive faith of Moses. For example, when Ramses reached Kadesh for the great engagement with the Hittites in 1275, he set his divisions in a pecking order according to the favor he accorded the denominations—Amun first, followed by Ra, Ptah, and Seth. See Bauer, *History*, 247.

3. Anderson, *Old Testament*, 198–225.

who provided conversation with God, until he should return at some distant future date.[4]

When new prophetic voices arose after Ezra delivered the Pentateuch to the Jews returning from exile, those writers (like the authors of parts of Daniel, the last chapters of Isaiah, and the superb yet apocryphal Wisdom of Solomon) had to deal not only with the tradition that had solidified around Moses alone (and now had a unified and finalized scripture to back them up), but also the scripture traditions that had solidified around each of the major pre-exile prophets, and perhaps a separate tradition coalescing around the Psalms. As we suggested above, each of the pre-exilic prophets had major hurdles to clear in the process of attracting sympathetic attention for a new word from God. Amos, for example, was banished from the northern community where he had traveled to prophesy against the political and religious establishment. The high priest in Bethel accused him of being a professional pundit and therefore having the same biased motive to direct partisan predictions against the north that others in the southern kingdom had. (Amos 7:12) Hosea, reflecting the language used against him by the haters of new light religion, often heard "The prophet is a fool, the man of the spirit is mad." (Hos. 9:7) As a man of oracles, he was shunned as "a snare of a fowler in all his ways." (Hos 9:8) One who should be loved is an object of "hatred in the house of his God." (Hos 9:8)

The prophets face regular persecution when they speak out to update the culture with their well grounded opinions about the direction society is headed. Isaiah is forced to give his "back to the smiters . . ." and his "face . . . (to) spitting." (Isa 50:6) God tells Jeremiah, "They shall fight against thee; but they shall not prevail." (Jer 1:19) Zechariah suggests the smiters and spitters should look for guidance directly from the one they scorn: "They shall look upon me whom they have pierced . . ." (Zech 12:10)

Ahab tries to kill Elijah (1 Kgs 18:9–16), Joash kills Zechariah (2 Chr 24:17–21), Asa imprisons a prophet (2 Chr 16:7–10), and Jehoiakim kills the prophet Urijah (Jer 26:20–23). Jeremiah, as well, suffers a long string of persecutions: the citizens of Anathoth plot to kill him, com-

---

4. See Bergen, *Elisha*, 171, 175. Bergen believes Elisha, Elijah's successor, demonstrates a diminished prophetic role because he does not warn the king or people against their evil ways using the direct utterance of God, but rather serves as a court-oriented adviser instead.

manding him to "prophesy not" (Jer 11:21); Pashur, the son of the high priest, imprisons him (Jer 20:2); the priests and princes of Judah nearly succeed in having him killed (Jer 26); Zedekiah imprisons him (Jer 37); and Jehoiakim destroys the scroll on which Jeremiah's prophecy is written. (Jer 36) Jeremiah laments "I am in derision daily, every one mocketh me." (Jer 20:7)

Ultimately, Jeremiah is involuntarily exiled to Egypt by his own people. Here his Judean captors ridicule the doctrine of new prophecy: "As for the word that you have spoken to us in the name of the Lord, we are not going to listen to you." (Jer 44:16 NRSV) Jeremiah had suggested it would be best to settle in Babylon, but they told him: "Thou speakest falsely: the Lord our god hath not sent thee to say, Go not into Egypt to sojourn there . . . the Chaldeans . . . might put us to death . . ." (Jer 43:2–3)

The mainstream rabbinic tradition of Jesus' day, which ultimately embraced prophecy several hundred years beyond Elijah, down to perhaps 400 BCE, still could not agree on an exact date of the termination of prophecy. Some assigned it to the destruction of the temple in 586 BCE, others to the work of Jeremiah, others to Ezra,[5] others to Haggai and Zechariah, or Malachi, yet others to the time of Alexander's conquests in the late fourth century BCE. In this view, late works like Ezra and Nehemiah, Chronicles, Daniel and Esther, included in the Judaic "writings,"[6] were significant remembrances of formative events rather than plenary revelations, and as such could be included in the final canon as documents supportive of Torah.

Israel was not oblivious to the ancient notion of "kenosis", the emptying out—almost bleeding out—of a god at a time of the decimation of a culture during conquest. An ancient god led his people into battle, and if the result was not good, the soldiers, the banner of the god, and the tokens and idols of the god's presence were taken into captivity. The remaining people of the nation were often severely humbled by means of sword, pestilence, burning and destruction of walls, cities and fields. At a time such as this, the god goes down with the ship. When the Amorites

---

5. Klaus Koch also supports this view. See Koch, *Prophets*, 2.187.

6. The Hebrew Bible follows a different sequencing of books than the Christian Old Testament. After the Pentateuch (Torah) comes "the prophets" (Neviim), which includes Joshua, Judges, Samuel and Kings, the three major prophets and the twelve minor prophets, and finally "the writings" (Kethuvim), which includes these later writings in addition to Psalms, Proverbs, Job and others.

invaded Sumer around 2,000 BCE, it could be written "Father Nanna, your song has been turned into weeping, . . . 'Where are you?' . . . How long will you stand aside from your city."[7] After the Philistines ravaged Israel in the eleventh century BCE, it could be written, "He forsook the tabernacle of Shiloh . . . and delivered his strength into captivity, and his glory into the enemy's hand." (Ps 78:59-61) Esarhaddon described the flight of Babylon's gods at the time of his father's defeat there in the early seventh century: "Gods and goddesses left their shrines . . ."[8] At the time of Babylon's conquest of Judah a century later, God's sovereignty was also surrendered in shame to imprisonment at that time, and his visible symbols—the temple utensils—were carried off to Babylon as well. (2 Kgs 25:13-17)

At such a time, even the god's nominal presence during the performance of liturgy and prayer seems severely attenuated. Individual spiritual relationship to the god is impaired by the undermining of civic security, peace and prosperity. There is a sense of the general unavailability of the god to the people, even abandonment of them altogether. In some sense, one possible adjustment to the decimation of spiritual religion is the development of intellectual religion. A formerly warm and immanent God is taken to be increasingly transcendent, distant, above it all. God speaks his will, sees that it is recorded once, and then goes away, leaving mankind to govern according to that original statement—a kind of ancient version of the watchmaker God of eighteenth century Deism.

This may have been the psychology behind those who rallied around the precursor of Ezra's Pentateuch, the so-called early "epic tradition" of Israel. After Moses' death, it seemed that God was clearly gone from the culture. (Judg 2:11-15) The best that people could do was remember those fine days when God was with the patriarchs, with Moses and Joshua and the pilgrims in the wilderness. Inspired Judges arose, but they did not leave oracular revelations. They merely acted in the names of the traditional prophets and did their best to imitate them. Even the church of Moses, which made its home at Shiloh upon settlement in Canaan, became as corrupt as the people themselves. (1 Sam

---

7. Susan Bauer's adaptation from "The Lament for Urim," in *The Electronic Text Corpus of Sumerian Literature* at http://www.etcsl.orient.ox.ac.uk/ (1998–), in Bauer, *History*, 143.

8. From an adaptation by Bauer, *History*, 401.

2:22–25; Ps 78:60) Later revelations from the hand of the great literary prophets came at times of great national hardship and predicted even worse outcomes than the present unstable conditions. Those revelations were derided as the misguided ravings of ignorant and unpatriotic individuals. They were not accepted by the mainstream churches because the leaders of those churches let Israel know that God no longer spoke to them.

All kinds of proof texts could be found to bolster this sort of view. God, historically it seemed, appeared only for brief moments, and then withdrew. He was not of a mind to stick around. In fact, because the world was generally so corrupt, God wanted to distance himself from it and even destroy it. (Gen 6:12–13) Where he had previously walked and talked directly with man as in the Garden and in the time of Enoch (Gen 5:24), he no longer wanted any part of that direct connection. Genesis 17:22, for example, seemed to give support to the idea that contact even with the great patriarchs was fleeting: "When he had finished talking with Abraham, God ascended and left him." (NEB)

A belief in the biblically unsupportable idea that God only addresses humankind in very early (Adam, Enoch, Noah), very fleeting (Abraham), and/or very foundational moments (Moses at Sinai), unfortunately clouds the legitimate notion that God strongly disapproves of a people who no longer respect the great commandments, and is tempted to leave them to their own devices. A people who accept both the above unsupportable and supportable notions perhaps tend to leave off trying to make a connection with God altogether. It is perhaps true that once they no longer believe in God's presence and no longer understand the laws designed to protect prophets and prophecy, there is not much he can do with them.[9] When a law promoting continuing prophecy is turned into a law prohibiting new prophecy, Lamentations can summarize: "The law is no more; her prophets also find no vision from the Lord." (Lam 2:9) But this unfortunate confluence of beliefs only hampers a people until one among them discerns in the ancient scripture God's ever-present desire to make vocal connection with them once again, and to re-establish human rights.

Ezekiel asserts that God himself will wield the sword against his own people when they have "despised the rod" of God's discipline given from the mouth of the prophet. (Ezek 21:8–15) Jeremiah offers a similar

---

9. We will review these laws in the next chapter.

sentiment. The professional priests seek only after a de-throated God: "For who hath stood in the counsel of the Lord, and have perceived and heard his word? Who hath marked his word, and heard it?" (Jer 23:18) "The pastors are become brutish, and have not sought the Lord; therefore they shall not prosper, and all their flocks shall be scattered." (Jer 10:21) The professional prophets are thieves and God protests their manipulations: "I am against the prophets ... that steal my words every one from his neighbor ... ye have perverted the words." (Jer 23.30, 36)

Isaiah remarks, as well: "Woe to the rebellious children ... they ... have not asked at my mouth." (Isa 30:1–2) The people "say to the seers, see not, to the prophets, prophesy not ..." (Isa 30:10) These pretenders—priests, scribes, court prophets—are responsible for the twists of doctrine that the legitimate prophets rail against: "This people draw near me with their mouth, and with their lips do honor me, but have removed their heart far from me, and their fear toward me is taught by the precept of men ...." (Isa 29:13)

When the people sin against the doctrine of the vocal presence of God, they will be rewarded with the desires of their hearts, the withdrawal of God's vocal spirit from their culture: "I will send a famine in the land, not a famine of bread, nor a thirst for water, but of hearing the words of the Lord ... they shall ... seek the word of the Lord, and shall not find it." (Amos 8:11–12). Also: "Ye shall not have a vision ... the sun shall go down over the prophets ... there is no answer of God." (Mic 3:6–7) But there is nothing about the temporary suspension or dormancy of prophecy that dictates that it will not arise again soon, when one or more individuals approaches God in the way the earlier prophets did.

The problem with a doctrine of cessation of prophecy, therefore, is that it is in some sense a self-fulfilling policy. The leaders encourage the people to disbelieve in new prophecy, and to read the ancient scripture that way, so the people do not seek after God's voice and hope to hear it as an earlier generation once did. They are asked to rely instead upon the institutional religious authorities for guidance. The people are tricked by their political and religious leaders. When things do not go the way the court prophets and high priests predict, the people feel betrayed by God. They turn away from the apparently disinterested ancient God and his sacred writ which the faulty interpreters of the religion have presented to them. Because the political and religious authorities present this God as one who shuns new prophecy, the people give short-shrift to any authentic prophet who arises in their midst and persists against the incredible discouragement of his efforts.

This was the situation with the group in exile with Jeremiah in Egypt. The high God of the high priests of Israel had abandoned them, since he had said all would be well with them in their relations with Babylon. They seemed to get more comfort from the pagan deity called the Queen of Heaven than from this Yahweh, whose promises of security had been so patently false. (Jer 43–44) Had they paid attention to Jeremiah at any time, perhaps even read his prophecies, they would have seen that Yahweh had not promised them security in their present course, but the doom that quickly overtook them.

In Israel, repentance from doctrinal sin, as from physical sin, had always allowed for the erasing of condemnation and the resumption of progress. The long dormancy of fresh word from God inspired groans from certain individuals who loved the original faith and socio-political principles of Israel. Those individuals understood the nature of God and revelation and wondered when the self-imposed curse of absence would be overcome: "How long, O Yahweh, wilt thou hide thyself for ever?" (Ps 89:46) "My heart remembers thy word: 'Seek ye my face!' Thy face, Lord, I seek. Hide not thy face from me." (Ps 27:7, independent translation)

Ultimately, however, the culture leaves most of the early readers of the ancient scripture with colorful, yet cold comfort—the replacement of new prophecy by priestly schools who claim to govern in natural succession to the prophets by providing liturgies, interpretations, and legal decisions. Scribal schools claim to govern in natural succession to the prophets by providing copying, translation and textual reconstruction services, historical information by which to discern the truth of the scripture, secular—even scientific—learning, and proverbs based on experience. One inter-testamental text measures the effect of the settlement of the canon: "Until then the prophets prophesied through the Holy Spirit. From then on, 'Incline thine ear and hear the words of the wise.'"[10] Indeed, princes and kings claim to govern in natural succession to the prophets by providing divine kingship characterized by (occasional) royal righteousness, civic ritual performed in temples, and regular consultation with court prophets. Office replaces oracle. The authority of kings, priests, pundits, scribes replaces the authority of God. A theology of might replaces a theology of right.

10. Seder Olam Rabbah 30.

Profile—Snow on Solomon's Porch (Jesus)

One of several heavily-clad temple worshipers and workers headed away from the Court of the Israelites stopped to listen to the rabbi-healer, dressed in the manner of the Galileans. "Healing the sick is a calling open to all," he was heard advising his listeners. The last of these now disengaged from the conversation and moved along toward the gate, due to the decided chill in the air and the stiffening wind blowing across the valley.

Having the master to himself, the worker drew close to the wall of the east portico where the teacher was propping himself. He resolved to address him. "But physician, if you are the one of whom I have heard, you seem to possess a special gift. Who taught you such medicine? Did you study in Damascus, or Tyre?"

Before answering, the lean doctor who had such mature definition in his young face, looked heaven-ward and, smiling, held out his hand to catch a snow flake wafting back and forth on its way down toward the stone block of the porch. "Such a gift, I suppose, is unusual . . . like snow on Solomon's Porch! Yet it still can still be found!"

Stepping back from his questioner after seeing his disciples, a distance away, motion for him to come, Joshua of Nazareth neatly punctuated a conversation he could not hope to continue. "The priests of old studied ritual, law and medicine . . . and truly these things come from God, my friend. A pleasure meeting you."

But the temple technician stepped away with him, having not yet obtained what he was looking for, for he had heard much about this rabbi and his teaching. As they walked, he continued, "I understand, good man, that you yourself are a teacher of the law, a student of medicine, and a supporter of ritual sacrifice. How is it then you are so opposed to the priests of Jerusalem?"

Joshua, seeing that his disciples were now engaged on some subject among themselves at least for a moment, sensed that he had an inquiring mind standing before him and stopped so he could reveal a bit more. "A good student need not travel to Tyre, but must travel in time. The greater part of the gift of healing, whether applied to a man or a nation, comes from acquaintance with God who acts in history. The priests study the priestly disciplines, but the prophets study all these, and also study the history of nations."

Sensing the worker's silence meant he wished to continue listening, he offered more. "The Sadducees and priests do not believe in a God who lives and breathes . . . and speaks." Seeing a quizzical look on the man's face, he explained, "I teach a God who reveals himself periodically to a prophet-physician who in turn resolves to heal the abased and cankered of the people and thereby the entire nation."

"You have had this experience like the prophets of old, then, rabbi?" The worker pushed for one last word from the popular miracle worker. "This experience must have put you in close touch with the God who once spoke to Moses?"

The Nazarene clasped the hand of the worker in an announcement of departure, "If I say I don't know him, I am a liar." (John 8:55)

PROFESSORS ARE PUPPETS OF THE PRIESTS

Isaiah's "precept of men" (Isa 29:13) suggests how transformation from vocal God to silent God can be navigated reasonably and justifiably. One such notion is presented by a modern scholar of the period: "At the outset of the Second Temple period prophecy had not yet ceased but inspiration in that era was not seen as fully equal to inspiration in the past."[11] The post-exilic prophets, for example, are not informed directly by God, as prophets once were (compare Jer 1:11–14), but now only by angels. Post-exilic Zechariah, for instance, refers to "The angel that talked with me . . . " (Zech 1:9) In addition, such prophets as Zechariah and Daniel have to have things explained to them, since they do not seem to easily or quickly grasp the significance of things. Zechariah says, "What are these? And the angel . . . said . . . I will show thee what these be." (Zech 1:9) An angel must explain to Daniel the meaning of Jeremiah's prediction of "seventy years" (Jer 25:11, 29:10): "He informed me . . . and said, 'O Daniel, I am now come forth to give thee skill and understanding . . .'" (Dan 9:21–22) Such a late Judaic figure does not speak new oracular words, but only reads and studies the old ones. Prophecy is not so much reception of revelation from God, as it is divinely inspired interpretation of previous revelation.

The post-exilic prophets also receive much of their inspiration through dreams, while sleeping. (Zech 4:1) Early on, God spoke directly with the high prophets, but after the captivity was far more likely to

---

11. Sommer, "Did Prophecy Cease?," 41.

speak in a vision or a dream. For example, God "spake unto Moses face to face, as a man speaketh unto his friend." (Exod 33:11) The same was said of Jacob. (Gen 32:30) Many of the classical literary prophets used the term "Thus saith the Lord," indicating that prophecy was not of man, but of God himself. On the other hand, revelation through dreams was thought to be an inferior means of communication, as attested in the book of Numbers. (Num 12:6–8) Dream revelation is even at times associated with false prophecy. (Jer 23:25–29)

Another point of separation between classical and post-exilic prophecy, in the view of the cessationists, relates to reference to activities of the council in heaven. Isaiah, for example, participates directly in the discussion of the council in heaven (Isa 6:1–13), while Zechariah seems only to observe the workings of the council. An angel explains to him the council's discussion about the investing of the high priest. (Zech 3:1—4:1) This suggests a secondary role for post-exilic prophets. Furthermore, the book of Chronicles, composed in the post-exilic period, uses the term "messengers" rather than "prophets," thus suggesting that only an attenuated gift is in force after the time of the classical prophets. This gift is expressed in occasional inspired utterances, or divinations related to specific issues, but not in a constant, day to day outpouring like that of the great prophets.

Chronicles relies heavily on the classical prophets, and does not detail any direct divine communications from many of the seemingly secondary "messengers," who have long-forgotten names such as Shemiah (2 Chr 11:2), Hanani (2 Chr 16:7–9), and Oded.[12] (2 Chr 28:9–11) A number of books are written in this period by authors using pseudonyms—the names of patriarchal and classical figures like Enoch, Abraham, and Baruch—so that these works might gain credibility with their audiences, who believe that divine revelation only came authoritatively in an earlier day.[13]

In addition, post-exilic literature seems to move firmly and substantially into the realm of apocalyptic eschatology—end-time disaster and miraculous renewal. Apocalyptic defers the return of legitimate prophecy to a time of world-wide war and reckoning, presided over either by a returning spiritual hero of the past like an Elijah or a Jesus, or a new one, if that be possible. This may stem from the sense of the over-

---

12. Schneidewind, *Word of God*, (forthcoming).
13. Sommer, "Did Prophecy Cease?," 43.

whelming impotence of Israel's political existence, forced as she was to subsist under the hand of powerful nations who dominated her for the next several hundred years after her return to Judea after the Babylonian exile. All the rationales mentioned above are brought to bear at one time or another against the feasibility of continuing prophecy.

One consequence of acceptance of the theory of cessation is that the scriptural text becomes a replacement for God. This kind of tradition requires fealty to the Bible and gives rise to a sort of "bibliolatry," or worship of the scripture. The Torah and its housing in the scroll become a sacred, almost divine object. The canon becomes a substitute for God and his representative, the prophet.[14] Many widely divergent interpretations of scripture become wildly popular, as God's true nature is divided and conquered by well-meaning priests and pastors. Those who want to find a proof of the ending of oracular revelation can easily find one. For example, a brief text from Isaiah, read out of context, can be read as a rejection of any new prophetic gift: "Truly you are a God who hides himself, O God of Israel . . . " (Isa 45:15 NRSV)

The setting of this verse, however, is not God's retreat to the top of Mt. Olympus, or a far-away galaxy, but rather his determination not to be reduced to a physical sham or idol. The verse contrasts Israel's God with polytheistic gods whom the people believe insert their spirits into ceramic or molten idols so they can be possessed privately and toted around to the benefit of the bearer. That belief earns the condemnation of Isaiah: "They that make a graven image are all of them vanity." (Isa 44:9) The sense of "hiding" intended by the author here is a sense of sovereign greatness. After all, God is creator: "Shall the clay say to him that fashioneth it, What makest thou?" (Isa 45:9)

Such a passage supposedly suggesting God's distance from man actually does the opposite. It celebrates God's ability and desire to draw near to man: "Drop down ye heavens, from above, and let the skies pour down righteousness; lest the earth open, and let them bring forth salvation . . . I the Lord have created it." (Isa 45:8) This verse is reminiscent of Jesus' encouragement for the people to ask that God's kingdom come to earth: "Thy kingdom come, thy will be done . . . " (Matt 6:10) Jesus' prayer is essentially a prayer for the return of belief in authentic prophecy, since God's kingdom operates on earth only through the vehicle of an able, anointed prophet-leader. For Isaiah and Jesus the sovereignty

---

14. Brueggemann, *Theology*, 573.

and highness of God does not distance him from man, but places him in direct oracular relation to man: "I have not spoken in secret in a dark place of the earth ... " (Isa 45:19) From such heights, he can speak to all, not merely a privileged few. In fact, God asks man to accept revelation as an ongoing fact of life: "I said not unto the seed of Jacob, seek ye me in vain ..." (Isa 45:19) In the same chapter as the preceding verse the prophet announces God's inspiration of King Cyrus, who will serve as God's anointed prophet to redeem the Jewish people from their captivity. This is to be an act of great providential import, to be felt by all of Israel. (Isa 45:1–7)

Profile—A Command to Persevere (Hosea)

Hosea sat with head in hands. Today he was once again struggling to process the fact that his wife Gomer had been promiscuous before their marriage and therefore unfaithful to him in their vows. (Hos 1:2, 2:2) He nevertheless had worked hard to forgive her trespass. (Hos 3) He reflected on the symbolic nature of his predicament. His problem was microscopic compared to that of Israel, the nation. But, still, it was symptomatic of the infidelity of the entire people to the political commandments of equality and justice. (Hos 4:1–3) Under conditions of mass wandering away from traditional moorings in local government and acceptance instead of the culture of aristocratic kingship (Hos 8.4), even a prophet's family could not help but be marked. Israel was as disloyal to God as Gomer was to the ethic of chastity before marriage.

Hosea had studied the early days when the tribes wandered in the wilderness, and then settled in hardly less a wilderness west of Jordan, and elected charismatic judges from time to time. In the time of her wanderings in the wilderness before entering Canaan, Israel finally came to trust in Moses and Joshua. It took an entire generation, but after forty years the rising generation knew what it was to live by the rule of ethical law, and under the daily guidance of a prophet of God. Now it was etched in Hosea's mind that it was the ethic of asceticism and the understanding of the danger of political dependency that sustained the ancestors during the early years of the republic and enabled them to inherit and build such a successful civilization in Canaan.

Salvation comes by three indispensible means: God and his providential work, God's fully human prophet who accepts and activates that work, and each individual penitent who understands he can rescue himself and who, once having accomplished that, intercedes with others to encourage them to save themselves. Those who teach this salvation are not those born into a hereditary line of kings, but those standing in a non-hereditary line of prophets.

But now success, abundance and recognition among the nations had gone to Israel's head, as Gomer's personal sexual power had gone to hers. How could he explain to the community that God chooses one son, a prophet, and one people, a nation, and works faithfully with them to make a fruitful relationship that can be an example for all? God is like a parent (Hos 11:1–4), and God is also like a spouse (Hos 2:1–9), accepting less of the breadth of all the earth has to offer, in order to make of a child and a partner the best of the depth that the earth has to offer.

He determined at that moment to name the child he and Gomer were expecting together in a way that would bring to mind the prophecy that God had given him to speak against Israel. He would name the child "Not My People." (Hos 1:9) Every time family, clan or neighbor would pronounce the name of this child, they would know the opinion of one who claimed intimate knowledge of the God of Israel. The generations might then know when they read his testament that there was one at least who cast his lot in favor of the commandments of Moses even in the modern day. There was one who understood the need to accumulate understanding and wisdom in a place of priority over the accumulation of property and wealth. Yes, that would be the name of the child.

THIS BOOK NEEDS A SERMON

As we have suggested, perhaps the most compelling of the rationales for cessation of prophecy is the existence of the momentous spiritual event in the history of a tradition when its interpreters compile and settle a canon of sacred literature. Surely this is an act of and an admission of "finality" in the dispensation of God's word and way. And, in fact, this is the way Jews view the Hebrew Bible and Christians the combined Old and New Testaments. When the book was bound, God's voice was ended.

Biblical historians have shown, however, that the Jewish and Christian canons did not take place under the clear auspices of a God who dictated an end of prophecy. In fact, those books were authorized as a part of the effort by priests and kings to consolidate their domains or to exclude competitors. Scholars have long suggested that Ezra's exilic codification of Jewish indigenous "torah" was promoted by Persian authorities to bolster the bureaucratic presence of settlers in Syro-Palestine, as against efforts of Egypt and others to overrun Persian territory.

One cannot escape the fact that the later post-exilic compilation of the Judaic canon, which added the prophets and other writings, was finalized at about the time the sayings of Jesus were being recorded for publication. Those sayings vehemently challenged the notion of a God whose voice could be stilled. When the Christ movement grew to such a degree as to hijack distinguished Pharisees such as Paul from the ranks of the mainstream Judaic church, the rabbis did a theological about-face and argued even more strongly the finality of the heretofore fluid Judaic canon and the inapplicability of the stories and words of any such messianic figure as Jesus Christ.[15]

In a similar way, the final authoritative compilation of the Christian canon took place at about the time new Christian revelators like the Montanists were challenging the notion that revelation had ceased with the deaths of the Apostles. The Christian book, of course, underwent its final settlement when Emperor Constantine directed that a book be published for his use in administering the new state religion.

A prophet is a simple seeker of peace and happiness through religion who at some point experiences an extraordinary moment of connection with an otherworldly Spirit. That calling, ironically, then makes of him a diligent student of history and a political activist and sets him on a course of criticizing and confronting all that is unethical and unjust in his own society and even in those societies and nations round about him.

A prophet, or his students, or his biographers, also produces a literature. In time, a community of believers fixes the body of that literature and uses it as a basis for activity and for worship and civic engagement. Israel encouraged the process of remembering the words and activities of her prophets and her laws supporting them by inserting them in the sacred scripture. She also allowed for the incorporation of the historical events of a prophet-inspired nation into a series of sacred histories of

---

15. Frederick E. Greenspahn argues that the cessation of prophecy promoted by the first century rabbis is directed against "the phenomenon of continuing Jewish prophecy," of which the new light Jesus movement is just one. He also suggests that the project to canonize the prophets in the Tanakh "protected them from its contemporary practitioners." See Greenspahn, "Why Prophecy Ceased," 48–49.

the nation. Each cultural, religious, academic or political party in the nation was apparently at liberty to publish the history of the nation from its own point of view.

Biblical scientists have substantiated the existence of a number of these histories scattered over the major periods of time covered by the Hebrew Bible and the Christian Testament. These include early histories of the nation from the point of view of the northern kingdom, the southern kingdom, the community in exile in Babylon, reform parties in the days of Judges and Kings, the communities grouped around each of the prophets, academic schools championing the so-called "wisdom" literature, and biographers, essayists, story writers and psalms anthologists.

In fact, today's version of the Hebrew Bible and the Christian Testament are each merely one literary product in a long line of such attempts to normalize the interpretation of the religious and political events of those periods of time. These "canons" of sacred literature, even when they include treatises which seem more secular than theologic (every literature is held to be sacred by its author or its publisher whether explicitly theistic or not), are then used to tutor constituencies in the true way of the world.

Of interest to this present work is the fact that canons of scripture are essentially political documents representing the interests of particular groupings of institutionalized power. These documents, while originally based on inspired remembrances or writings, have undergone such a process of development—addition and exclusion of sources, physical editing, interpretation, translation manipulation of wording to suit specific favored doctrines—that they are ultimately used by their publishers primarily as a tool for the training of belief and thinking among their own targeted memberships.

While this may seem like a sinister purpose, I maintain that most of it really is not. It is the right of the individual, or the party, or the institution to remember the prophet and the history as they please and to use what sources they believe are germane to their views. On the other hand, it is misleading when priests and politicians add to, or delete, material from the author's work, or change the interpretive spirit of it, especially when they have an authentic version of the author's work in front of them. This is precisely the sort of thing the prophets warn against, apparently since the practice of corrupting ancient texts was well known to them. (Deut 4:2; Rev 22:18–19) Indeed, historians eventually uncover such malicious undertakings.

The canons of the Judaic, Christian, and Islamic religions were each gracious enough to include a number of prophetic traditions handed down and known to them before the time of their own canon-making. The Judaic tradition included the earlier threads of divergent tradition we mentioned above, including the highly stylized prophet movements and communities, the wisdom work of the scribes, and the variant histories of the northern and southern nations. The Christians included the whole of the (Alexandrian) Judaic canon in their own. The Islamists repeated much of the story of the Judaic and Christian traditions in their own sacred book.

But Judaism did exclude the Christian tradition, and the Christian fathers, after suffering under the circumstances of exclusion of their literature from the Hebrew Bible, amazingly undertook the same suffocation of the voice of the Spirit that the Jews undertook before them. For example, they excluded many minority and dissenting voices in Christianity, and then they excluded the revelation of Islam.

The Islamic people suffered under the lash of conformity mandated by the Judaic and Christian canons. For example, one verse in the Quran states: "You hate us only because we believe ... in what has been revealed to us ..." (Quran 5:58) Nevertheless, the guardians of the tradition of the Quran bequeathed to those divines who came after Muhammad the same exclusionary fate that Muhammad suffered. They taught that Muhammad was the last of the prophets and that any after him claiming a message from God must be impostors.

In sum, first the rabbis of the Pharisee wing of Judaism, then the patristic fathers of Christianity, and finally the caliphs and mullahs of the major sects of Islam each concluded that there could be no more inspired literature produced after their own was compiled and published. Each western monotheist institutional tradition asserted that it, and it alone, had the latest, best and last word from God available anywhere on the face of the earth.

Each of the three traditions refused to understand what its own founders had learned, that God's voice cannot be stilled by the actions of men. It is as though the sacred history of the world came to an end after each new canon was published. God neither would nor could speak

Cessation of Prophecy 77

to man ever again, after he gave his word to a particular people in a particular time and in a particular place on the earth.

That this continues to be a real and not an imagined policy is underscored by the fact that in the past 2,000 years mainstream Judaism has not added a single major new prophecy to the canon of the Hebrew Bible. In 1,600 years, the Christian mainstream churches and their offshoots have not added any new prophecy to the canon of the Christian Testament. In 1,350 years the Islamic tradition has not added any new prophecy to the book of the Quran.

This policy has had extraordinary repercussions in medieval and modern times. It has produced a regularized and highly provocative animus and jealousy between and among the three monotheist traditions that has led to distrust, misunderstanding, and war. The sealing off of each of the canons has provided a smug assurance of superiority and finality that is not found in the sayings of the founders of each of the religions. While the religion of Moses was engendered in the idea of the passing of the torch of God's firstborn (most sophisticated) nation from Egypt to Israel, Moses and his visionary successors never intended or suggested that God's election of them would, or could, reside with them forever. While Jesus proclaimed the advent of a new kingdom based upon his understanding of life and death, and continuity of life after death, he did not teach that his disciples would, or could, hold on to and supervise the essence of his teaching forever. In fact, he taught that within a short while after his passing there would come many false prophets. He gave no indication about how to sort them out except to look for an inspired "Son of man," whom many interpret as his own second coming. While Muhammad suggested that he alone provided the proper "seal" or authentic stamp of prophecy in his own day, he never suggested that his followers alone would or could automatically understand and propagate exactly what that stamp represented to the world for evermore.

In fact, Moses is reported to have mused, "Would God that all the Lord's people were prophets . . ." (Num 11:29) Jesus promised, "I will pray the Father, and he shall give you another Comforter . . ." (John 14:16) Jesus, too, taught his followers to pray that God allow his will to be "done" (and thus certainly newly *known*) in the future. (Matt 6:10) Muhammad, as well, renounced the idea of the cessation of prophecy with the words, "Children of Adam, when apostles of your own come to proclaim to you my Revelations, those that take warning . . . will have nothing to fear or regret . . ." (Quran 7:35)

Each of the closed canons of the Judaic and Christian religions also shunned works produced before the canon project was finalized, which today's historical insight might encourage us to include. For Jews, such candidates include Philo and Josephus and some of the more formidable rabbis. For Christians, those candidates include very early leaders of the church such as Barnabas, Clement, Ignatius and the Montanists.

The Judaic and Christian traditions continue to exclude inspired pronouncements of God coming in the tradition and in the names of each of their own founders during medieval and modern times as well. Thus the Judaic tradition excludes from evaluation such divines as Abraham Abulafia, Sabbatai Zvi, and Isaac Abravanel, and the Christians such prophets and prophetesses as Jan Hus, Emanuel Swedenborg, Joseph Smith, Ellen G. White, and Mary Baker Eddy.

The closed canons of Judaism and Christianity also exclude inspired or important works by ancient expounders of the faith which were exhumed by archeology during the twentieth century, such as the documents found at Qumran (the Dead Sea Scrolls) and Nag Hammadi, although some of them, such as the Book of Jubilees, were well-known and refered to in ancient times and are frequently cited in theological works now. Other documents of prophetic importance were known at the time and have circulated continuously (though barely) since then, such as the Jewish and Christian apocrypha and pseudopigrapha, and yet have never been seriously evaluated for inclusion in the canon.

Finally, those closed canons also exclude the stories of monotheist prophets in the Far East, such as Zoroaster, Buddha, Confucius, and Nanak, whether those divines lived before or after the publication of the canon. It must be said that exclusion of a new prophet by the traditional canon of a legacy prophet or prophets does not always hamper the new tradition. The term "canon" means "measure." A new prophecy becomes what the rest of the world and its literature must measure up to. Every word from a new and different prophet is essentially its own canon, and is respected as such by its followers. Unfortunately, the often inspired words of a new prophet are usually held out of the sight of other traditions by the small-spirited keepers of those older movements.

The canons of the major Western religious traditions must be read, even in their stunted capacities, as precious proclamations of human rights and promotions of perpetual dissent against tyranny. That is the good news. But the theory of finality which surrounds the canon of each one of the big three traditions undermines God's prospect for finding ways to bring those rights to nations. It does so by limiting the number of ears that can potentially be exposed to hearing a new message, updated as such a message is in terms of the language and technology understandable by the people of the day. The rabbis, the priests and ministers, and the caliphs and mullahs, together with their scribes, ultimately, then, undermine the God they claim to represent. That is the bad news.

Without a clear understanding of religious liberty as the foundation of faith, and without generous recognition of and even incorporation of new revelation into the traditional canon, orthodox traditions narrow the range and depth of God's vocal pronouncements to outdated periods and dim interpretations with respect to which they exercise exclusive hegemony. They become like the Samaritans of ancient Israel who did not accept a single prophet after Moses or a single inspired work beyond the Pentateuch, and who still hold to such a narrow view down to this day.

Profile—"Finalizing" the Canon (Ezra)

Ezra crossed "the river" of Babylon holding the laws of the ancestors firmly clenched in his arms. This grand work of scholarship must not be damaged, as it had a most important function to fulfill once its bearer finally reached and crossed "the river" of Judah. The work of the most astute of the elders, scribes, priests and prophets of the community in exile had accomplished just what the Persian king had commissioned them to do. They had reconciled the competing interests of the north and the south of Israel, as well as those of the priests and the people of the land, whose records and stories had heretofore clashed with one another. They had produced a new version of the unified history of the ancestors, staking out the claim of the Hebrews under the sun since the beginning of time. These five books had been broadly acclaimed by the community in exile. Representatives of the peasant remnant left in Judea some 150 years before had also examined it and made improvements as well.

Ezra now dictated a missive to the Governor of Judea, the esteemed Nehemiah, whom he would be shortly joining. His intention was to survey the ecclesiastic mood and ethical standard of the people, and then to draw the people together to accept and implement the provisions of the law which the congregation of interests had found in the ancient ways that ought to be recovered in the land of Abraham. His would not be an easy task. The Samaritans were determined to resist any return to endogamy, necessary to re-assess and re-assert the land holdings of the exiles. But the Five Books of Moses, and the further genealogies he brought with him, were the key to the redemption of the land and the happiness of the people. Ezra was conscious of the mantle he now bore, that of a second Moses, delivering his people from a second Egypt, meeting and negotiating with an ethical people of Canaan long in settlement there during the second exile. As soon as he crossed the Jordan, he was Joshua too, and must do his best to establish proper settlement in the land and maximize reconciliation by means of the law of mercy in his hands.

The scrolls he carried with him constituted a literal history of the freedom concerns of his ancestors. Its authorization for use among the people would provide a virtual manifesto for the national renewal of the land. He marveled that the Persians understood this, and yet still facilitated its development. The heart of their God Mazda was surely at one with the heart of Yahweh.

5

A Thoroughly Modern Law was Found in the Mound

THE DECALOGUE IS SEEN by many as the foundational—in modern terms, constitutional—law of ancient Israel. After God spoke the Ten Commandments "with a loud voice," the Hebrew Bible says "he added no more." (Deut 5:22) For this reason, it was important for Jews to tie the law-making that occurred subsequent to the Sinai event to the authority of those initial ten, broad laws. This is the reason the medieval legalist Saadiah Gaon catalogued all 613 laws of the Torah/Pentateuch under one or another of the ten foundational precepts.[1]

If there is legal basis for continuing revelation as a cultural phenomenon, and religious liberty as a principle to undergird it, we would therefore expect to find it in the Decalogue. In this chapter we outline a general theory of the Ten Commandments as purely secular law, rather than the mixture of cultic and civic law it is usually thought to be. In them, there is no mention of priest, prayer or pilgrimage, cult, creed or confession, shrine, sacrifice, or song, altar, ancestor or afterlife. We also present a number of laws which plausibly enact Israelite forms of religious liberty pursuant to the statutory authority of the Decalogue.

Israel struggled in Egypt against religious oppression. Ten times Moses requested permission for the children of Israel to undertake a pilgrimage into the wilderness for purposes of worship. (Exod 7–12) It would be curious indeed if, once free of Pharaoh's proscription on free worship, at Sinai they would then neglect to enact some provision to sustain such freedom in their new governing covenant.

Once Joshua led Israel across the Jordan, Israel surely faced city-state establishments of religion which threatened her own mainstream

---

1. Diamond, "Ethical Encounter," 5.

Yahwist cults. These religious confrontations likely played a role in tribal decisions about whether to peacefully co-exist with or militarily engage such cities. For example, Jebusite Jerusalem apparently did not challenge Israel's right to govern herself and worship as she pleased, whereas Jericho, which shut up her gates in a confrontational mode and sent no emissary to talk, apparently did. (Josh 6:1) During the time of the Judges, threats from neighboring Philistines, Amalekites, Amorites, and Ammonites must have been based at least in part on religious animus. Their sensibilities might well have resembled Moab's motivation, when she confronted the children of Israel by using the prophet Balaam, hired by King Balak to cast aspersions on them on behalf of the heavenly powers. (Num 22-24)

The Egypt-like experience of economic and religious confrontation and captivity was a pattern of oppression familiar to tribes and cults throughout the ancient Near East, and from time to time laws were enacted to broaden labor and worship rights of these oppressed cities and groups by reformist kings, as we shall see below in the section on proclamations of freedom. For her part, Israel seized the bull by the horns and made room for ethical dissent within her own ranks by means of constitutional law.

While most modern scholars confess they do not believe ancient Israel made any distinction between the secular and sacred spheres, we argue here that they clearly did. The very root of religious freedom is separation of church and state, or, in ancient terms, cult and crown. The Bible, for example, describes a process typical of both ancient and modern times, for investiture of priests under the authority and power of the state. After such licensing of cultic personnel, priests then proceed to operate in a functionally and organizationally different sphere than that in which the officials of state operate. (Exod 29) In fact, after Moses inaugurates such an investiture process, he enacts what may be called the "Levite policy," which effectively assures that secular officials cannot usurp the clerical role, and priests cannot usurp the political role. (Num 3-4) Judges and kings subsequently are censured for making any attempt to bridge this separation between priest and prince, cult and state, shrine and palace. Gideon, Saul, and Uzziah, for example, overstep this boundary and incur the wrath of contemporaries or of their historians. (Judg 8:24-27; 1 Sam 13-15; 2 Chr 26:16-21) While Levites do not get directly involved in matters of secular administration of government, it is understood that Levites have freedom in religious matters. They may officiate at religious denominations of their own choosing. (Deut 18:6) One notable Levite does just that as he first affiliates himself with Micah's new family cult, based around a molten idol, and then later affiliates himself with an independent tribal denomination of Yahweh at the new northern shrine site of the migrating tribe of Dan. (Judg 17–18)

While the Decalogue mentions God several times, most secular documents and treaties of the ancient world mention one or more gods as well, without compromising their civil character. In Israel, as in most nations of the ancient world, many civic activities were couched in a kind of religious terminology which makes them appear like religious practice to modern readers. For example, when two parties went to court on a civil matter, they were said to be appearing "before God," (Exod 22:8 NRSV) because, like God, the court had an interest in establishing the truth of the matter. But the judge did not rule according to cultic law, but rather based on the secular statutes that concerned the subject matter.

The first five commandments, the so-called First Table, arguably outline a legal principle of devotion to the God of the Exodus. But this devotion is intended to commit the people to the civil rights obtained by means of the Exodus rather than to any particular liturgical rites to be enjoyed by religious factions within the new nation. In particular, we see the First Commandment (no other gods) as a law enfranchising political rights of speech and participation in local government and shrine activity, and the Fourth Commandment (keep the Sabbath day holy) as a right to rest from labor so that the citizenry may pursue work in government and worship in private.[2] The Decalogue relates to the place of religion and labor in society, rather than the specific content of those agencies, and accords both free expression and free rest a high priority. For example, it deals with religious liberty and separation of cult and state, but not with matters of animal sacrifice or religious doctrine. It enforces the civil rights of laborers, but does not prescribe their occupations.

The Decalogue also provides a foothold for the institution of social prediction, that is, consciousness of history. If the Bible's readers honor the

---

2. There has been much scholarly work done aimed at analyzing possible sources for or analogues of the Decalogue (such as the Hittite treaty document), cataloguing the variety of forms in which it appears in the Bible, re-counting its continuing importance in the New Testament, and elucidating the variety of possible meanings, applications and connections for each of the "words" or laws contained in it. See, for example, Nielsen, *The Ten Commandments*, 1968.

historical memory of Israel's sojourn in Egypt, they will know what to do in contemporary situations. The book contains a straightforward key to its interpretation that points to the Egyptian problem and the Exodus/Sinai solution: "And when thy son asketh thee in time to come . . . what mean the testimonies, and the statutes . . . Then thou shalt say unto thy son, We were Pharaoh's bondmen in Egypt . . ." (Deut 6:20–21) The purpose of the law is "to preserve us alive . . . " (Deut 6.24) A people stay alive and free by means of human rights and local government of the sort enshrined in the Decalogue. Furthermore, if Israel screws up and doesn't watch out for religious liberty and free labor, back to Egypt they will go, to religious and economic servitude: "Ephraim shall return to Egypt." (Hos 9:3)

The Decalogue deals with what religion is not rather than what religion is. For example, it sets constitutional boundaries on acceptable varieties of religion by means of the second commandment (no idols), and outlines civil, criminal and socio-ethical prohibitions and encouragements in the rest of the commandments, rather than theological ones.

The Decalogue enacts a foundational or constitutional law for the organization of political society, and includes within its corpus a variety of human rights. The whole of the legal ramification of the code, while it may be termed early, cannot be termed primitive. It is rather progressive even by today's standards, for it moves ancient Israel away from socio-political practices which continue to plague the "enlightened" western world to this day.

The balancing precepts of the Decalogue in respect of legitimate versus illegitimate religion may be compared with the constitutional law of modern nations. For example, the Constitution of the United States, and those of its states, enact freedom of religion, but at the same time provide the people with a means or a context by which to limit certain religious practices. In the Reynolds case in 1878, the U. S. constitution was construed so as to prohibit polygamy, a religious practice of Latter Day Saints (Mormons). Bigamy, as well, was outlawed in the colonies before the federal Constitution was written, and continued to be outlawed in the states after it was written. In like matter, Israel enacted religious liberty with one precept (the First Commandment) and enacted a criminal law against religious "idolatry" with another (the Second Commandment). Politico-religious idolatry was a cultural practice thoroughly discredited by virtue of the experience of the Abrahamic people in Mesopotamia,

Canaan, and Egypt, and so it was severely curbed in the foundational national law.

TEN COMMANDMENTS IN THE LIGHT OF DAY

The first five provisions of the Decalogue—the so-called First Table—are commonly thought to relate to matters of individual and corporate religious behavior because, in contrast to the laws of the Second Table, they mention the word God. The First Commandment—"thou shalt have no other gods before me"—is easily taken as a law making an establishing of religion, specifically requiring worship of the denominational God of Moses. In fact, it is the opposite. It is a law allowing for the structuring of belief and worship according to the dictates of conscience, as long as conscience does not lead to criminal activity associated with pagan idolatry—such practices as sorcery (prohibited by the Second Commandment—no idolatry), child sacrifice (prohibited by the Sixth Commandment—no killing), and temple prostitution (prohibited by the Seventh Commandment—no adultery). Jesus, as well, supports the same ancestral political prohibitions related to manipulation (Matt 6:24, 7:7-12; 12:38-39), killing (Matt 5:38-39), and adultery. (Matt 5:27-28) By means of this law, Israelites were required to respect the religious consciences of monotheists among their midst who worshiped gods with different names than their own. Depending upon the interpretive tradition, the governing authorities and the people were even presumably required to honor the religious beliefs of polytheists, so long as the behavior of such religionists comported with the precepts of the Decalogue.

The content of the Ten Commandments is roughly the following. The state and the church must promote academic, political and religious freedom and must eschew superstition, ignorance, force and inequality (first commandment). The state and the church must accomplish the first commandment by means of law-related education and curbs on economic exploitation, accumulation and luxury such as are common with idolatrous kingship (second commandment). The two great sectors of society must promote constructive contractual relationships between parties in political, social, economic, and religious matters (third commandment). These contracts, most often entered into with God as witness to them, are not to be treated lightly, that is, broken without civil repercussion. The nation must enforce a human right to rest from labor and laws which promote redemption from slavery and dependence (fourth commandment). Israel must ensure decentralized political governance of a type that respects gender equality and places substantial governing power in the grasp of families, in much the same way the Tenth Amendment of the Constitution of the United States reserves considerable power to local and parental government (fifth commandment).

The polity must forbid and decry any expenditure of life that is not consonant with the aims of the first five precepts or which is required in the service of despotic, imperial central government (sixth commandment). The communities of the nation must prohibit sexual conduct which upsets the solidarity of family government (seventh commandment). The agencies of society must prohibit theft of people and property and must prevent any exaction of individual, family, and clan property by government which derails the interests of local home rule described in the first table of laws (eighth commandment). The citizenry must prosecute any expression or testimony which obscures or subverts honest factual inquiry in the courts and in the other institutions and agencies of society (ninth commandment). Finally, the people are to act responsibly as citizens by taking no covert action to disenfranchise a neighbor, and, are not merely to maintain but positively promote the social, health, and economic status of that neighbor at all times (tenth commandment).

The great commandment—"Thou shalt have no other gods before me" (Exod 20:3; compare Deut 5:7)—is at root a law establishing religious liberty and political pluralism in Israel, and thus allowing for the periodic return of authentic prophecy. It would not do for Israel to promote prophecy in its broad religious worldview, as attested by the many independent books of prophecy in its sacred text, without making a place for it in its civic law. Prophecy is generally critical of institutional, political, and religious interests, and is based on a progressive socio-scientific world view. Early Israel wanted to guarantee the vitality of such a critical tradition. She did so by means of her foundational law. The Decalogue constructed a democratic principle and a democratic power by guaranteeing freedom of belief, inquiry, and discovery. Believers must first be *free* to place a God of ongoing democratic prophecy above all others before they can effectively proceed to do so. Thus they must be free of national, and even regional political and religious proscription in order to honor the constitution. Those who would inquire after the varieties of political governance possible in the ancient world, and after the natural laws of the cosmos, must first be free to seek after political and natural wisdom before they can effectively do so.

In terms of political organization, the law might be viewed as an early form of election law for free speech and free election. It encourages the people to periodically acclaim a new leader for the nation based not on heredity, but on ethical qualification for office. Judges and kings were elected according to the law. Jephthah, for example, insisted upon a vote of confidence to undergird his assumption of power (Judg 11:9–10), and David stood for election in the north and south, and also after the usurpation of his throne by Absalom. (2 Sam 19:9–15)

In terms of church or shrine organization, individual citizens must be free to organize society around the extraordinarily masculine God of Moses once he is properly re-introduced to a people who have lost sight of the liberties he provides. Thus it is not surprising that the First Commandment is provided with a language of legislative intent, located only a few verses after the law itself appears. This intent language clarifies the process of political re-organization necessary to enthrone the God of free inquiry above all others. It essentially encourages the people to follow a new prophet and cleave to the original Sinai program of constitutional justice and righteousness whenever God's "name" is "recorded" (KJV) or "remembered" (NRSV) by a bidden prophet of God arising after Moses: "In all places where I record my name I will come unto thee, and I will bless thee." (Exod 20:24) It is likely that this early "altar law" statute—so-called because it specified the building not of a temple, but a simple altar of earth—governed the incorporation of new denominations of Yahweh which sprang up based on oracular experiences during the period of Judges. This law, for example, suggests a largely voluntary transition of memberships from stale or corrupt denominations of religion at old places to lively new ones at new places, of the sort that occurred in the day of Gideon. (Judg 6–8) This law was later re-stated in terms of the Deuteronomic legal material which encouraged the activities of prophets, and inspired kings such as Josiah to play a role in the cultural and religious revitalization of the nation. (2 Kgs 22–23; Deut 12–13, 17–18)

Transition in cult membership to a new "place" where God recorded his "name" also happened during the time of the Babylonian captivity. Ezekiel, for example, chronicled God's abandonment of the Jerusalem temple and the deity's journey with the prophet to Babylon. (Ezek 8–10) At some time in the future, Ezekiel wrote, God would take up residence in the "New Jerusalem" once the new temple was built, a place where it would be said, "The Lord is there." (Ezek 48:35)

The canon of the New Testament certainly portrays Jesus as one who believed prophecy had been extended to his own day. He well exemplified the ancient itinerant prophets who took their critical teachings on the road, with the mobile Spirit in tow. He experienced an extraordinary calling from a powerful God, directing that a message be delivered to a people and to their leaders: "He gave me a commandment what I should say and what I should speak." (John 12:49) This recalls the virtual kidnapping of the Old Testament prophets discussed in chapter 2.

Jesus couches the details of "what I should speak," particularly in Matthew, in terms of Israel's foundational law. He gives support both to the Decalogue in the Sermon on the Mount (Matt 5) and to a popular reduction of the Decalogue into two great commandments by quoting verses in Deuteronomy and Leviticus. (Matt 22:34–40; Deut 6:4–5; Lev 19:18) This recalls the laws/commandments/words given by God through Moses to the people at Sinai. (Exod 20; Deut 5) Jesus took seriously his own personal constitutional right to express religious belief and interpret the scripture. A part of this freedom is the freedom a prophet has to claim new light revelation from God, and criticize or judge existing political and religious institutions, using speech and press and assembly. Jesus defines proper political action as the "sword" of truth, not use of the actual sword—courageous speech and the predictive power of the published word rather than violent and coercive means. (Matt 10:34, 26:52) The truth of the existence of God-given human rights makes for freedom, not violence. (John 8:32)

Jesus made a clear connection between the great first commandment and the preservation and promotion of prophets, and thus positioned Mosaic law squarely in the realm of religious freedom. He said, "Did not Moses give you the law, and yet none of you keep the law? Why do you go about to kill me?" (John 7:19)

Not long before Jesus' time, during the time of the Greek usurpation of religious rights in Palestine in the late Second Temple period, Onias IV built a temple at Leontopolis in Egypt, based on the same kind of ancient de-legitimizing/re-legitimizing scenario that those before him and after him would use.[3] He understood that the high priesthood and temple in Jerusalem had become corrupt under Hellenistic influ-

---

3. Vaux, *Ancient Israel*, 341.

ence, and believed it was time for God and man to set up a more pristine priesthood and temple in Egypt.

In the altar law passage in Exodus, the writer places God in the position of taking the initiative, as though he were unilaterally recording his name. There is a basis for this as we will see in the next chapter, but it is also understood that God works through a human medium to accomplish a remembrance of the capacity of man for independent government and worship. If the people want the blessing—to see the mighty arm of God at work in their own day—they must allow the prophet to speak.

In order to accomplish and effectuate this blessing, the people must have freedom to promote political and religious ideas by instructional and devotional means. Citizens must be free to assemble at sacrifice and pilgrimage sites, and must be free to speak, instruct and worship at those shrines. The history of Israel makes clear that the people exercised these prerogatives. They must also be free to publish sectarian histories about the nation and its peoples. The existence of the Bible itself, and the evidence of its multiplicity of early sources, is the best witness of the availability of this freedom.

That the people hold and exercise these several freedoms is demonstrated, for example, in the wilderness when they challenge the leadership of Moses and Aaron in their respective spheres, and in the settlements of the Promised Land when they immediately experiment with Baalism. (Judg 2) Gideon (Judg 8:24–27), the parents of Sampson (Judg 13), Micah of Ephraim (Judg 17), and the tribe of Dan (Judg 18) all exercise their right to start separate and independent denominations of Yahwism during the time of Judges.

Israel during the time of Kings, David, Solomon, Ahaz, and Manasseh, among others, gave birth to or gave place to new religious denominations. During Jeremiah's day there is an expectation that politico-ethical prophets have a right to function and provide heterodox and independent interpretations of God's will apart from the institutionalized priesthood and court prophets, since we learn that citizens pestered Jeremiah and other prophets with requests for discerning the "burden of the Lord." (Jer 23:33–40) A variety of ecumenical, or syncretistic, or denominational worship of Yahweh is also instituted at various "high places" such as Gezer, where Samuel himself had worshipped. (1 Sam 9:6) Archeological excavations and biblical scholarship demonstrate that the great literary prophets each started either political, ecclesiastic, or academic/scribal movements around their own cultural restorationist interests, and document the stunning proliferation of independent religious denominations in Israel over the 600 year period after crossing Jordan.[4]

By the time of Jesus the record demonstrates the existence of a wide variety of Judaic/Palestinian cults, including the Pharisees, Sadducees, Essenes, Samaritans, Baptists, movements forming around Theudas, Judas, and others, the Jesus movement, and the several dozen Christian denominational movements which arose soon after Jesus.

A constitutional mandate to honor and obey God can be understood in three basic ways and was likely enforced in all three ways during this formative 600 year history. First, it can be seen conservatively as a duty of all citizens to conform to a state specified, "established" or monopolistic form of denominational worship—in effect, mainstream "Yahwism only," to the exclusion of almost all others.[5] Alternatively, it can be seen liberally as a civil right to worship Yahweh in a land given over to many forms of ethical worship, specifically all those which resemble the original form of Yahweh worship founded by Moses and Aaron. This second interpretation carries with it a mandate for citizens to conform to the ethical and democratic human rights originally specified by Yahweh, which necessarily excludes worship of such nature gods as Baal. A third interpretation is that which invites Yahwism to compete with any and all forms of worship in Israel, including against whatever brand of religion is preferred by the king. Under this scenario a king may specify a state-mandated religion that marginalizes Yahwism.

The best way to envision the intent of the First Commandment is the second, and this was probably the original intent of both the Sinai legislation enacting religious freedom and the Deuteronomic law re-enacting it during the time of Josiah.

It may be observed, with respect to the third interpretation, that Yahweh's place at the table was usually not in question in Israel. However, there were times when mainstream Yahweh worship was badly treated. This happened in the day of Manasseh and at the time of Ahab/Jezebel, when Yahwists were persecuted and killed. But arguably it happened, too, at those times when legitimate prophets of Yahwism were denied free expression.

4. Zevit, *Religions*, 2001.
5. Smith, *Palestinian Parties*, 15–56.

The second interpretation provides a civil right for citizens to live in an environment of Decalogue-based secular ethics. It also provides a religious right for citizens to seek out the oracular God of the Exodus, to express political and religious sentiments characteristic of that God, and to re-organize society according to the original intent of the constitutional law given by that God. It is, then, a dual right to revelation and revolution. The second interpretation explains why Gideon overthrew Baal culture in the time of Judges, why Jehu overthrew Baal culture in the time of Kings, and why the Deuteronomistic historian excoriated Solomon for allowing worship of Chemosh and Moloch at the same table as Yahweh.

The margins of Decalogue ethical acceptability were not always clear, however. The so-called "high places" at times seemed to fit comfortably inside the ethical religious sphere, and sometimes were found to be outside it. While most kings judged them to be within the margins of acceptability—i.e., they "ordained (priests) to burn incense in the high places in the cities of Judah" (2 Kgs 23.5)—Hezekiah (2 Kgs 18:4) and Josiah (2 Kgs 23:5) understood them to be outside those margins and "put down" those priests.

Profile—Matters of Sacrifice (Moses)

The family of three and their retinue paused by the side of the road leading to Heliopolis (Pithom). They wanted to rest the child whom they had subjected to a minor surgery earlier on the journey. (Exod 4:25) The boy was still irritable, and both parents hoped he would sleep.

The father, Moses, supposed that the debacle that made him an escaped felon some years before would now be a cold case, well outside the memory of a new Pharaoh's administration. Today he traveled slowly and during the day when once before he traveled this road speedily, only at night, and in the opposite direction.

The now middle-aged man was the one who as a youth had the audacity to try to incite insurrection among the slave workers of Pithom (Exod 2:11–15), those people who counted Abraham as their ancestor as he did. Two decades, and family responsibility, had bred in him undeniable maturity. He could see now that overthrowing a dynasty was not a task that could be accomplished by an ethnic minority faction.

But the passing of years and the responsibility of a wife and children did not temper his sense of how to rescue his people as much as did the event on Sinai Mountain. There a flame engulfed the bush without consuming it. A voice not of this world encouraged him and provided him with a way to intervene on behalf of his oppressed people. If his goals were still the human right to work and worship as one wished, the means to achieve them was now political conversation, negotiation, and stratagem, not violence. In Midian he had continued his long-time medical and legal studies, but on Sinai he had learned possibilities of a different order.

The youngster's eyes bobbed gently shut as he lay beneath a lean-to tent braced by Moses' staff. He turned to his travel companion, the physician whom he had married. "I am at peace Zipporah," he whispered. "The god of my fathers and yours is a merciful God. He will move Pharaoh when the time is right." "Yes," she answered, "but he will not react easily to such a challenge to his authority in matters of sacrifice and corvee." He sensed deeply the wisdom of her words, having spent a period of time at court as a young man. "True, dear wife, but I would shirk my duty of silence before the face of Pharoah long before I would put off my duty to God's express intention."

As he turned to stroke the child's hair and his wife rooted about in a bag for some medicine, the thought struck him once again about the link between medicine and motivation in the cause of political freedom. Yahweh had convinced him that one important means to convert the Hebrew people to their own cause was by a demonstration of new treatments for baneful threats to health for people living in a river environment. (Exod 15:26) To this end he brought with him from the Arabian peninsula a variety of physical substances which could be used to ameliorate such nefarious natural threats as the venom of a snake.

God had used a metaphor: authority in the world about him was symbolized by the possession of a staff. Their prospect of organizing around his own staff must rest in this new sophistication he could bring to the people as a healer. If the world could unleash snakes upon human society, Moses was in a position to stem the effect of their bites. (Num 21:4–9) He was constantly to remember that the respect he sought from his own people and also from the Egyptians rested on his ability to deal with their down-to-earth health problems. (Exod 4:1–5)

And if his ability to cure snake bites were not enough to move palace and people to action, then God provided him with a cure for yet another baneful disease, "leprosy." (Exod 4:6–8) If the people were still not convinced that he could lead them to organize a society having greater ease and sophistication than the one to which they presently were bound, while at the same time relieving them of the burden of rigorous slavery, he was to rely upon yet a third suggestion of health care sophistication. This was his ability to produce a physical reaction in water which would turn it into a red liquid like blood. (Exod 4:8–9) This symbolic action would lend further credence to the prospect of God's ability, and the ability of a wisdom-oriented prophet-physician, to extend life.

As a youth Moses blinked, he doubted, he feared, and he ran. But now there was no doubting his course. He must risk all, even his fledgling family, and trust in the God who spoke with unmitigated authority and gave him such means for recovering his people from both every-day illness and long-term oppression.

A MOBILE ROTUNDA FOR GOVERNMENT

The commandment to "have" no other gods before Yahweh is tantamount to a requirement that the people elect no other leader over Israel than a high prophet-judge like Moses. Moses heard the voice of God, and some of the Judges, Deborah and Gideon, for example, heard that voice as well, and led according to God's dictates. The book of Deuteronomy (Deut 17–18) actually places this principle of ongoing national charismatic leadership into an article of civil government. While biblical scientists believe this law was written in its present form by a scribal school around the time of Josiah, it certainly reflects the pattern which held throughout the time of Judges and to a degree during Kings as well.

This law anticipates a prophet leader will appear at an unexpected time and at a "place which the Lord thy God shall choose." (Deut 17:8) It is hoped that such a political leader will demonstrate the historical and politico-social perspicacity Moses demonstrated as the nation's first Judge, and be accorded respect and authority by the people. Such judges are empowered by the law to reform the secular/civic system, in part by re-setting constitutional parameters for the religious sector. Each may also organize a denomination within those parameters himself, if so inclined, as indeed any citizen may do.

The Israelite people who settle in Canaan are devoted to a decentralized, confederate system of tribal government. Threats to the security of one or more of the federated tribes occasionally demands stellar national or interregional leadership. These are the times when an enlightened national judge is especially needed. When such a judge is acclaimed by the people, he chooses a place of "judgment," that is, government. Thus, government during the settlement period turns out to be much like the mobile place of government during the wilderness wanderings. Neither the government nor the church are static, institutionalized, aristocratic, localized, hereditary, captive to special interests. The two great sectors of society, instead, must be malleable, de-institutionalized, democratic, term-limited, transitory as to location, free of the interests of unethical powers, and separated.

Government court officials act on two levels. Lower court secular judges/elders and ecclesiastic priests and Levites carry out both administrative and judicial duties specialized to their independent spheres, as presumably they did in the day of Moses and Aaron (Lev 1–9) and in the early days of settlement. (Num 35; Josh 21; 1 Sam 16:4–5)

However, there should be a higher court operating at the place of judgment established by the prophet-judge. "If there arise a matter too hard . . . arise, and get thee up into the place which the Lord thy God shall choose . . . unto the priests the Levites . . . and unto the judge . . . and inquire; and they of that place . . . shall show thee . . ." (Deut 17:8–10) A variable "place" for appellate judgment is mentioned twenty times in the Book of Deuteronomy.[6] Both the priestly sector and the government sector have civic responsibility, but those two sectors, roughly equivalent to private and public, are separated so they can serve as a check and balance on each other. An assembly (qahal) of the people of the land (am hares) serve as the legislature and maintains responsibility for acclamation of the popular leader. The people thus exercise the ultimate and final check on power.[7]

In fact, there are several "places" of historical oracular judgment in Canaan recognized by Israelite historians, even before the final settlement. These places have what may be called "oracle names"—names which reflect the association of those places with God's vocal presence. The well of Lahoi-Roi is the place where God spoke to Hagar. The term means "The Living One who Sees."[8] Kadesh, the place where Moses and the children of Israel encamped in the wilderness, was earlier called En-Mishpat, meaning "The Spring of Judgment or of the Oracle." (Gen 14:7)

---

6. Vaux, *Ancient Israel*, 327.

7. Albertz, *Israelite Religion*, 201.

8. Ibid., 278.

Indeed, pre-Islamic Arabs consulted stone idol-oracles near the Sheik's tent as they wandered in the wilderness.⁹ This same kind of tradition is associated with the Tent of Meeting in Moses' day. (Num 18:22)

The high judges, and presumably those at all levels, must pay particular attention to enforcement of the constitution against elements within and without the society who seek to diminish its strength and vitality. There is mandated a type of perpetual reform in Israel, activated through the exercise of the rights of ethical speech and action granted by the Israelite constitution to all the people. Thus, it is the job of patriots of the constitution to rally around inspired leaders like Deborah, Gideon and the most capable school of Levitical priest-lawyers that can be found. These leaders not only make case law relative to the constitution, but also raise armies to defend against aggressors and lead educational and political campaigns to overthrow cultural menaces within society itself.

But charismatic claimants to the office of prophet-judge, and presumably even hereditary priests and kings who claim the prophetic gift, must fit the criteria specified in Deuteronomy if they are to be accorded sustained authority in the community. In order that the idea of prophecy be held before the eyes of the people, the searching eye of the Torah, and the consummate gaze of God, historians accord all men who claim political and ecclesiastic wisdom as "prophets." But the same scribes also reserve the right to call them "false" prophets. Some make efforts to provide what the liberation commandment hopes for, but most do not succeed.

Two sections in Deuteronomy add further clarifying detail to the First Commandment-induced "law of prophets." The people are to elect and follow only a prophet of the stature of Moses. They shun such leadership only at peril to themselves: "I will raise them up a Prophet from among their brethren, like unto thee, and will put my words in his mouth; and he shall speak unto them all that I shall command him. And it shall come to pass, that whosoever will not hearken unto my words which he shall speak in my name, I will require it of him.¹⁰ (Deut 18:18–19) On the other hand, the people must case aside all other political figures than such a prophet: "But the prophet, which shall presume to speak a word in my name, which I have not commanded him to speak, or that shall speak in the name of other gods, even that prophet shall die." (Deut 18:20)

9. Ibid., 296.
10. Halpern, "Kingship and Monarchy," 415.

In the day of kings, it may happen that the prophet, unlike the judge, has to work outside the political establishment in order to effectuate the work of God. In the case of prophet-prince tandems like Elijah/Jehu, Isaiah/Hezekiah, and Jeremiah/Josiah, the prophet may act like a shadow government or citizen overseer who funnels policy initiatives to the king, who may or may not implement them. Together they try to muster enough support in the great "congregation" (edah) of citizens to reform the political and cultural institutions of society. (Ps 7:7, 107:32)

The law in Deuteronomy also provides criteria to help the citizenry recognize the difference between true and false prophets. (Deut 13:1–5) From time to time the citizenry apply these rules to prophets whose status with God is under dispute. (Jer 26:16) The fact that Deuteronomy publishes grounds for judging between true prophetic leadership and false prophetic leadership presupposes not only the existence and expectation of continuing prophecy, but also its constitutional legality in Israel.

Jesus acknowledges the importance of popular political leadership in the sacred tradition, but offers a caveat: "Not every one who saith unto me Lord, Lord, shall enter into the kingdom . . . have we not prophesied in thy name?" (Matt 7:21–22) Here Jesus underscores the doctrine of Deuteronomy regarding illegitimate prophets. (Deut 13) He also suggests the people should be more discriminatory in their choice of political and priestly leaders. The fact that there are illegitimate prophets means, by extension, there are legitimate ones too. Prophecy is not dead.

Israel is bidden by her tradition and by her ancestral laws to embrace the legitimate prophets. However, in olden times the people had problems doing this and they still have problems in New Testament times. Luke's Jesus laments over Jerusalem like the prophets of old. Jesus says "It is impossible for a prophet to be killed outside of Jerusalem." (Luke 13:32–34 NRSV) This is a wry statement recalling the mainstream church's typical intolerance of new light religion and new light politics, as the stories of Elijah, Amos, Jeremiah and others demonstrate. Certainly it is physically possible to kill a prophet outside Jerusalem, but it is not politically possible, not even legal, without the encouragement of the blind guides of Jerusalem and their relegation of the First Commandment to the constitutional dustbin. The people love the prophets and their bold speech, but the ecclesiastic and other political leaders kill them, and in the process kill free speech. "Jerusalem . . . the city that kills the prophets." (Luke 13:33 NRSV)

It is not a stretch to theorize that one reason the book of Deuteronomy, or at least the ancient source used as its basis, was at one point marginalized by the keepers of the Mosaic tradition, as we mentioned in chapter 1—perhaps shunted off to a dark and inaccessible corner of the temple archive—was that it required that those keepers be supplanted from time to time by prophets who have a fresh word from God!

Profile—The King's Chapel (David)

David lay in hiding in a cave among rocks frequented by the wild goats of Ziph. (1 Sam 23:14) These caves, the ancestors said, were created in the southern part of the Judean wilderness by an unusually large number of earthquakes common to the great north-south rift of the Jordan River valley. He himself had known the shaking loose of rock on the slope downward toward the Dead Sea during one of these episodes.

As he climbed through the mouth of the cave on all fours to reach the dusky evening air, he sat on a boulder and reflected on the course of his life as a peasant prophet. He mused on the words he heard when God spoke to him, words which would later serve as the coronation liturgy of the kings rising in the House of David: "I will tell of the decree of the Lord: He said to me, 'You are my son; today I have begotten you.'" (Ps 2:7 NRSV) That is the voice he heard when Samuel anointed him to lead Israel. Of that moment it was eventually written, "And the Spirit of the Lord came upon David from that day forward." (1 Sam 16:13)

But the expectation of instant glory turned to the foul stench of ridicule, plots on his life, and exile. Today, he thought, "I have become a stranger unto my brethren, and an alien unto my mother's children." (Ps 69:8) "What good is a word from God," he mused, "if few are able to hear of it?" He had hidden away Samuel's prediction and the voice of the Spirit, almost as if they had never happened. "What good is a word from God if its dictates never come to pass?"

He wet his finger in his mouth and put it to the soil and returned to his mouth a bit of the chestnut red dust. He could taste a slight hint of salt which his body craved just now. He carried with him some barley bread, garlic, and young nettle he had gathered, which he would cook as a vegetable this evening. He also had some dried chamomile in his knapsack with which he planned to steep some tea from the spring water nearby to help him rest from his pursuers. His body today seemed as badly depleted as his soul.

Yet, he thought, buoyed by the prospect of a meal, the patriarchs and the founders had spoken of a mobile spirit that frequently departed from the long houses of kings and could present to the humblest of servants and shepherds in the places where they trod. Deborah, Gideon and Manoah with his wife had demonstrated the power, relevance, and closeness of that God. Perhaps one day the administration of God's kingdom would move from a cave near Ziph to more exalted quarters, and crown daisies and lilies would replace the briars among which he now stepped.

At this moment he felt the rising of a positive sensibility within the depths of his frame. If God would give him the plurality of the people necessary to carry the day, he knew a place where he would judge all Israel. In this city he could inspire a renovation of the priestly families and a recommitment of the people to the high torah of the ancestors. This evening David resolved, as the Judges had before him, to avail himself of the right to re-furbish the tarnished mainstream shrine and re-incorporate the ancient political constitution of Israel.

He would move the ark to Jerusalem, where the Jebusite priests had lived in holy harmony with Israel for so long. Such a place would serve a grand political purpose too. Its walls belonged historically neither to the northern tribes, nor the southern. No Hebrew prince ensconcing his camp there could invite a charge of favoritism.

In Jerusalem the high priests of the renewed denominations would assist with the administration of the new chapel of a nation whose large boundaries had been demarcated in Abraham's vision three quarters of a millennium before. Here he would educate and invest his own sons in the priesthood and perhaps find one capable of following in his steps as a governor serving at the pleasure of the people. After all, the prophet Nathan had encouraged him that the promise of righteous posterity given to Abraham could be his as well.

THE FIRST LAW OF REAL NATIONS
(OR, LAW SCHOOL FOR DUMMIES)

It is the position of this book that the First Commandment was understood by ancient Israel and its great prophets as an explicit directive to look for new political prophets on the intellectual and ethical pattern of Moses and for citizen action in society on the pattern of Exodus. Israel enacted the Nazarite program/law in order to support this priority.

(Num 6) Nazarites are individuals who combine priestly and political learning in preparation for prophetic leadership at court, or at the head of the nation. Sampson serves as a model for how a leader can come out of the ranks of a Nazarite school for prophets. (Judg 13:4–5) Samuel undergoes a similar process of vowing and dedication to learning and service. (1 Sam 1)

That a commandment to put the Exodus God before all others is both a theological commandment to seek out and heed new revelation of a high oracular type, and a secular constitutional provision directing attention to the socio-political sphere, is conceptually rather direct and easy to understand. It is because the people of Abraham are so prone to backsliding—turning away from both God and limited government—that prophets, and the surest support of prophecy, religious freedom, are needed. These provisions allow Israel to regain her political footing. The sons of Jacob demonstrate a propensity toward worldliness and aggressiveness toward family and neighbor in the days of the patriarchs. In fact, the new nation of Israel loses focus on the democratic objective at the very moment of the drafting of the national constitution at Sinai. Instead of reaching for the heavens, she stoops to the depths-bound culture of idolatry and fashions a golden calf to symbolize her inclination toward kingship. After chastisement and subsequent reception of the new law with great enthusiasm, she nevertheless continues to murmur against Moses when things get hard. Some, like Korah, not only murmur but rebel.

Backsliding is a prominent feature in the book of Joshua and Judges as well, and in the subsequent history of kings. (Joshua 22; Judg 2:11) Only a handful of kings in Israel did not "do evil." The prophet Hosea describes the strength and duration of the faith of the people who chose those kings in terms God would approve of: "Your goodness is as a morning cloud, and as the early dew it goeth away." (Hos 6:4; compare Deut 31:16) It is clear the priestly leaders of the plural worship traditions did poorly as a rule, too. (Ezek 22:26; 1 Kgs 12:31; 2 Chr 15:3; Jer 2:8)

The intent of the First Commandment is to build egalitarian and ethical social institutions. In New Testament days, God directed that the ancient law be honored in the present day in both speech and action. Jesus, then, self-consciously spoke pursuant to an ancient law whose force and effect had never been repealed, and urged a kingdom whose spiritual leader had never been deposed. His ministry was complete only when the apostles understood that prophecy had returned to Israel, and that men were fully licensed once again to leaven change in the political structure of society. (John 17:3-8, 18)

That Jesus understands the First Commandment as a law to undergird a prophet-led nation is seen in his adherence to the notion that God is the real king, and an authentic prophet the rightful political ruler. (Matt 25:34, 40) Though he could not exercise actual political leadership in Palestine in the time of a powerful occupying force, he nevertheless emphasized this de facto leadership by entering Jerusalem in the manner predicted by Zechariah for the messianic king. (Zech 9:9; Matt 21:1-9; Mark 11:1-10; Luke 19:28-38)

Prophecy is necessary, probable, and encouraged for God's people because it is the only really effective instrument by which they regain their magnificent original moorings and apprehend the blessing promised to them. Yahweh and Moses understand from the beginning that Israel will periodically need new, persuasive prophetic leadership to bring them back from the brink of ignorance and disaster to knowledge of history and to the prescient way of God. They will need these leaders in the same way Israel captive in Egypt needed Moses.

Given the predictability of moral, spiritual, and political decline, it was necessary and inevitable that God send another prophet, if one could be found, to restore the conditions and doctrines of secular salvation understood and practiced in the earlier day. That voice is not available unless communicated through a clean and sentient vessel, one who is able to receive a calling and perform it.

To love God and put none other before him, then, is to provide an institutionalized way to encourage and allow the report of his voice in society. In the ancient Near East, a law commanding "love" was understood not as a provision related to thinking or feeling, but as a provision related to doing or acting. Ancient suzerainty treaties required one head of state to "love" the other by faithfully enacting all the agreed upon treaty obligations.[11] In Israel this kind of international legal provision was made an article of domestic government. God served as suzerain, and the people enacted the primary obligation found in the constitutional law, a provision paving the way for dissident prophets to rise and serve as leaders of the nation and intermediaries for God.

---

11. Milgrom, *Leviticus*, 218.

The love of this God is a matter of legal action and political obedience to enlightened government. If the people failed to be obedient to such common sense, the sovereign could abrogate the blessings of protection and support he promised them in the covenant, just as the suzerain would do in the event of non-compliance by the vassal. If the sovereign God mentioned equitable treatment of aliens as a provision of his covenant with the people, it was not to be thought of as a suggestion, but as a legal mandate. Thus a provision stating "If a stranger sojourn with thee, ye shall not vex him . . . thou shalt love him as thyself . . ." (Lev 19:33–34) is a mandate to enfranchise the alien with the highest and best rights enjoyed by the citizenry. This idea is stressed elsewhere as well: "One law and one manner shall be for you, and for the stranger that sojourneth with you." (Num 15:16) Israel's sense of "love" of God and stranger is deferential in the same sense of a vassal obligation to put the interests of the suzerain above even that of his own. He must be willing to abase himself and exalt another. If he comforts the stranger, it is as though he comforts God as well. (Matt 25:40)

Jesus re-iterated the great Sinai law—"Thou shalt have no other gods before me"—when he stressed its importance in preventing the oppression of minority views. Speaking on behalf of God "the King," he indicated God would say to the righteous at the last day, "I was a stranger and ye took me in . . . I was in prison, and ye came unto me . . ." (Matt 25:34–36) When the righteous answer "When did we see thee a stranger and take thee in? . . . when saw we thee . . . in prison and came unto thee?", God responds by saying "Inasmuch as ye have done it unto one of the least of these my brethren, ye have done it unto me." (Matt 25:37–40) God, by means of the "stranger" law of Israel, requires obedience to the very commandment of religious liberty that Leviticus and Jesus speak of here: equity afforded to strangers. Those who enact and protect it will be favored. Those who do not "shall go away into everlasting punishment . . . " (Matt 25:46) It is God's voice through the prophets that is most often the one impaled on the cross of religious bigotry. His prophets are treated as the least of all the pundits in the nation. Prophets are welcome only where religious liberty is practiced, and Israel embraced such liberty for most of its long early history.

Jesus maintains that the legal doctrine of protection of the rights of others is the warp and woof of the Decalogue: "This is the first and great commandment ["love the Lord thy God with all thy heart" Matt 22:37] and the second is like unto it, 'Thou shalt love thy neighbor as thyself.' On these two commandments hang all the law and the prophets." (Matt 22:38-40) The first commandment requires blessing or securing the beliefs of the neighbor, and the tenth commandment blessing or securing the family and property of the neighbor. The duty of securing the interests of all the people is the duty of all in Israel.

The whole experience of Israel is about the importance of this law. Jesus thus underscores that God's ancient law is still the pre-eminent law of the present day. A true prophet defends both God and himself in promoting this law: "If ye love me, keep my commandments." (John 14:15) When Jesus' disciples report to him that the Pharisees are offended by some of his sayings, Jesus does not take the bait of provocation. He does not take any action against the Pharisees, or enjoin with them a battle over doctrine, but says "Let them alone." (Matt 15:14) The proper way to handle religious difference is to let people's beliefs play out by means of natural consequence under the protection of law. He suggests that those who try to provoke others might well "fall into a ditch." (Matt 15:14)

The First Commandment, in one or another guise, is thus the pre-eminent political policy of the Bible. Each of the great figures of the Bible is associated with a slightly different version of the commandment.

The First Commandment was known in early form in the Garden in the admonition to avoid the tree of knowledge of good and evil, which tree essentially was associated with experimentation with evil. (Gen 2:16-17) Man was to hold rather to the tree of life, associated with clear-eyed observation of the consequences of evil and prevention of such a spiral of degradation in one's own life and in the life of the community. The primeval Adam understood the commandment as a law to listen to the voice of God above all other voices and to follow its intimations so that it bore the fruit of life, rather than decay and death. (Gen 3:17-19) In order to follow God's voice, it was necessary to establish the sort of tolerance for economic, intellectual and religious differences (Gen 4:2-7) and civil and religious rights which the Adam community then demonstrated in the matter of handling the manslaughter of Abel by Cain. (Gen 4:1-16) Significantly, Adam and Eve are given free choice as to whether to listen to this God or to shun his advice, or for that matter the advice of any other god as well. While at first they set aside the civic religion of God for the religion of the serpent, they later understand the consequence of this decision and apparently use the same free exercise to return to the God of the Garden.

The promise made to Abraham of numerous offspring was contingent upon the upkeep of a social environment in which individuals and groups "blessed" one another in their beliefs rather than "cursed" one another. God promised Abraham that he would be on the side of those who do the blessing but not the cursing: "I will bless them that bless thee, and curse him that curseth thee . . ." (Gen 12:3) Here, then, God expects Abraham to establish and promote an environment of tolerance for prophetic leadership of society and intolerance of an environment of suppression of it. While seemingly rudimentary, here is the First Commandment in stunningly pointed and effective form.

The Psalmist also retains this key concept: "As he loved cursing, so let it come unto him: as he delighted not in blessing, so let it be far from him." (Ps 109:17) We find the same kind of natural law expressed some 2,000 years after Abraham in the Book of Revelation: "He that leadeth into captivity shall go into captivity." (Rev 13:10) The book of Jude in the New Testament extols this same legal condition and cultural practice. Jude suggests that the earthly law stems from a prototypical law in heaven. In heaven the archangel Michael did not "bring a railing accusation" even against the devil. Instead, Michael said, "The Lord rebuke thee." (Jude 9) Thus, religious toleration is found even in heaven. The Psalmist literature, for its part, is not content to merely draw parallels. In words un-minced, it states: "Touch not my anointed, and do my prophets no harm." (Ps 105:15)

Hebrews, as well, expresses a similar sentiment to that of Jude: "See that ye refuse not him that speaketh: for if they escaped not who refused him that spake on earth, much more shall not we escape, if we turn away from him that speaketh from heaven . . ." (Heb 12:25) The same principle that activates free speech on earth exists as well in heaven.

Yahweh commissioned Moses to establish a constitutional law for Israel and then gave him the Ten Commandments. The first precept of this political constitution is a provision for political and religious freedom found both in Exodus 20 and Deuteronomy 5. (Exod 20:3; Deut 5:7) However, yet another form of the law is expressed in even more palpable form in Deuteronomy 6. Here "love the Lord God with all thy heart" is both preceded and post-scripted by mention of the method by which this love can be accomplished: "Hear, O Israel . . . thou shalt love the Lord thy God with all thine heart, and with all thy soul, and with all thy might." (Deut 6:4–5) The word "Hear" is highly suggestive of oracular listening, and the word "might" is highly suggestive of government power. When the factual existence of oracular revelation is given protection by human right through law, one does then love God effectively. When the Pharisees asked Jesus which was the greatest commandment, he answered quoting this very passage from Deuteronomy 6. (Matt 22:34–38)

Love in Deuteronomy is a love that can be commanded, as one scholar notes.[12] Freedom is to be enforced by government. To love God is to walk in his ways (Deut 10:12), keep the commandments which dictate human rights and human responsibilities (Deut 10:12), heed both the law and his voice. (Deut 11:13, 30:16) To love this God is to listen to those who speak about him and who convey his instructional message and interpret his law. In Jesus' view, the commandment relating to "love" of God is one mandating support of the liberality of this God in matters of political and religious conscience. When political leaders stray from enforcing such human right, citizens may rebel against them.

The Bible presents a cultural history which demonstrates the existence of many religious points of view, whose political propagation and historical publications apparently had some kind of protection under law. Increasingly, scholars have been getting closer to the idea presented here that a seemingly private, cult doctrine admonishing love of God is actually better understood as a public statute enfranchising a variety of acceptable forms of such devotion.

THE FREEDOM LAWS OF ANCIENT ISRAEL

At the moment of commitment to the law and the land after Israel crosses Jordan into Canaan, Joshua reminds the people of the tremendous freedom the law gives them to choose between a variety of ways of cultural life: "Choose you this day whom you will serve . . . but as for me and my house, we will serve the Lord." (Josh 24:15) This passage serves essentially as an executive branch proclamation of religious freedom, which enacts and mirrors the constitutional law the ancestors committed themselves to at Sinai with one voice. (Exod 24:3) It perhaps then serves, in the minds of the Deuteronomistic historian, as a basis for pe-

---

12. Moran, "Love of God," 103–115.

riodic, perhaps annual covenant renewal celebrations held at a national holiday of varying type, location, and date during the time of Judges and Kings.[13] These festivals celebrate and re-commit Israel to political and religious freedom.

The law of intellectual freedom can be found in Israel in a variety of legal forms, cultural practices, and intimations. We have mentioned above the law relating to enfranchisement of the rights of resident aliens. (Exod 22:21, 23:9; Lev 19:34; Num 9:14; Deut 10:19, 24:17) Law protecting free exercise was also extended to household servants. (Deut 12:17–18; 16:10–12)

The law in Israel required all meat to be sacrificed (killed and prepared) at a religious shrine rather than at home. (Lev 17:1–9; Exod 20:24–26) Since altar law understands each cult shrine to be a place of independent denominational worship, the law relating to sacrifice is thus another ancient way of enacting religious liberty. It assumes the availability of numerous denominational worship centers and priestly offices within a short range of travel from widely dispersed villages across Canaan. These sites were presumably serviced by the Levites dispersed about the territory of the nation. (Josh 21; 1 Chr 6:54–81) Even during the days of the constitutional reform of King Josiah, Levites worked locally "in the gates" in such shrines. (Deut 12:18; 16:11; 26:12) Josiah's reform established that people could kill and prepare meat in their homes rather than at a local shrine, because many constitutionally marginal local priests were put out of business by the reform. (Deut 12:15, 21)

The early Covenant Code law of Exodus provides a statute which rabbis of the Pharisaic period understood to promote religious pluralism: "You shall not revile God . . . " (Exod 22:28 NRSV; "Thou shalt not revile the gods" KJV) In the context of the polytheism of the period, this law aims at achieving religious liberty for whatever name is given to God, not a sort of orthodoxy based on protecting one particular concept of God over another. None of the gods worshiped by the people of the Exodus wanderings or of the settlement can be cursed, reviled, or disrespected, nor their adherents persecuted, unless such religion violates the ethical laws of the Decalogue. Isaiah understands such reviling of God as a condition of a benighted people who have forgotten their original commitment to liberality in religion: "To the law . . . if they speak not

---

13. Anderson, *Old Testament*, 518–19.

according to this word, it is because there is no light in them ... They shall ... curse their king and their God ... " (Isa 8:20-21)

The Covenant Code in Exodus contains verses which mandate sacrifice to the singular God of the Exodus: "Whoever sacrifices to any god, other than the Lord alone, shall be devoted to destruction." (Exod 22:20 NRSV) Interestingly, the provision does not specify the sacrificial location, the appurtenance used for the sacrifice, the animals to be used, nor the specific liturgy to be followed. The verse cannot be read, then, as a provision mandating the specifics of worship or faith, but only as a statement of the ethical boundary which hedges in the practice of religious sacrifice in Israel. The sacrifice must be made within the context of political freedom and the social ethics of the commandments.

The verse following this one, in fact, mandates that Israelites not oppress a resident alien. (Exod 22:21) It would be curious indeed to enact a provision mandating the establishment of a specific religious denomination and then supplement it with a provision forbidding religious oppression. The second verse, in fact, provides a sort of legislative intent or clarification of the first, and the first provides the same for the second. Sacrifice in Israel is singular in the sense of the necessity of its ethical context, and resident aliens must respect that. The unorthodox religion of resident aliens is permissible in the land of religious democracy, as long as those religions manifest in the ethical way of sacrificial religion mandated in Israel.

During the time of the political and religious revitalization campaign of Josiah, many converted to worship at the central shrine at Jerusalem. Because many of these could not eat meat under the earlier law unless butchered at the shrine of their choice, permission was given in the law for people to prepare sacrifices at home rather than at the Jerusalem shrine. (Deut 12)

Rather than ultimately limiting worship to one central shrine, the law thus actually broadened sacrificial worship to home-based shrines, so that these could be used as family, clan and village places of worship in addition to the great denominational temples outside of Jerusalem and the temple at Jerusalem. The Jerusalem temple itself, we must remember, while serving as a mainstream denominational center, also served as the king's chapel for use by his court staff just as the northern temples were used (Amos 7:13), as a non-denominational center for national citizen holiday pilgrimages, and as a place of shared use for other denominational groupings. (Ezek 8–10)

The law relating to blasphemy clearly can be construed as protecting legitimate religious denominations from libelous excoriation and thus civic submersion. Israel's first "supreme court" test of First Commandment religious freedom is narrated in Leviticus 24. Here, Moses, serving as high court judge, distinguishes between a defendant who calls into question his own denomination's beliefs (Lev 24:15), and one who speaks against God's political program of religious liberty by reviling the "name" of God. (Lev 24:16) In the first situation, the member may be dealt with by the denomination (presumably ex-communication), but the second case is to be prosecuted as a felonious offense against the constitution of the land.[14] We mentioned above that law relating to blasphemy is also outlined in Exodus, where the law states a man "shalt not revile the gods . . ."[15] (Exod 22:28)

The law relating to vows demonstrates the political latitude and social depth accorded religious variation even within the microcosms of the family union and the marital union. Fathers and husbands may overrule vows of religious dedication and piety made by their children and wives, but must do so immediately or else they give tacit blessing to those actions. (Num 30) This is as much to say that parents and husbands must be vehemently opposed to religious choices of those in their care, or else religious liberty cannot be interdicted. That even in this patriarchal society women have considerable latitude to make choices about religious affiliation is seen in a reminder of that latitude given to Jeremiah by the women in the diaspora in Egypt: "We will certainly do whatever goeth forth out of our own mouth . . . " (Jer 44:17) They have the power, and have exercised it for a long time, to make their words deeds!

The law of vows, understood in light of the Fifth Commandment (honor parents), would appear to give parents the power to decide the religion of the family. In fact, the archeology of Iron Age Israel demonstrates the existence of many home-based shrines of the type Micah set up in his own home.[16] (Judg 17–18)

Not just at the lowest social level, but at the highest social level of government, authorities in Israel are under mandate of law to act with

14. See also Milgrom, *Leviticus*, 292.
15. Phillips, "*Criminal Law*," 42.
16. Zevit, *Religions*, 541–42, 554–55; Albertz, *Israelite Religion*, 99–103.

"equity", "justice", and "righteousness" in all of their decision-making. There is no exclusion mentioned for religious equity. (Isa 9:4, 7; 11:1–5; 16:5; Ps 89:14, 99:4)

The laws barring severe economic treatment (usury, indenture) of Israelite "brothers" (Lev 25:39, 46) and economic rescue or redemption of clan members (Lev 25:47–55) are a species of first commandment law, since matters of conscience have a close relationship to matters of financial indebtedness. That relationship is nowhere better demonstrated than in the twin deprivations of economic and intellectual freedom in Egypt and in the importance of the Sabbath day of rest in response to those deprivations. The periodic days and seasons of "rest" in Israel—every 7 days, 7 weeks, 7 years, 70 years, and 7 times 70 years—are those times when Israel obtains legal relaxation from work and debt and therefore time to engage in developmental study, worship and other intellectual pursuits, such as study of the constitutional law of liberty. (Deut 6:4–9) There seems to be an implicit understanding, based on the Decalogue, that the tribes are free to enter into regional religious denominational groupings, and that they must remain hospitable to one another's intellectual and ethical interests, the violation of which brings substantial reprisal. (Josh 22; Judg 19–20)

That tribes and clans have sovereignty in matters of religion is seen in the story of the two and a half tribes. These tribes set up their own system of worship even before the conquest of Canaan is complete. (Josh 22) Thus, the situation in Israel was not unlike that in classical Greece, where Plato outlined a scheme for setting up model cities based on twelve pie-shaped sections of town, each of which would be devoted to a different god or religious denomination of the Greek pantheon.[17]

Even before entering Canaan, God admonished wandering Israel against any economic or religious repression of groups with whom they had ancestral ties, such as the Edomites and the Moabites. "Meddle with them (Edomites) not, for I will not give you of their land." (Deut 2:5) "Distress not the Moabites." (Deut 2:9) That overrunning a neighboring nation's land typically brought about religious oppression in addition to annexation of land is observed in Israelite treatment of the Gibeonites after conquest of Cannan. The Gibeonites were made slaves of the Israelite shrine at Shiloh. (Josh 9:23) This sort of ill-treatment of neighbors was to be kept at a minimum. Indeed, Israel's concern for political

17. Weinfeld, *Social Justice*, 236.

independence of land-holding citizenries plays out during settlement in the form of numerous laws, stories and statements relating to release of political and religious captives. (Gen 14:14; Deut 30:3; Judg 5:12; Ps 68:18, 85:1; Jer 22:3, 29:14; Isa 61:1; Luke 4:18)

The holding of land is the surest cornerstone of religious liberty, for one may believe and do as one wishes on one's own land. Therefore, laws which tended to keep land in a clan or family line, such as endogamy— marriage within the faith or within the clan (Ezra 9–10)—and land and labor redemption laws (Lev 25; Deut 15) are a support to religious freedom law as well. As did Israel's law, Plato's Laws indicate that land in Greece devoted to a particular god should not be alienated or sold outside the faith, so as to not incur the wrath of the god.[18]

Each of the prophets exercised their own distinct way of couching the foundational human right of the constitutional law. Hosea wrote, for example, "By a prophet the Lord brought Israel out of Egypt, and by a prophet was he preserved." (Hos 12:13) By the law of freedom which enfranchises prophets Israel was founded, and by the same law she existed as a nation for 500 years down to Hosea's time.

Ezekiel received a distinct oracle from God relating to religious toleration: "Thou shalt say unto them, Thus saith the Lord God; He that heareth let him hear; and he that forbeareth, let him forbear." (Ezek 3:27) The key term here is that the law must "let him hear," that is, allow men to organize around a prophet's new revelation. The author of Lamentations wrote in searingly modern legal terms when he announced, "To turn aside the right of a man before the face of the Most High . . . the Lord approveth not." (Lam 3:35–36)

Jeremiah was also concerned about providing theological support to the notion of new prophecy and thus religious freedom: "Am I (not) a God at hand, saith the Lord, and not a God afar off?" (Jer 23:23) He also provides his audience with the quintessential "canon within the canon" of the Judaic scripture. God's gospel is none other than that he is accessible to all those who seek him and desire to come to grips with his laws: "Thus saith the Lord . . . 'Call to me, and I will answer you.'" (Jer 33:2-3)

The New Testament does not slack behind the Old Testament in outlining the concept of First Commandment-based ongoing revelation and religious tolerance in terms understandable in the time of Roman Palestine. Jesus taught, "Love thy neighbor as thyself." (Matt 22:39; Mark

---

18. Ibid., 236.

12:31) He also instructed those who were at religious odds with one another to "worship in Spirit and in truth." (John 4:23) For Jesus, the Holy Ghost and the liberty of thought which allows it full expression teaches tolerance and progression toward truth. (John 14:26) At the Pool of Bethesda, he chided his audience for having lost touch with both the principle of revelation and the precept of law once cherished by the nation: "Ye have neither heard his voice at any time, nor seen his shape. And ye have not his word abiding in you." (John 5:37–38)

Profile—The Egyptian Connection (Jeremiah)

Only days after his release from the dungeon, Jeremiah found his way into the safekeeping of one of the homes of the sons of Shapan. To the brothers gathered there he reflected, "The people call my predictions treason. How can that which is inevitably coming . . . how can the truth . . . be made treason? Egypt tells the people what they want to hear, while Babylon does nothing but spit fire and brimstone."

"Do the scribes have no understanding of the heart of Nebuchadrezzar? It is dark, unremitting, unrelenting. The people will have to learn to live under the yoke of the Chaldean, because the hand of Egypt is effeminate and cannot prevail. Her sorcerers and enchanters beguile our princes and priests, none of whom has for years darkened the door of the temple archives to examine our long history. We have too much history with both nations to suppose that the days of Shishak have returned to Egypt."

Jeremiah paused and read the faces of his hearers. Their eyes were open wide, their countenances wrapt, believing, interested. "Besides, I have received a confirmation from the God of our fathers. We must absolve ourselves of ignorance and shame and submit to the East. The day of Yahweh by the arm of Assyria is gone. The day of Yahweh in which Egypt will join in holy devotion to God along with Assyria and Israel, as the prophet Isaiah has prophesied (Isa 19:24–25), is not yet here. The Day of Our God in the hands of Babylon is upon us. What say you O Sons of Shapan?"

KNOCK ON THE KING'S DOOR... WHO KNOWS, IT MAY OPEN

Bible students have made much of the notion of the Exodus as liberation from slavery. But they have not been so careful to discuss the most fundamental kind of slavery, that of religious slavery. Liberation from physical slavery is surely what is necessary to establish occupational rights, physical health and other social benefits. But an even more significant form of liberation is that of liberation from the shackles of forced conscience. Without the exercise of free thought and belief, even economic freedom cannot mean much, as citizens of communist China well understand today.

It is somewhat self-evident, but still not a small matter, that if God's word in a given day and time comes afresh by the mouth of a new prophet, that new revelation must be given free expression in order for it to be truly effective in reaching large numbers of the citizenry. Human rights such as free speech, free scribal copying of books, and free assembly are an essential pre-condition for free revelation and free religion. Bringing the prisoners out of both intellectual and physical dungeons is necessary so that more people can approach God on their own terms, independent of vested interests. Release of the prisoners of conscience and promotion of religious, political and academic diversity allows the people to be exposed to new light leadership and trusts that the people will choose the best to affiliate themselves with, as Deut 17: 8–10 expects.

In Israel's day, except in times of oppression of rights of expression, there was freedom to preach, teach, publish and assemble for purposes of advancing fresh ideas about the original doctrines of Abraham and Moses which had lost currency in the society. David and other ardent religionists published psalms indicating the dimensions of their own specific individual beliefs and their belief in religious rights, because they were allowed freedom of worship in a competitive marketplace of religious ideas.

But in those all-too-frequent times of deprivation of rights or of backsliding into nature worship, proclamations of devotion to freedom and of overthrow of oppression, in one variety or another, came not only through Moses but also through princes and princesses, prophets and prophetesses, paupers, physicians, pundits and provocateurs. They came in one form or another through Joshua on Mt. Ebal, Deborah, Gideon, David, Jeroboam, Elijah, Jehu, Isaiah, Hezekiah, Josiah, Jeremiah,

Zedekiah, Ezekiel, Second Isaiah, Cyrus, Haggai and Zechariah, Nehemiah, Ezra, Esther, Daniel, and Judas Maccabee in Old Testament times, and by way of John the Baptist, Jesus, Peter and Paul and others in New Testament times.

Proclamations of religious freedom came from foreign sources as well, which impacted Israelites either indirectly or directly. Seti I, for example, issued a proclamation of religious liberty about the time when Moses was a child,[19] but that proclamation either fell short of protecting the Hebrews who worked the brick factories of Goshen, or perhaps was reversed by Seti's son Ramses II. That very oversight or reversal may have given impetus to Moses' efforts in their behalf, and raised the sympathy of the Egyptian public for their troubles. (Exod 12:35–36) A proclamation of freedom came from the throne of Cyrus as well, when Israel was captive in Babylon, which freed them to return to Palestine and rebuild their culture. This is noted on the famed Cyrus Cylinder and in the Book of Isaiah. (Isa 41:25–27; 45:1–7)

The problem of economic and religious captivity and the means for release from it is the pre-eminent politico-cultural problem of the ancient world. This is attested in extra-biblical sources and in the Bible itself. Abraham's journey from Ur to Haran to Canaan, for example, is couched as an effort to avoid or disengage from captivity. (Gen 12:1) There was a constant threat of overrun of Chaldea by neighboring city-states, Elamites, and barbarians from the far north. Extra-biblical sources make it clear that the religion of moon worship was a deeply established state religion both in Chaldea and in Haran during the range of times suggested by scholars for Abraham's residence there. In fact, while Terah's family have names associated with such worship,[20] some in the party may well have wanted to dissociate themselves from it. The tradition of Canaan as a destination for religious dissidents did therefore not likely originate with Moses' group.

Joseph, the son of Jacob, was held captive by his own brothers. (Gen 37) The story of the Exodus is clearly a response to the problem of captivity. Israel during the time of Judges falls into temporary captivity at the hands of the Mesopotamians, Philistines, Midianites, Moabites, Ammonites, and the Canaanite King Jabin. (Judg 3–16) In the time of

---

19. Weinfeld, *Social Justice*, 16, 136.
20. Bauer, *History*, 128.

Rehoboam, Solomon's son, Israel has a near brush with total captivity at the hand of Shishak of Egypt. (1 Kgs 14:25–26)

The northern kingdom, after a period of vassalage, ultimately falls into Assyrian captivity, and the southern kingdom eventually succumbs to Babylonian captivity. After the return to Palestine, Judea is taken captive by the Seleucid Greeks, and then by the Romans. In this kind of environment, it is easy to see why a law related to freedom of conscience came to be of such importance to the Hebrew tribes of Canaan.

The picture we have painted of the ancient importance of the right of free worship is not limited to Israel, but is a canvas known from time to time elsewhere in the ancient Near East as well. Egyptian Proclamations from the Fourth Dynasty onward (about 2500 BCE) freed farmers in the vicinity of the temple from slavery so that their labor and their beliefs could be devoted to a deity of choice.[21] During the time of early Assyrian ascendency (1900–1700 BCE), the inhabitants of its colony of Cappodocia were extended rights of freedom as well.[22]

In ancient times it was considered bad form to haul away the idols or "gods" of a conquered nation. Aggressive nations who did so were thought to be cursed, either by means of retribution by the communities whose gods were thus blasphemed, or by means of a natural karma whereby the barbaric nation earned the enmity of decent nations throughout the region. Thus when Naram-Sin of Assyria desecrated the Temple of Enlil in 2150 BCE, the so-called Curse of Agade insured that another nation would soon enough return the disfavor.[23] The curse was fulfilled when the Gutians invaded Assyria and captured Agade not long after. When Hammurabi hauled off the gods of Susa from Elam, he understood he had made a mistake and sought counsel from his advisers on the best way to return them.[24] In similar fashion, when the Philistines realized they had made a mistake in hauling off the sacred Israelite ark, they quickly returned it. (1 Sam 5–6) Assyrian citizens rebelled against their King Tukulti-Ninurta when they saw he removed the sacred statue of Marduk from Babylon. Their next king returned the statue.[25] Jesus understood the ancient tradition associated with religious freedom, and

21. Weinfeld, *Social Justice*, 101.
22. Ibid., 92.
23. Bauer, *History*, 121.
24. Ibid., 175.
25. Ibid., 271.

announced at the outset of his ministry that it would be his mission to release the prisoners of religious conscience. (Luke 4:18)

Profile—On Free Expression (Solomon)

Solomon draped himself over the low stone wall ringing the porch of the palace he had built long years before, the blue fringe on his short sleeves noticeably setting off the bright white garment from his dark arms. (Num 15:37) To his trusted adviser in the natural sciences he complained, "The priests condemn the prophets and scribes. The scribes condemn the priests and prophets. The prophets condemn the priests and the scribes. But my father taught that God is responsible for and interested in everything under the sun. Each power in society must learn from all of the others. The laws of nature, of the heavens and of the animals, are the same as the laws that men live by. Those laws can be transgressed by the unruly and ignorant, the hungry and the fat of each kind under creation, just as the laws of man can be broken and reviled by the unmerciful of those who are nevertheless still created in the image of God."

Without giving his hearer a moment to respond, he continued, "I empower the religious practices of the representatives of the nations to the Jerusalem court. I have given them leave to worship at their own shrines opposite the temple on the Mount of Olives. But because the names which they use for their gods are not the same as the name for our esteemed God, the nay-sayers condemn me for enfranchising idolatry." Pausing, and gathering breath, he gazed across the Kidron Valley.

"Do not the priests and prophets understand what David taught when he spoke in the great congregation of Abraham? Our God is a God of free conscience. The suppression of conscience is a greater mischief than the dilution of the pure practice of it as handed down to us by our ancestors. The doctors of the law who embolden themselves in the temple daily do not look past their own noses. They take no thought about the practical requirements of nations and in particular their ambassadorial policies. Besides, our own people step further afoul of the boundaries of true Yahwism than even the foreigners do."

HE SAID WHAT?: THE NEGATIVE EVIDENCE ABOUT RELIGIOUS LIBERTY

Any interpretation of the Decalogue as a manifesto for political and religious liberty must grapple with what might be termed the negative evidence of such a theory—indications and incidents which seem to argue the opposite. Here we very briefly review arguments suggested by the Korah story, the concept of idolatry, the "conquest" of Canaan, the problem of the "high places," and Josiah.

The incident of Korah's rebellion in the wilderness at Kadesh (Num 16) and Moses' response to it may be interpreted as evidence of a Sinai-based legal structure promoting intolerance of religious diversity rather than the tolerance we have suggested above. After all, Korah's group argue for democracy in prophetic leadership and complain about Aaron's exclusive priesthood, after which God and Moses together exterminate their entire party. But theoretically equal access *to* God is quite different than equal authority *from* God. If Korah's intent were merely to assert religious diversity, clearly his right to do under the charter, he might have simply siphoned off a group of followers and co-existed in peace. His intent, however was to commandeer the entire operation and undermine the popular (that is, elected), representative government established at Sinai with Moses as its administrative head. Korah suggests, as an alternative to that form of government, a radical sharing of prophetic political gift and leadership in a sort of mass collective of the people, the same kind of mob democracy shunned in most proto-democracies of the ancient world. This is prohibited by the covenant of government made at Sinai and amounts to overthrow of that charter. When Moses puts down the coup attempt, he acts not against human rights, but in defense of them, and in defense of the form of government the people chose unanimously only shortly before. (Deut 29:10–13)

Some worry that Israel's own Second Commandment (no graven images) enshrines religious bigotry as an article of government. We argued at the beginning of this chapter, that certain limits relating to legitimate content of worship and relating to general social concourse are an inherent part of any political charter of government. While the First Commandment enacts freedom of worship in the largest of print, the Second Commandment is the small print that takes away some of it—that portion of the panoply of possible religious choices which Israel considered to be either criminal, politically oppressive, or primitive.

Israel's system of free religion drew a bright line between proper moral religion and nature religion, with its emphasis on symbolic licentious sexuality; between properly independent priesthood and divine kingship, which fused cult and state; and between proper religion and sorcery, with its emphasis on intimidation, deceit and violence in human commerce. Any religion which suppressed the land-working populace, discouraged broad-based citizen participation in government, or stultified the interests of the poor by pointing them toward salvation in the next life rather than in this life (ancestor worship), was not good religion and was not to be tolerated in Israel at all.

Many biblical scientists have challenged the popular notion of Joshua's thoroughgoing conquest of Canaan, and the supposed extermination of competing religious systems thereby. Archaeological evidence supports military destruction at some late Bronze Age sites at Canaan, but finds a lack of such destruction at many other locations. Some biblical reports claim broad based conquest (Josh 11:16—12:24), while other biblical reports indicate only selective engagements with the populations there. (Josh 13:1-6, 23; Judg 1:1—3:6) Most likely Israel cooperated and intermingled with communities and tribes who accepted their way of benevolent consensual government and agreed to abide by it, and only confronted those city-states whose monarchic form of government was incompatible with their own way of socio-cultural living. For example, four cities lead by Gibeon voluntarily become a part of Israel (Josh 9), but Israel felt it necessary to confront Jabin, a king of Canaan whose capitol was in Hazor. (Judg 4-5) Israel's political claim to a substantial inheritance of land in Canaan is bolstered both by the claim of Abraham's prior purchase of land there (Gen 23), and by the sheer numbers of pilgrims who squat on available land in the sparsely-settled Canaanite highlands and commit to the rule of law there.

It must be observed that the Israelite "high places"—dissident, syncretistic or minority places of religious worship—were loudly judged to be illegitimate places of worship in Israel. The writer of the Deuteronomistic history (the books of Joshua, Judges, 1 and 2 Samuel, and 1 and 2 Kings) condemns them, even though they were readily and broadly patronized by the people. Surely this is evidence that Israel intentionally promoted and enforced only a single national cult, based in Jerusalem, and perhaps a separate national cult at Bethel after the monarchy divided, say some. However, the history of the Israelite confederacy during the time of the Judges, the brief period of united monarchy, and the period of the separate monarchies in the north and south, demonstrates an expansive and extended tolerance of independent denominational worship at the high places. For example, only two of the forty kings of Judah and Israel can muster sufficient support to suppress them under an appeal to the original intent of the Israelite covenant, while the other thirty-eight apparently tolerate them. Thus, it is not appropriate to deem the animus against these shrines to be representative of a general theocratic tendency among all in Israel. That concern represents instead only a category of thinking that sees some of the shrines at times as falling outside the standards set for legitimate worship under the law.

Josiah makes his move against the high places after a book revealing the original intent and practice of the Mosaic laws comes to light during his administration. (2 Kgs 22) His many and varied reforms result, it seems, in what has come to be called a "centralization of cult" in Judah. While it is clear that there is a de-licensing of many priests laboring in rural Yahwist cults, those cults had slipped into a syncretistic modality of accommodation with nature religion, involving polytheism, sexualization of the deity(ies), promotion of a feudal-like economic class system, and ancestor worship. It was this kind of heavily watered-down Yahwism about which the literary prophets leveled such criticism in their written testimonies. A better way to view Josiah's reform, therefore, would be as a political populist movement working in tandem with a religious revival devoted to the old local ethical ways, one by-product of which was a beefed-up chaplaincy at the national shrine in Jerusalem.

6

Jerusalem's Gang of Twelve

EACH BIBLE PROPHET'S OWN peerless reflection upon history, analysis of contemporary events, and predictions about the future certainly serve as a primary kind of Bible evidence of God's ever ongoing interpenetration into the culture. But the literary prophets are not willing to leave well enough alone. They are fond of taking a polemic jab or two at the opponents of continuing prophecy, as we have seen in chapter 4, and the major and "minor" prophets together develop the theme of continuing revelation in a variety of ways. We will examine the musings of one of the prophets on the topic at the start of this chapter. Amos seems to have been the path-clearer, the first after David to have raised the assertion in literary form that human Godliness extends to others than kings and high priests. We will also review a few common idioms, including prophet as watchman, servant, and shepherd.

THE CAT OF HEAVEN: AMOS' POLEMIC ABOUT ONGOING REVELATION

Amos is widely regarded as opening a new era of prophecy and influencing those prophetic voices roughly contemporaneous with him, including Hosea, Isaiah, and Micah. This group of prophets had to contend with a priestly establishment which had essentially declared no new oracular revelation should ever again come from God. Amos laments, for example: "Ye . . . commanded the prophets, saying, Prophesy not." (Amos 2:12) This lament presupposes widespread satisfaction of the culture with the sacred literature current at the time. It also gives a sense that optimism and unanimity was the preferred temperament among politicians and historians of Amos' day, rather than pessimism and dissent.

Indeed, scholars have found evidence, not that the entire Pentateuch existed in its final edited version at that time, but that separate versions of the early sacred history of Israel were available both in the south and in the north at this time, and that those separate political communities had strong reasons for holding to their own views. For example, the so-called "Yahwist" or "J" source, which reflects the concerns of Judah, seems to have been compiled in an early form during the time of Solomon's enlightenment, around 930 BCE. The so-called "Elohist" or "E" source, which reflects the concerns of Samaria to the north, was compiled perhaps in the ninth century, in the time of Elijah/Elisha. Alternatively, it may have been composed in the eighth century since it reflects themes common to the literary prophets. It is also possible that it might have been written as early as the late tenth century in order to justify and undergird Jeroboam's political and religious schism after Solomon's death.[1] Whatever its precise date, it is clear that these sources all have their own polemical angle which new revelation had the potential to upset.

Amos apparently felt a heavy sense of responsibility to correct the idea that the sacred word of God could be encapsulated and stored in final form in an archive jar. God's spirit held an interest not only in the fortunes of the heretofore elect people of the settlement in Canaan, but of all people. For this reason Amos took aim, in the first two chapters of his book, at all the nations around Israel who knew better than to be doing what they were doing. Having initially dispensed with the politicians of those nations, he next offered to those willing to reflect more deeply on a specific subject some six verses into which is compacted one of the most cogent and potent explanations ever given in Bible literature about the reasonableness of perennial oracular revelation. His argument is both philosophic and theologic. It stems from nature itself, with its laws of cause and effect, and also from the nature and providence of God. Not only is new word from God reasonable in terms of its civic emphasis, but it is also necessary for contemporary political and religious salvation. Furthermore, Amos admits that he himself has been asked to convey the new material to the people. (Amos 1:1) The verses comprise a distinct text, but also form a portion of the larger literary unit often entitled "The Prophecy of Doom," found in the first four chapters of Amos. The argument in question occupies verses three through eight:

---

1. Pury, "Yahwist ("J") Source," 1012–1020; Jenks, "Elohist," 478–482.

(3) Can two walk together, except they be agreed? (4) Will a lion roar in the forest, when he hath no prey; will a lion cry out of his den, if he have taken nothing? (5) Can a bird fall in a snare upon the earth, where no gin is for him? Shall one take up a snare from the earth, and have taken nothing at all? (6) Shall a trumpet be blown in the city, and the people not be afraid? Shall there be evil in a city, and the Lord hath not done it? (7) Surely the Lord God will do nothing, but he revealeth his secret[2] unto his servants the prophets. (8) The lion hath roared, who will not fear? The Lord God hath spoken, who can but prophesy? (Amos 3:3–8)

Through the pairing structure of this text, Amos argues that God and his prophet are connected logically, like the roar of the lion and his kill, and the bird taken in its snare. They go together. They are inseparable. They are linked for a reason. There is a powerful, almost mechanical force involved when God calls a prophet. God takes command of the situation like the lion its prey and a snare its fowl. The prophet becomes entangled with God forever more.

When the bird's flight is stopped, it is because it has flown into a snare. When the lion roars, it is because it has captured meat. When a man interrupts the settled life of work and family and begins to rattle the cages of the high and mighty about him, it is because he has had an experience with the Almighty. And, furthermore, God does not finally act for great good or for great evil, according to Amos, until he causes a prophet to prophesy—until he provides the people with a searing condemnation and last-ditch hope of a message. Apparently, human beings, like animals, do not act in consequential ways unless and until they are goaded, prodded, almost forced to act. This metaphor of God as lion and prophet and people as prey is remembered three hundred years later by Joel: "The Lord also shall roar out of Zion . . . and utter his voice from Jerusalem." (Joel 3:16)

The larger text of Amos's book summarizes several of the theological arguments we develop in the next chapter regarding the nature of God. Amos' argument for continuing revelation is that God lives and is still and always will be sovereign. (Amos 4:13) Because he is a benevolent sovereign and loves his subjects, he continues to act providentially throughout history, even if he must send punishments to turn them from their ways. (Amos 4:4–13) He sends a new prophet to give a last-minute

---

2. Translated "plan" in the NIV

warning—a call to political, religious, economic and social repentance. The onrushing catastrophes playing out in the day of Amos are linked to former prophecies. (Amos 4–5) When the people make an excuse out of the idea that their religious leaders have led them astray, the prophet opines that God provides them with a way out of the mess even at this late moment. (Amos 3)

Amos's story makes clear that a prophet is not necessarily a priest in an established religion, but an ordinary person going about the business of life, seeking God as the scripture invites. Amos admits he is not an ordained ecclesiastic—only a simple landholding herdsman. However, he has had the life-changing experience of having the lion of heaven roar in his ear. (Amos 3:8, 7:14) God has found meat for his cause. That message from God is so clear and so loud that he can ignore it only with great shame to himself and great indifference toward his own people.

Amos's prophetic career demonstrates the larger chain of causation to which Bible texts speak as well: the people make a covenant to walk with God (i.e., live peacefully and ethically); the people and their political and religious leaders go astray (begin to dissemble and lust after conquest); because God loves his people, he speaks loudly from heaven in the direction of anyone humble and worthy enough to hear that voice; the prophet, going about his business (in this case, tending his herd), hears that voice and feels strongly compelled to pass along a message; the people hear or read the message but fail to hearken to it; a nation (in this case the community of the northern tribes) are soon afterward destroyed by an advancing army and the survivors permanently scattered. In sum, the people sin, God warns one last time, the people ignore the warning, and then the people are no longer.

Profile—On the Road to Bethel (Amos)

The trip had been a pleasant one in terms of the amenities of travel. Amos left Tekoa, only ten miles south of Jerusalem, and traveled straight north along the road to Bethlehem. From there he turned onto the national highway which linked Beersheba far to the south in the Negev with Jerusalem and Shechem much farther north. From Jerusalem he headed to Bethel, only another twelve miles, some of it atop the watershed ridge, which provided a view to the east and west. He had the satisfaction of leaving his flocks in good order, securely watched in the folds which dropped toward the lowlands of the Jericho Valley, littered with rocky stretches where little vegetation thrived. He had left only after the fodder of sycamore figs for his cattle had been harvested and stored for the winter.

Now he was leaving his comfort zone and stepping into precincts of northern power, confronting the religious and political establishments of Israel at a time of unprecedented prosperity and power. Israel had not long before reclaimed Gilead, and thus now controlled the great King's Highway running to the east and parallel to the national road. It ran through that territory linking the Tigris and Euphrates valleys with the Gulf of Aqaba. With such wealth, the north had re-established much of the former glory of David. There seemed few threats to her smugness and opportunism, but Amos saw the situation differently. He was an advocate of the interests of the people.

Along the road he encountered diplomatic runners, tradesmen, pilgrims, social travelers headed for weddings and funerals, and a few servants and new settlers. His conversations with his fellow-travelers only heightened his sense of purpose. To one somber artisan traveling with his attractive wife he boldly remarked, "Enjoy the road while it is pleasant and passable. The Assyrian will soon crowd out all traffic and tear down all that your countrymen have built. Their god Asshur will take all the crops and wealth you have stored."

The worker raised his brow. His wife withdrew a few paces away so the two could talk. He responded, "You are a southerner and yet you are familiar with our plight?"

Amos rejoined, "I dare say your problem will soon be our problem in the south as well. Many of the people of Samaria will flee to the south and invade our cities once Assyria decimates the gods of the region."

Amos's combination of neighborly concern and bold analysis now triggered the northerner's own tongue. "How can the monarchy not see what its policies have wrought." His cheeks reddened and he began to gesture with his hands. "The rich care only for riches. The king's men care only for power. The common people have little to eat, and a man's cloak is not returned to him by his creditor."

Amos, evidently sympathetic with the artisan's view of domestic matters in the north, continued: "Citizens are taken into indenture, a brother of means charges interest to a brother of his own clan . . . the laws of civil humanity of olden days are being threshed like winter wheat. A Day of Yahweh's power is coming, and a time of falling for those who now stand proudly." Amos paused to size up his listener, and then continued. "If your destination is Bethel like mine, may we meet again after we settle our purposes there? I have obtained a word from the Lord, and desire to share it with any like yourself who will listen."

His eyes opening wide, the woman's husband retorted, "I, too, have seen the folly of Israel by the hand of God. God once again speaks to his people, and offers his love by the hand of a prophet. Hosea is my name."

ZION'S NEIGHBORHOOD WATCH

Several important prophets explain the phenomenon of continuing revelation using an analogy of the civic sentinel. In very ancient times, city-state governments set night watchmen upon the fortifications to warn of threats against the people of the town. In a similar way, God set up prophets who were turned inward on the walls, to watch for ethical threats to the people from within their own communities. In fact, the analogy existed long before the eighth century prophets used it. The city of Mispah, whose name means watchpost,[3] is associated with an oracular experience which made that place a holy city, to which persons like Samuel often resorted to pay respect. We have seen that Amos uses the metaphor (Amos 3:6), but Hosea, Isaiah, Second Isaiah, Jeremiah, and Ezekiel all use it as well. (Hos 9:8; Isa 21:11–12; Jer 6:17; Ezek 3:17, 33:1–9) In their view, prophets are watchmen, set by God at the outskirts both of the town and of the nation to warn of intrusions against the peace and tranquility of the people.

In the view of these writers, God would no more not send prophets than city elders would fail to set night watchmen to guard the city in times of peril. Isaiah's later namesake summarizes God's view: "I have set watchmen upon thy walls . . . which shall never hold their peace day nor night." (Isa 62:6) Notice that here God uses a plural noun . . . one night watchman is not enough. Also, notice it is the duty of the watchmen to sound out during the night if there is danger. This later Isaiah followed the notion first outlined by the original Isaiah, who wrote: "Go, set a watchman, let him declare what he seeth." (Isa 21:6)

God asks Ezekiel, as well, to serve as watchman: "I have set thee a watchman . . . therefore thou shalt hear the word at my mouth and

---

3. Vaux, *Ancient Israel*, 305.

warn them." (Ezek 33:7) Ezekiel develops the idea further by discussing the shared responsibility of the watchmen and the people who hear the prophet-watchman's outcry. If the watchman successfully warns the people, but they do not respond, the responsibility for the outcome is on their own heads. (Ezek 33:4–5) If the watchman fails to warn the people, the ensuing disaster is the responsibility of the prophet. (Ezek 33:6) Both must act in concert for the outcome to be truly healthy.

Profile—The Spirit Packs Its Bags (Ezekiel)

Ezekiel looked at the flimsy fortifications of his adopted hometown. Who would stop to bother such a village, or to take such walls seriously? The people went about their business here secure in the same way of thinking. Surely no aggressive army would cause it any harm. Yet that is what his native Judea had thought as well, and all that land had been ruined.

In Jerusalem and in the exile the people would not listen to an ordinary mortal such as himself, a mere "son of man," as God had designated him. He was not a member of the royal family—a potential "son of God"—and thus was not worthy of attention. Ezekiel had thought often about what he was to make of the designation that God had rubbed his nose in. It surely must be that even the most genuine student of life is but mortal, relatively inhumane, and ignorant compared to the author of all knowledge and creation. Man's sons are always man. Man sprouts, grows, glories, withers and then dies like a blade of grass.

But then he thought, God also gave me a more glorified title. God called me to be *responsible* man—a "watchman" at the city gate of Israel in exile. How curious, Ezekiel thought, to be seen as one proudly strutting upon a high stone edifice and gazing out over a vast expanse of hill and vale from a protected spot on a fortress wall. In fact, he stood on no wall. He functioned daily more like one hiding underneath walls. In fact, he lived unpretentiously in a hut dug several steps into the clay-like soil deposited by the near-by River Chebar.

Chebar was an ancient canal cut from the waters of the Euphrates just north of Babylon and running in a great semi-circle south and eastward to water the fields about Nippur, before rejoining the Euphrates near Erech.[4] Here in the town he was rarely even noticed by the gro-

---

4. Thompson, "Chebar," 893.

cers and buyers of dates scurrying about in the busy market outside his home. From a small room that his group had constructed, he relayed clandestine messages and tidbits of God's word to his associates in the reformist priestly school which he now headed. Perhaps, he reflected, his humble position helped to show what can be accomplished when a prophet's associates listen to God, even when God's headquarters is in such a hovel, that truly distinguishes man from the beasts. Then, those "sons of man" might mean a great deal, indeed. They might become even more helpful than those few hereditary sons of God.

Ezekiel's messages to his disciples took account of the history of Babylon he had learned from stories and texts given him by the locals. That account spoke of the shifting sands of liberty in Babylon—how Nabopolassar had led the freedom fight to expel Assyria and then returned to the Elamites the statues of gods abducted from them by the Assyrians.[5] Nabopolassar had been succeeded by his son, Nebuchanezzar, who took the opposite view, that it was a king's prerogative to favor a deity and marginalize others. Moses and the ancestors despised primitive nature worship of the type Nebuchadnezzar imposed upon his people in Babylon. Ezekiel, identifying closely with the progressive thinking of those honorable ancestors, had been working feverishly to write a new political constitution for a future community of Israel, which would re-enthrone religious liberty for all Israelites. One day, someone like Nabopolassar or the Elamites of the highlands would come to power in Babylon and allow Yahweh's people to return home.

Today the message to his compatriots was an exultant one. The covenant charter for the re-establishment of the nation of Israel was now complete. If his colleague Jeremiah foretold the end, it was Ezekiel's job now to decree a new beginning, as Moses and David had done once before. A spirit of rights and values and cultural independence would one day consume the fabled city and free its captives. At the very least, a new monarch would see the wisdom of establishing a small people like Israel in its ancestral homeland as a bulwark against great power advances from the south and west. The new imperium could possibly come from the Zagros mountains to the east where the followers of the prophet Zoroaster informed the zeal of the people there. And Israel would be ready, then, to resume her civilization in the land of Abraham.

---

5. Grayson, "Mesopotamia," 764–65.

A PRINCE IN THE CAFETERIA LINE: THE SERVANT NARRATIVES

The Bible text frequently uses the metaphor of the faithful servant to suggest the re-appearance and unusual diligence of a messenger of God. The most trusted servant of a king, after all, is often the diplomatic messenger he sends to a fellow prince to communicate urgent matters. A landholder in ancient Israel, too, typically had one or more particularly well trusted servants. Most servants were free employees of the household. But there might also be individuals indentured to the landowner for the payment of debt, or young servants apprenticed for learning a trade. The father's children had the legal status of servants, as well, bound to honor and serve both parents. As surely as Israel has servants, she also has prophets. Servants labor for their earthly masters, prophets their heavenly masters.

The prophet, as servant, carries out functions performed both by the indentured or bound worker, and the free employee. The force of his calling, as we have seen in chapter 2, binds him for service to God his entire life. On the other hand, he is free in many situations to exercise his own judgment. Like the servant in Abraham's household, he is free to use his experience and learning to accomplish difficult and lengthy tasks given him by his employer.[6] (Gen 24)

God's binding of the prophet into a life-long indenture is underscored by the fact that the word "servant" is used in the utterances from God's own mouth, and not as utterances of the prophet's own mouth.[7] For example, in Isaiah, the term is usually used in situations where God has made a decisive calling.[8] The decision to be "servant" is one almost taken out of his own hands, arranged by virtue of circumstances not necessarily his own. Once indentured, the prophet can leave God's service, but only at the expense of the future, even the lives, of many others. (Ezek 33:6, 8)

The servant, despite the fatalistic beginning of the relationship between God and prophet, ultimately enters into a close personal relationship, an intimacy, between instructor and instructed. The office of servant-prophet implies a heartfelt trust between servant and master

---

6. Zimmerli and Jeremias, *Servant*, 10.
7. Ibid., 16.
8. Ibid., 27.

of the type known by Moses. Of him it was said, "My servant Moses" speaks "mouth to mouth" with God. (Num 12:7–8) God negotiates with Moses, his "friend" (Exod 33:11) in much the same way God's servant Abraham negotiates the terms of the disposition of the city of Sodom. (Gen 18:16–33) In fact, the servant loves the "name" of God because that name "Yahweh" conveys the concept of ongoing conversation with man, conversation which each servant can testify of having heard directly from the mouth of God: "The seed also of his servants shall inherit it [Zion]: and they that love his name shall dwell therein." (Ps 69:36) Moses, as the seed of the servant Abraham, learned to love that name as his predecessor had.

But also there is an expectation of diligent performance on behalf of both parties, a holding to the honor of the name and the office. (Num 11:11; 2 Kgs 16:7; Ps 143:11; Isa 65:8) The active political dimension of the performance sought by God is exemplified by God's servant Moses. Moses is law-giver (Josh 1:7, 8:32; 2 Kgs 18:12), divider of the land (Josh 1:13, 15), and organizer of the church. (2 Chr 1:3, 24:6) The very definition of a diligent servant of God after Moses is one who upholds the Mosaic law, like David. (1 Kgs 11:38) Prophets are to be veritable missionaries of the law. (Isa 49:5–6)

Israel's legal system of local, social, and financial rescue is based upon the responsibility of designated relatives to assist family members in sorrow, oppression, trouble, sickness or debt. The "goel," or redeemer, is like a living guardian angel, a God-parent of a child. The prophet-revelator serves as the last line of defense in this legal system. If all other designated local citizens fail to step in to aid their own, and the government fails to step in to aid the poor, the feeble, the innocent, and the strangers of the land, the prophet is the one who will stand up to do so.

The linking of the concept of servant to the prophet-messenger is intended to convey the idea of the universal assignment of prophets to human societies. Society cannot work without servants, and neither can God. It is also intended to indicate the diligence with which God and the prophet serve society. Second Isaiah makes explicit the link between the idea of national service and the prophetic message: "I am the Lord . . . that confirmeth the word of his servant, and performeth the counsel of his messengers." (Isa 44:24, 26) The duty of the messenger is to provide a platform God can use to perform his historic work among the people.

The story of David's ambassador to the Ammonite Hanum (2 Sam 10) demonstrates how closely the servant messenger and his master are associated in the ancient world. The party who receives the embassy is sorely temped to treat the innocent messenger with the same hostility he holds for the figure who sent him.[9] They want to, literally, kill the messenger. If the receiving court has respect for the King, they will receive his servant well. If not, then poorly. Perhaps one reason prophets are received so poorly in the courts of Israel and the ancient Near East is that they embody a different personality than the one demonstrated by most institutional leaders—one that is honest, humble and learned.

The servant recalls God's own nature. He is one who does not discriminate between one human being and another. He must act professionally and politely, like a well trained representative of his master. Impartiality is a firm criterion for the character of a prophet: "Who is blind, but my servant." (Isa 42:19) His calling also is to encourage, heal, comfort. (Isa 61:1) Also, he often must often suffer great indignity in the process of bringing salvation to his people.

Within the scholarly community and the Judaic tradition, a number of candidates have been suggested for the identity of Isaiah's suffering servant, outlined in Isaiah 49–53. Among possible kingly candidates are Uzziah, Hezekiah, Jehoiachin, and Jerrubbabel. Candidates for a prophet figure range from Moses, Isaiah, Jeremiah, and Ezekiel, to Second Isaiah himself. Second Isaiah fits the bill of the suffering servant, for example, because of the considerable opposition by Jews of the exile to his prophecy that Cyrus is called by Yahweh.[10] (Isa 45:1–3) The Christian tradition, of course, sees Jesus as the suffering servant, one called to be scourged and to die on the cross.

But the job of the servant is also to get things done in society, and in particular to clarify what is going on. If the job of the servant is to persuade, the job of the audience is to listen and to heed the message, because it sheds light on the present situation: "Who is among you that feareth the Lord, that obeyeth the voice of his servant, that walketh in darkness, and hath no light?' (Isa 50:10)

The "servant" title is applied in scripture to prophets in Canaan earlier than the time of the Israelite monarchies and throughout the time of the monarchies as well. The term is applied to Abraham (Gen 26:24),

---

9. Zimmerli and Jeremias, *Servant*, 21.
10. Zimmerli and Jeremias, *Servant*, 30.

Jerusalem's Gang of Twelve 129

Moses (Num 12:7; Josh 1:1), Joshua (Josh 24:29), David (2 Sam 3:18; 1 Kgs 11:13; Isa 37:35; Ps 89:20), Ahijah (1 Kgs 14:18, 15:29), Elijah (1 Kgs 18.36; 2 Kgs 9.36), Amos (Amos 3.7), Isaiah (Isa 20.3), Jonah (2 Kgs. 14.25), Second Isaiah (Isa 42:1), and Job (Job 1:8).[11]

Jesus uses and thus honors the two idioms we have mentioned above to refer to legitimate prophets—watchman (Ezek 33, Luke 12:37); and servant. (Isa 53; Mark 10:44) These are epithets or nicknames for new prophets, and Jesus' use of them throughout his ministry bespeaks the effort he must make to convince his hearers that prophecy is not dead in Israel, as the Pharisees and Sadducees believe.

Jesus sees himself as fulfilling the role of the suffering servant written about in Isaiah 53.[12] (Mark 2:20, Isa 53:8; Mark 9:12, Isa. 53:3; Luke 11:22, Isa 53:12; Mark 10:45, Matt 20:28, Isa 53:10–12; Mark 14:8, Isa 53:9) His silence before the various authorities reprises Isa 53:7. Even the divine baptismal declaration about Jesus connects him with the servant mentioned in Isaiah 42:1. (Matt 3:17; Mark 9:7; Luke 9:35) The fact that a prophet inevitably suffers is characteristic, in Jesus' view, of all those servants who come before him, for example from Abel to Zechariah (Matt 23:35), down to and including John the Baptist. His identification with the plight of the suffering servant reflects Jesus' understanding of the hostility expressed by political and religious institutions with respect to the idea of new prophecy. It also motivates dire predictions about his own death.[13] (Mark 8:31; Luke 18:31–33; Matt 26:5)

LAMB STEW ON THE MENU: SHEPHERDING PEOPLE IN THE ANCIENT WORLD

In ancient Mesopotamia and Egypt, heroic political figures, law-givers, and reformers were given the title Shepherd. So it was with Ur-Nammu, who at the end of the third millennium before the common era formulated the first known law code.[14] Some 300 years later Hammurabi wrote in an autobiographical statement: "Hammurabi, the shepherd, called by Enlil, am I; the one who makes affluence and plenty abound."[15] In Egypt pharaohs are pictured holding the shepherd's staff or crook.

11. Coogan, *Old Testament*, 411; Zimmerli and Jeremias, *Servant*, 19–23.
12. Zimmerli and Jeremias, *Servant*, 98–99.
13. Ibid., 30.
14. "Ur-Nammu Hymn," ANET, 583.
15. "The Code of Hammurabi," ANET, 164.

The work of shepherding describes the regularity and care with which God, righteous king, and prophet dispense their duties among mankind. The shepherd guides his flock to food, water, and safety. The political or religious leader guides his followers to the same physical comforts, but also may lead them to figurative food and water, the bread of life (John 6:51) and living water. (John 4:10)

God himself served as shepherd to the patriarchs, as they wandered about Canaan looking for food and water. (Gen 48:15, 49:24; Jer 13:17; Mic 7:14) He carried them as one would a young or sick lamb. (Isa 40:11) He also served as shepherd of the people wandering in the wilderness after the Exodus. (Ps 78:52–53)

Moses set an early example of an expectation that the nation's human prophet-shepherd should be spirit-filled. He prayed that God appoint a man to serve as shepherd over the nation after his death. (Num 27:15–17) God then prescribed that it should be a man "in whom is the spirit" (Num 27:18), an expectation later re-iterated by Isaiah: "And the Spirit of the Lord shall be upon him . . . " (Isa 11:1–3) Cyrus of Persia, as well, served as an inspired shepherd of God, when he assisted Israel's return to Canaan after the exile. (Isa 44:28)

The job of a political shepherd is to serve as the oracular intermediary between God and the people, but most such leaders shirk their responsibility: "The pastors are become brutish, and have not sought the Lord . . . all their flocks shall be scattered." (Jer 10:21) Like a watchman on the city walls, the shepherd must not be asleep while on the job. (Isa 56:10–12; Nah 3:18) Isaiah suggests that a "deep sleep" has overtaken all those in Israel who no longer turn to oracular prophets like himself. (Isa 29:10) In fact, the prophetess Deborah is asked to "awake, awake, . . . utter a song," which suggests a level of heightened awareness of history and good judgment possessed by one who regularly watches for the safety of the people. (Judg 5:12) The song she writes is an oracle of scripture known as "the Song of Deborah and Barak." (Judg 5) Without such an oracular leader, Israel strays like a flock without a leader. (Isa 53:6)

One Psalmist reflects upon having once gone astray "like a lost sheep." (Ps 119:176) However, once he understood that "Thou art near, O Lord," (119:151) he became God's "servant." (119:125) David, as both actual and figurative shepherd of Israel, is the prototype of other prophet-shepherds to come: "I will set up one shepherd over them, even my servant David . . . and he shall be their shepherd." (Ezek 34:23)

There is a time when the powers in society give up the notion of oracular shepherding. Zechariah, the prophet and author of the last book of the Christian Old Testament, finds he is on the cusp of that momentous change in his day. He has seen the notion of prophecy go from a place of some favor in society to a place of disrepute and disrespect. God asks Zechariah to act out the part of two different shepherds. In the case of the first, or good shepherd, he acts the part of one called to protect and teach the sheep of the nation. As time goes on, he understands these are only headed for slaughter. He realizes the futility of his efforts and abandons them to the fate which their owners, the priests and politicians, have consigned them. (Zech 11:4–17)

Zechariah is then asked to understand the point of view of the owners, themselves once lowly shepherds, but now foolish herd owners. (Zech 11:15) Those owners earlier paid him his wages for the job he did while he was caring for their sheep (Zech 11:12), but later they turn fully against him and seek to violently end his life. (Zech 13:7)

The disciples saw the images of the "strik(ing of) the shepherd that the sheep may be scattered" and the payment of final wages to the shepherd in the event of the crucifixion. (Zech 11:12, 13:7; Matt 27:9) Jesus had identified himself as "the good shepherd." (Num 27:17; Jer 23:4; Ezek 34:5; Matt 9:36; John 10:11, 16) He was clearly remembered as such after his death. (Heb 13:20) Jesus claimed to "enter in by the door" of the sheepfold, that is, to follow in the path taken by ancient prophet shepherds. His sense of duty to God, law and man is such that he will give his life for the sheep. (John 10:11) He will do so because he has been given a prophet's or owner's authority over them, unlike the "hireling" who "cares not for the sheep." (John 10:13) As one who cares, he has taken time to "know my sheep." His job is to be a shepherd to whomever he exercises responsibility for, for all those about whom he can say, "I am known of mine." (John 10:14)

Profile—Monotheism and the Diviner's Cup (Joseph)

Joseph, son of Jacob, stood restively near one end of the hallway outside his chambers, observing one of the vases recently set on stands there. He admired its handiwork, but was disturbed by the petulant royal boasting inscribed on it by a long-dead Pharaoh. Having long before been released from the dungeon, he still remembered the twin feelings of elation upon obtaining his physical freedom, and suffocation as he sensed a different atmosphere of foul air—the social conformity emanating from the pressured precincts of political power. Pressed into service as Pharaoh's vizier, he had accepted an invitation also to wed into a priestly family. (Gen 41:45)

His wife Asenath was as great a challenge to him as Pharaoh's frequent dreams. She was independent-minded in all her ways. Today they exchanged comments about her selection of artwork as they stepped from one piece to another. Her maid servants awaited her wishes, perched just out of hearing distance at the other end of the hall.

Joseph sported a clean white tunic of fine cloth, and she bright red colors suiting her mood. "My dear Asenath," he intoned, "I sense you believe as I do that there is but one God, whether his name is Neith, the god of your ancestors, and the god after whom you are named, or Shaddai, the God of Abraham, or Pahad the God of Isaac."

"My Lord," spoken with a playful bit of sarcasm in her voice, "I believe only in a God of all the people. I worry that your policy to divest the people of their lands in exchange for food from the king's storehouses will not be easy to reverse, even in a time of plenty." She continued, "It matters not to me how the God is named as much as how he honors his people."

Joseph now smiled and considered her words. "My dear, you are brilliant and courageous at the same time." He then reached for a retort which might answer the question at the back of her mind. "We must not disturb the estates of the main, or even the minor, high priests of Egypt. Their lands will provide a balance of power against the king's interests. The house of Pharaoh will then be well advised to see to it that our policy will only be temporary."

Not willing to drop an opportunity to pursue the debate a bit further, Asenath stepped further away from her servants and looked her husband in the eye. "If the God of Jacob is one who discerns the future out of diligent study of the past, why then do you accept Pharaoh's divining cup as an instrument for discerning God's will? Is not that a mere continuation of the primitive policy of the ruling houses of Egypt? Ought not the diviner's prerogative to be the possession of the priest rather than the prince?"

Joseph, not lacking confidence in either his position or his belief, stepped with her further away from the attendants. "The cup, sweet Asenath, is but a cup. It reflects only the image of the person who looks upon its shiny surface. I rely on the annals as much as any in the king's court, and my God . . . our God . . . must provide some room for negotiation and variation in policy to meet the special needs of the day." She allowed her face to melt with pleasure at hearing this. He continued, "I worship a god of history and progress as you do. We must divine our daily actions and our policies based on God's universal ethical laws. Then there is much less room to go astray than there is for magicians and courtiers who peep and twitter, shake and convulse."

This answer his bride swallowed with satisfaction, as she took his arm and headed back through the door to greet the late afternoon air.

EARTH, AIR, FIRE, AND WATER: THE LINGUISTICS OF PROPHECY

The Bible uses nature idioms like "cloud," "cherubim," "fire," and "rock" to describe God's oracular mobility and recurring presence amidst the people. In Moses' day the "cloud" by day and "fire" by night expressed God's dark and brooding presence.[16] (Exod 13:21) Elsewhere, Yahweh rides on clouds (Ps 68:34, 104:3; Deut 33:26) and manifests himself in thunder and storm. (Ps 18:14–15; 77:18) In the ancient Near East a "cloud" or stormy sky is a symbol of theophany, so perhaps early writers and readers of the Pentateuch understood this idiom in a way modern readers insulated inside office buildings cannot. The great storm and subsequent flood in the early literature of Mesopotamia is associated with the advent of half mortal/half god Utnapishtim as well as the Bible's own prophet Noah. A storm is a powerful image, derived from nature's ability to force men to retreat under rock overhangs and contemplate their own powerlessness, and, perhaps then, to achieve the humility necessary to entertain the voice of God.

Part human/part animal winged creatures, like the sphinxes of Egypt and of Mesopotamian art, are guardians of places of revelation.[17] Cherubim served this function in Israel's temples, where they guarded not so much the priests of God, but the constitutional law of the Decalogue. That law, by means of its free speech provision, assured periodic emergence of legitimate prophetic oracles perhaps originating at those disparate mountain crags where shepherds cringed from the ele-

---

16. Coogan, *Old Testament*, 393.
17. Ibid., 389–90.

ments. Winged creatures are important in Ezekiel's concept of deity as well. (Ezek 3:13)

The term "fire" is used to describe Moses' initial encounter with God: "Behold, the bush burned with fire." (Exod 3:2) "The Lord descended upon it (Sinai) in fire." (Exod 19:18) At night God provided Israel "a pillar of fire, to give them light." (Exod 13:21) Isaiah used the oracular words "storm" and "fire" to describe future advents of judgmental prophecy: "Thou shalt be visited of the Lord of hosts with thunder, and with earthquake, and great noise, with storm and tempest, and the flame of devouring fire." (Isa 29:6)

The cloud and the fire give impetus to the "glory" of Yahweh, a term associated with the ark which houses the freedom tablets, which in turn allow the prophets to ply their trade. (Exod 40:34–35) When the ark is stolen by the Philistines, the wife of the high priest, dying in child birth, cries out in anguish not for her son, nor for her own life, but for all the sons and daughters of Israel: "The glory is departed from Israel: for the ark is taken." (1 Sam 4:22) But the best manifestation of "the glory" is the nexus of God's spirit, God's law, and God's prophet. In Ezekiel's vision, all three travel from Jerusalem to Babylon in the first deportation of 597 BCE. (Ezek 9:3; 10:4, 19; 11:23; 43:2–5)

The metaphor of a mighty rock or mountain is associated with the phenomenon of revelation throughout the scripture. Jacob spoke of God as "the stone of Israel." (Gen 49:24) During the time of the transition to kings, David wrote: "The Rock of Israel spake to me . . . " (2 Sam 23:3) About a future time of God's ascendency throughout the world, Isaiah writes, "And many people shall go and say, Come ye, and let us go up to the mountain of the Lord . . . and he will teach us of his ways . . . " (Isa 2:3) In New Testament times we find: "That spiritual rock . . . Christ." (1 Cor 10:4)

The Bible also uses anthropomorphic idioms like "name," "face," "voice," "word," arm," and "image" to suggest God's revelatory character. We will see in chapter 7 that the "name" of God in the ancient Near East not only identifies him with some kind of localizable characteristic (see Isa. 55:13) but also describes something about his character (Exod 34:6; Ps 138:2), his goals and his modus operandi. Israel's God is one who condescends in order to remove oppression (Exod 3:8, 15:3), who moves from place to place (Exod 20:24), and speaks. (Exod 23:21)

The Hebrew word "panim" translates "face." The face is the body part from which vocal communication issues forth. It is used in the Bible to indicate God's ongoing revelatory work among mankind. When a prophet meets "face to face" with his God, as Moses did with Yahweh, he invariably receives a verbal communication. For example, it is said, "And the Lord spake unto Moses face to face, as a man speaketh unto his friend." (Exod 33:11) Admonitions given in the Bible to "seek his face" (1 Chr 16:11; Ps 27:8, 105:4) are exhortations to believe in and seek direct oracular communication with God. The historians of the Bible, such as the Chronicalist, tie successful connection with the face of God to Israel's success as a people: "If my people, which are called by my name, shall humble themselves, and pray, and seek my face, and turn from their wicked ways; then will I hear from heaven, and will forgive their sin, and will heal their land." (2 Chr 7:14) Ezekiel, as well, suggests the connection between God's face and his revelatory spirit: "Neither will I hide my face anymore from them; for I have poured out my Spirit . . . " (Ezek 39:29)

The term "voice" rather directly suggests God's mode of operation. God's voice is his express verbal communication to man by means of prophetic messengers. "And when Moses was gone into the tabernacle of the congregation to speak with him, then he heard the voice of one speaking unto him from off the mercy seat that was upon the ark of testimony . . . and he spake unto him. (Num 7:89) That voice is essential for an elect people: "Now therefore, if ye will obey my voice indeed, and keep my covenant, then ye shall be a peculiar treasure unto me above all people: for all the earth is mine." (Exod 19:5)

When Israel doubted her place in the world, she could ask "Did ever people hear the voice of God speaking out of the midst of the fire, as thou hast heard . . . " (Deut 4:33) That voice came again and again in Israel and was heard by David, for example: "The Lord thundered from heaven, and the most High uttered his voice." (2 Sam 22:14) For Elijah, the voice was less thunderous in actual volume—"a still, small voice" (1 Kgs 19:12)—but still consequential in terms of social reform in Israel.

Indeed, the "voice" of God is associated with the history-bending efforts of the prophet who hears the voice: "Thou shalt therefore obey the voice of the Lord thy God, and do his commandments and his statutes, which I command thee this day." (Deut 27:10) That effort results, as it did in Moses' day, with the success of a new people establishing themselves in the world.

John records a theophany after Jesus' entry to Jerusalem and about the time certain Greeks sought him. Jesus' soul was "troubled" and he prayed "Father, save me from this hour . . . Father, glorify thy name . . . Then came there a voice from heaven, saying, I have both glorified it, and will glorify it again." (John 12:20-26) The saying seems to suggest not only the reprisal of Ezekiel's glory in Jesus' day, but the likelihood of its ongoing recurrence in days to come.

The term "word" is also associated with revelation. The "word" is rare, precious, and must be preserved and not adulterated. (Ps 12:6-7) Man should not temporize with it by changing its meaning. He must not "add unto the word" (Deut 4:2) but should elucidate it correctly. (Job. 6:10) Men should not be content with economic advantage in life, but should instead live by every word that proceeds forth from the mouth of God. (Deut 8:3; Matt 4:4; Luke 4:4) The word is the message given to a prophet. (Ps 119:11; Jer 15:16) It often comes in the form of ethical law (Ps 119) and patterns of right conduct. (Isa 45:23) The word from God is durable: "Heaven and earth shall pass away, but my words shall not pass away." (Matt 24:35) The "word" is often rendered in the phrase "word of the Lord" to suggest a body of communication received from God. (Gen 15:1; 1 Sam 3:1; Isa 1:10; Jer 1:2; Hos 1:1; Joel 1:1; Jonah 1:1) The literary prophets themselves do not speak of Spirit (ruah), but only of the "word" given from God.[18]

When great deeds are accomplished subsequent to the prophet's calling, it can be said that the powerful "arm" of God has been bared on behalf of his people. The term "arm" connotes not just presence, but the salvation, often military, that results from God's presence. (Isa 63:5-6; 59: 16-17) Isaiah believes the arm follows after the voice and the two, together with the fire and the storm, will be seen again and again in history: "And the Lord shall cause his glorious voice to be heard, and shall show the lighting down of his arm, with the indignation of his anger, and with the flame of a devouring fire, with scattering, and tempest, and hailstones." (Isa 30:30)

The writers, editors, and compilers of the Old Testament and New Testament leave us with the impression that any individual who ardently seeks God may actually find him and have the experience of epiphany or theophany. The Old Testament term "image/likeness of God" is one that suggests this promise. This term, used in Genesis to describe man's

---

18. Mowinckel, "'The Spirit' and the 'Word'" 199-227.

important role in the created order (Gen 1:26–28; 5:1–3; 9:6), is also used in Egyptian and Mesopotamian literature as well.[19] In this wider cultural milieu, an "image" is a statue, often a molten idol, where deity manifests itself to the priest or Pharaoh and communicates his will to those sacred authorities. The Hebrew view of heavenly manifestation, in contrast, represents a much more democratic view that all human beings are "images" of God and thus are capable of revelatory conversation with deity.

The Bible also uses the term "angel" (malak or ruhot) to describe the form God takes when he communicates with a prophet. This seems to be a way of interposing a bit of distance between God and prophet, as though the messenger-prophet requires a messenger himself. Angels function as part of the divine council in heaven. (1 Kgs 22:19–23; Gen 28:12, Ps 89:6–9) In the beginning, each nation is assigned an angel, "son of God," or god to look after it. (Deut 32:8 NAB, NEB, NRSV) Angels perform a variety of revelatory functions, including announcing a birth (Gen 18:1–10), giving reassurance about a promise or performance of a vow (Gen 31:11–13), commissioning a specific thing to be accomplished or prevented (Gen 22:11–12), revealing the future (2 Kgs 1:3, 15), acting as an agent for protection or for punishment (Gen 48:15–16), guiding personal actions (Gen 16:7–8), and, most often, communicating God's word to prophets. (1 Kgs 13:18)

This word is often used as a template like the following: "The angel of the Lord [interacted] with man." In the Bible the "angel of the Lord" "appeared" (Exod 3:2; Judg 13:3), "called" (Gen 21:17, 22:11), "found" (Gen 16:7), "hastened" (Gen 19:15), "spoke" (Gen 31:11), "stood" (Num 22:23), "met" (Gen 32:1) "came" (Judg 2:1), "encamped" (Ps 34:7), "touched" (Elijah, 1 Kgs 19:5), "said" (to Elijah, 2 Kgs 1:3), and "talked with." (Zech 1:9, 4:5) These deliberate anthropomorphisms are designed to underscore that God is like man in that he is communicative, intentional, and intimate in his behavior.

One unnamed prophet of the Bible living in Bethel makes the connection between the angel and oracular revelation explicit. He says: "I am a prophet also as thou art; and an angel spake unto me by the word of the Lord, saying . . . " (1 Kgs 13:18) An angel communicating God's word also came to Gideon. (Judg 6:11–12) Achish mentions to David, ironically, that he is as refreshing as the appearance of "an angel of God,"

---

19. Curtis, "Image," 389–391.

which suggests some affinity with the Greek notion that God's angels are often merely men acting to do God's will in God's place. (1 Sam 29:9)

An angel's appearance in a new and different place from the last appearance of an angel roughly equates with the movement of the oracular God from one denomination or prophet to the next. Joshua has a theophany at Gilgal. (Josh 5:13-15) But Gilgal declined as a place representative of God's favor: "And an angel of the Lord came up from Gilgal to Bochim . . . " (Judg 2:1) Here a new revelation was communicated "unto all the children of Israel . . . and they called the name of that place Bochim: and they sacrificed there unto the Lord." (Judg 2:5) Later an angel appeared and spoke to Gideon (Judg 6:11), still later to Manoah and his wife (Judg 13:3, 9, 11, 16, 21). Wherever God's voice is heard anew, the people rally to that place and that leader. Such a leader is often termed simply "a man of God" who delivers a message "by the word of the Lord." (1 Kgs 13:1)

The prophet Isaiah reminded Israel that the oracular presence of God was the very vehicle by which the nation avoided disaster time and time again: "For he said, Surely they are my people, children that will not lie: so he was their Saviour. In all their affliction he was afflicted, and the angel of his presence saved them . . . he bare them, and carried them all the days of old." (Isa 63:8-9)

Often it is not clear whether the angel is a messenger, or actually Yahweh himself. For example, in one text God says "I will send an angel," but in the same sentence then goes on to say "and I will drive out the Canaanite . . . " (Exod 33:2-3) This passage seems to suggest that God sends some sort of emanation of himself to carry out a specific purpose. It has been remarked that God uses a surrogate like an "angel" to buffer the individual from too close contact with his searing presence, and the text in Exodus above could be conveying that. In the New Testament, an angel serves as a go-between as well. For example, an angel serves the charitable function of releasing Peter, (Acts 12:6-11) and also other apostles (Acts 5:19-20) from prison.

Jesus extends an invitation to Phillip and Nathanael to join his movement, recorded in the Gospel of John. (John 1:43-51) Nathanael agrees to meet Jesus, but before they can discuss things, Jesus hails Nathanael to his face as "one in whom there is no guile." (John 1:47) Nathanael immediately questions how Jesus knows something like this. Jesus answers that he has observed Nathanael while sitting (and perhaps speaking) under a fig tree. (John 1:48) Nathanael acknowledges that such power of quick discernment is befitting a revelatory "Son of God." (John 1:49) Jesus, for his part, answers "Thou shalt see greater things than these... Hereafter ye shall see heaven open, and the angels of God ascending and descending upon the Son of man." (John 1:50–51)

Here Jesus associates new oracular knowledge with a communication link between God and man that was well understood in the ancient world, the angelic messengers of heaven. He draws a direct link to the patriarchal period story of Jacob's revelatory experience, which also draws on the image of angels ascending and descending. (Gen 28:12) He thus aligns his own ministry with that of the founding prophet of Israel, the patriarch Jacob, who left his descendants a culture of prophet-initiated democratic human rights. Jesus implies that the acceptance of prophetic wisdom, of the sort Nathanael demonstrates, assures that he will be learning much more about life than he now knows. In fact, the story leaves the reader with the impression that those who believe in new prophecy and follow Jesus will see an outpouring of heavenly revelation and knowledge attending the prophet and marking the era.

7

A Theology of Continuing Revelation

THE BIBLE IS A witness to acts of revelation, just as prophets are bearers of them. Rationales for continuing oracular revelation spring not only from the callings, teachings, and universal occurance of prophets, (chapters 2, 3 and 6) and the laws of the early settlement and of Deuteronomy (chapter 5), but also from the overall theology of the Bible. We define theology here as ideas about the nature and attributes of God. In the ancient Near East, the name of a god provides a shorthand summary of his personality, and such is true of Israel's God as well, as we will see below.

The God of Israel is by nature an unceasingly vocal God. It was an integral part of Israel's election as a people that she should have regular conversation with God, for God wanted a people who would not merely be mute objects of his providence, but would speak and act like he does, in a never-ending process of exercising responsible dominion over the earth. (Gen 1:26) Thus we see that God is content only when and where he finds a leader and a group of followers who bear up under his vocalized requirements.

If God can find such a group within Israel, that is good. But if he cannot, then he will look for a group outside of Israel, as we saw in chapters 1 and 3. (2 Chr 16:9) "The voice of the Lord is . . . upon many waters . . . The Lord sitteth king forever." (Ps 29:3, 10) God is one Lord, and his responsible personality can manifest anywhere and everywhere amongst human communities throughout the entire earth. (Deut 6:4) He can be found on the shores of oceans and by the rivers and rivulets of all of creation. We will see that the Psalms underwrite both the realities of actual life mediated by the presence of prophets and the hope for the return of such life somewhere on earth, based on the dependability of a vocal God.

A Theology of Continuing Revelation   141

The overriding theology of the Old Testament mirrors the story that unfolds in the pages of its history. It is one of the in-breaking of God's universal ethical personality into a world presently bereft of adequate social, political, and ethical moorings. That renewal of presence is accomplished by the use of a human mediator or messenger. The first part of the message is simply "God speaks again," and the second part is the instructional message itself.

God's presence in the Bible has a cyclical aspect. His earliest presence on earth comes as he overcomes chaos and creates man. The first man is the first prophet—the first to hear God's voice and to evaluate its meaning and importance for his life. (Gen 2:16) The first word given to the first couple establishes that they have a sovereign choice as to whether to partake or not to partake of evil—to have "knowledge of good and evil" (to acquaint oneself with how it works), or keep one's hands off of it. (Gen 2:16–17) The temptation to do as he pleases quickly overcomes Adam, as he succumbs to the alternative point of view that has been given to Eve and relayed by her to him. (Gen 3:6) Soon enough, both man and woman together hear the voice of God (Gen 3:8), and are made to understand that their devaluation of the revealed law concerning what is presumably the most beneficial lifestyle for them now brings consequences. The experience of God's close presence in their lives ends swiftly. When the first couple choose to exercise the same kind of agency that God exercises, but without the wisdom to undergird such decision-making, God responds by banishing them from the primeval environment in which they are originally placed. (Gen 3:22 23) They then experience the hardships of life, which play out at the whim of their willful natures outside the place of their beginning.

Outside the garden, the children of Adam and Eve exercise freedom to worship. They bring sacrifices of their own choosing, thus indicating a society governed by a law permitting such variation. (Gen 4:3–4) In the new world of toil upon the ground (Gen 3:23), mankind understands it can petition God and receive an answer tailored to specific situations: "Then men began to call upon the name of the Lord," that is, ask for new revelation. (Gen 4:26)

The Bible narrative is clear about the course of primeval history, the period before the time of Abraham. It is a time of periodic individual encounters of men with God, whose presence, it turns out, is available even outside the Garden of Eden. These men who "walk with God," like Enoch

(Gen 5:22), or find "grace in the eyes of the Lord" (Gen 6:8), like Noah, labor to bring those they can into conformance with God's will, which often counters their own. Others, like Cain, go "out from the presence of the Lord" and deny or diminish that revelatory possibility. (Gen 4:16)

The stories of the later patriarchs provide some geographic and chronological detail as to the far-flung places of God's recurring presence. In due time, God speaks to another prophet, Abraham, and gives specific instructions for him to emigrate. (Gen 12:1) The heads of each of four generations of family beginning with Abraham, whose migrations take him through a half-dozen nations, remarkably, also become prophets. There are others about them, too, who know God's voice—women like the Egyptian Hagar, who migrates to the south with her son, and possibly certain of the Canaanites, like Melchizedek. The oracular experiences of all of these individuals are meant to stress the relative ubiquity of God's presence and the availability of his counsel in societies open to receiving them.

The theological linchpin of this period, of course, is the choosing, or election, of Abraham and his offspring for a great destiny. Their immediate circumstances apparently make them suitable for the frequent in-breaking of God's direct revelation. The long-term prospect for continuing oracles, given the early commitment of the Abrahamic people to right action, and the commitment of those same people to historical memory, is apparently good as well. But the middle part of their experience is not so remarkable. Upon the descent into Egypt, the oracular dimension of social and political life among the family of Abraham's grandson Jacob disappears from the record for 400 years.

With the advent of Moses, the community of Hebrews is exposed once again to the mantic or numinous experience known by their ancestors. By this time, there is more historical detail available to the Bible writers. The initial Abrahamic election to a social life so progressive and democratic that it enfranchises women such as Hagar as prophets is now available to large numbers of Israelites on substantially the same terms. They can attain the same kind of equality, land, security, and long life attained by the patriarchs, if they will but follow the new Abraham and his ethical God.

Moses, like Abraham, left a place of political, economic and religious oppression and fled into the wilderness to find peace and happiness. In the wilderness Moses hears God's voice, returns to organize his people, and negotiates a pilgrimage to the place where he had initially heard the voice of his God, a pilgrimage known as the Exodus. His ancestor Jacob had a similar experience. Jacob returned to his ancestral home to find a mate who would help him inaugurate a political clan, one that would be devoted to the God of liberal, social, and political values he had met in Canaan. At the base of Mt. Sinai, Moses and the pilgrims decide against return to Egypt and instead take steps to found a confederated society based on loose regional tribal government and strong clan and family controls. Some forty years later they cross Jordan and in Canaan they join a mixture of ethnic and political kin who have been eeking out a degree of local autonomy there as the Bronze Age city-states of the region waned in power. Their new society is to be situated in the still sparsely settled hill country of Canaan, based on a mixed economy of farming and herding, and governed by charismatic central leadership, which is decidedly non-hereditary.

In the time of Moses, there are more details given too, about the instruments of free and independent living. Abraham had entered into a covenant with God to live tolerantly and deferentially among the neighboring communities rather than aggressively. He was specifically admonished to be a blessing to others: "In thee shall the families of the earth be blessed." (Gen 12:3) The blessing of Abraham's own descendents is also made contingent upon the enforcement of positive, ethical clan government. All the people of this land will fare according to how they treat others. Laborers and warriors who make up the retinues of Abraham, Isaac, and Jacob are to respect the right of occupation and of intellectual expression, not only of their own number, but of neighboring tribes and city-states as well. They are to promote, not deny; bless, not curse. (Gen 12:3)

Moses enters into a similar covenant, which outlines in greater detail how that way of living is to be accomplished in a much larger society. That later covenant is the Decalogue, the ten words/commandments/statements revealed by God to enable ethical government and human rights. The blessing of Abraham's people in Moses' day, if they should live according to his covenant words, includes assurance of God's favor should hostility break out across settlement boundaries. It thus assures ongoing possession of whatever land they find themselves on, and the continuing presence of God on that land in the same way the Spirit was present with Abraham, Isaac, Jacob, and Joseph.

The narrative theology of the Bible, then, begins with a description of epiphanies experienced by primeval and patriarchal prophets, then Exodus and conquest leaders. It next moves to a description of epiphanies experienced by the Judges of Israel, like Gideon and Samuel, action prophets like Elijah and Elisha, whom we hear about from biographical materials, and the literary prophets who wrote essays and autobiographies. During the period of Kings the narrative remembers the northern kingdom as expecting an unstable institution of prophecy, subject to the whim of God and man, like the pattern given in the time of Judges. The southern kingdom, on the other hand, is remembered as one where prophecy is tied to a hereditary lineage of messianic princes, somewhat like the pattern in the days of Abraham's lineal successors. Thus both polities develop reasonable models for inviting ongoing oracular governance during the course of Israel's long and illustrious pre-exilic history.

All of these activities and ideologies stem from what is implied by the "name" of God in Israel, his basic hands-on nature, and his desire to be known by all the nations.

However, after Moses and Joshua, not one of the Judges left a psalmic or prophetic oracle that we know of, except possibly Deborah. (Judg 5) Hence, of the 200 year period before David it was said, "The word of the Lord was precious in those days; there was no open vision." (1 Sam 3:1) Of such a time it is said, "Where there is no vision, the people perish." (Prov 29:18) Such a long time without re-iteration of the fundamentals of human self-consciousness left Israel begging for an answer. Samuel's vision of things was too little too late. The people opted for the customary retreat from self-government—kingship.

David ended the 200 year drought (1200–1000 BCE) of in-depth heavenly revelation since the time of Moses.[1] After David and Solomon, who lived around 950 BCE, 200 years passed before another literary prophet arose. First came Amos in 740 BCE, then a flowering of such voices and champions of free exercise in the next 200 years: Hosea, Isaiah, Micah, Jeremiah, Ezekiel, and Second Isaiah, who wrote around 540 BCE. After Nehemiah and Ezra around 440 BCE, and Malachi and Joel, who labored around the same time, there was no open vision for another 200 years until revolutionary apocalyptic, canonical voices like Daniel,

---

1. This period of time is less, of course, if we consider the revelation song of Deborah. (Judg 5)

non-canonical voices like Enoch and Sirach, and historical chronicles like that concerning the Maccabees, surfaced around 150 BCE.

Some 200 years later, at the time of the adult Jesus, the mainstream Jews of the Pharisaic sect had concluded that the rabbis alone were sufficient to interpret god's will. Oracular prophets were no longer needed. Messengers like John the Baptist and Jesus were once again not welcome in and around Jerusalem in the Jewish tradition. But early Christian converts understood that Jesus and Paul taught that God is capable of new revelation not only through the first apostles, but through subsequent visionaries, many of whom were not officially sanctioned interpreters in the mainstream denominations of the church. Thus in Palestine, Syria, Asia Minor, and Egypt there was an explosion of new gospel stories, many dozens, that were not pared down for a couple hundred years to the official list we find today in Catholic, Eastern Orthodox, and Protestant bibles.

IS POLYTHEISM MONOTHEISM IN DISGUISE?

Prophecy is not static, unreasonable, un-negotiable. It is iron-clad only in its general ethical framework, but not in its exact application to every circumstance. God's word is geared, instead, to a particular time, place and circumstance. In fact, God himself is defined, or at least refined, by the prophet who reveals him. Israel remembers the time of the patriarchs as a time when God was revealed, not just once in a single static version, but three times, each in a slightly different profile. He was the God of Abraham, the God of Isaac, and the God of Jacob, each of these prophets emphasizing a different aspect or attribute of God relative to his re-occurring presence. (Exod 3:6) Jesus emphasizes that God must be reconstituted in the same way each generation in the culture of the present, in order to underscore that a living God speaks continually in the present to living people. A dead prophet speaks to dead people. God cannot speak long using the decaying words of buried prophets. (Matt 22:32)

The theology of continuing revelation is nicely encompassed by and expressed in the names by which God is known both in the time of Abraham and Moses. In each case the name is suggestive of an attribute that provides Israel with the security and independence they come to be known for. In patriarchal times, God is known either by the generic term "El," translated "God" or "Lord," or "Elohim," a plural synonym meaning essentially the same thing. This general name is often supplemented with an epithet, or nick-name, to form combination names like El-Shaddai, El-Elyon, El-Roi, El-Olam, El-Bethel, El-Berit. Shaddai means "Almighty" (Gen 17:1), Elyon "Most High" (Gen 14:18–22), Roi "One who Sees" (Gen 16:13; compare Gen 22:14), Olam "Everlasting" (Gen 21:33), Bethel "House"[2] (Gen 31:13), and Berit "Covenant." (Judg 9:46) In addition, God is referred to in early times as Pahad, or fearful (1 Sam 11:7), and as Sabaoth, "host" or "power to recruit into service."[3] (Exod 12:41; Zeph 2:9)

Abraham's God El Shaddai is one of strength, one, who is like a rock, or a mountain, which, because of its higher location, is capable of revealing the view to those at a lower level. (Ps 61:2) Hagar's El Roi is a God who sees, acknowledges, and recognizes those in trouble or in need. He "sees" or "appears" in the sense of "looking upon" or "raising up" one or many from obscurity and abasement. He removes their anonymity, gives them identity, rectifies their situation, levels the playing field. El Berit is one who makes covenants relating to oracular protection of a people.

Isaac's God "Pahad"[4] is a God whose presence is near and thus numinous, dreadful, powerful to make change. Sabbaoth is a name associated with one who commands intense loyalty, who has force, weight, might, like a king who recruits many to the national workforce. In the case of Yahweh, however, the king does not so much rule with a rigorous hand over the workers of a nation, as inspire mass volunteerism in a good cause. For example, he leads people out of rigorous slavery to economic freedom and national independence among the community of nations. (Exod 12:41)

Moses knows God as "I am that I am." (Exod 3:14–15) Many translations of the Hebrew consonants "YHWH" have been suggested. For example, the word can be rendered "I will be whoever I will be,"[5] or "I cause to be" (compare "I cause what comes into existence"[6]). The name seems to say that Israel's God is one who truly exists, who causes all existence, and who is responsible for all of history. We further learn that

2. Dalglish, "Bethel (Deity)," 706–708.

3. Rose, "Names," 1002–1010.

4. Some interpreters prefer a translation of the word "pahad" as "kinsman" rather than "fear."

5. Terrien, *Elusive Presence*, 119.

6. Albright, *Stone Age*, 198.

God has a specific interest in promoting life—profitable life, not death, or self-defeating life. (Deut 30:19; Jer 21:8) The way he does this is by establishing an intimate relationship with a progressive people. He causes good things to happen by means of his motivational communications with man.

When Moses worries whether God's presence would be with him as he undertook to lead the people out of oppression, God promises Moses: "Certainly, I will be with thee." (Exod 3:12) Some 1,200 years after the Exodus, God is still delivering the same message to a people: "I am with you always . . . " (Matt 28:20) God's immediate, alarming presence is not always available to the prophet or the people on a moment by moment basis. However, God's name suggests a kind of ongoing intimacy which supports from a distance one who makes an ethical journey along a difficult route. The name suggests "I see you and will be with you in your struggles," or "I live above, but I choose to condescend to be with you when you especially need me."

In the ancient world the personality or character of a human being was expressed in the name given the person.[7] When that character changed or matured, the individual was given, or took for himself or herself, a different name. Thus it was that kings took on honorific "throne names" when they ascended to kingship or after they made particularly notable achievements. So it was too that Jacob took the new name Israel, which means "God rules." (Gen 32:27–28) This happened after Jacob decided that there is a spiritual and political power higher than that of a king, and that this Spirit would govern men directly and vocally. The names of devotees of a specific God, too, as the name Israel suggests, often incorporate the name of the God into the name of the person—in this case "El."

In the ancient world, the character of the deity was also expressed in the deity's name. In order to cram as much information about the god as possible into the name, the followers of a particular god might well use an acronym to extend it. Some have suggested that YHWH might also have been such an acronym whose letters represented a longer description. In Sumer of Babylon, for example, the name of the god of animal husbandry was abbreviated from the phrase "He who assists bearing mothers."[8] Yahweh was known in a similar way as one who pro-

7. Anderson, *Old Testament*, 52.
8. See Albright, *Stone Age*, 198.

vides practical support to his people. He is one who uses his strength to assist oppressed people; he serves as midwife of political freedom and independence. Of him it is said: "I am Yahweh your God, who brought you out of the land of Egypt, out of the house of bondage." (Exod 20:2) He is the God who provides an independent way of life to those who follow him. The second clause of this critical verse gives clarity and definition to the name itself, extending it like an acronym might do, and thus might properly be part of the name itself.

After the time of Moses, the ark containing the law of Israel becomes the symbol of God's presence and the also of the freedom he inspires. When the ark arrives in the Israelite camp during a time of war, the Philistines say: "God is come into the camp." (1 Sam 4:7) Most of the Israelites themselves would have disagreed. Under no circumstances would they dare to assert that their God could be kept in a box. In order to avoid reducing God's presence to a simple icon like the ark, and thus incur a charge of idolatry, when Israel remembered the time the ark was placed in the precincts of the brand new Jerusalem temple, it was said that it was God's name only which dwelt in the ark, and not in any sense God himself. (1 Kgs 8:17, 29; Deut 12:5, 11)

This made clear for those who cared to read the history of the nation that the nation's God itself was not subject to control and manipulation. God did not reside in a container, in the way that foreign gods in human form resided on a litter when paraded in public or were stood up on a pedestal when returned to the shrine. What made Israel's God different was the behavioral pattern that distinguished the people of Yahweh from the nations round about. That behavioral pattern was promoted and enshrined in a constitutional law document, which *was* positioned in a box to protect it. God, in this view, was only as strong and humane as the people who worshipped him. Their laws, and the enforcement of them, were what determined their happiness, and their remembrance of the God who gave those laws to them.

The character and quality of Israel's God, his aspiration for all people, was given representation in both the document and in the name. While the document and the name properly resided on earth, the ennobling spirit of God, which provided Israel's strength, resided in heaven and could not be contained on earth. He and they were devoted to local free exercise of religious, political and economic power. Israel's was a moderate, modest way of life devoted to social, economic, and political happiness and self-determination. This way of life was represented best by the political statements carried inside the box, and not by a gold or silver statue of a greedy god or king carried into battle by other cultures. It was a freely accepted and periodically re-enacted constitutional law which best represented their God, and not any metal statue of an earthly king or an oppressive power in heaven.

In the language immediately following the Exodus version of the Decalogue, Yahweh suggests that he plans to speak to man again and again in order to re-iterate the meaning of his name. Accordingly, he directs those who revere him to "make an altar in all places where I record my name." (Exod 20:24) If by this means the people will take care to re-assert the original progressive freedom culture established at Mt. Sinai, Yahweh will "come unto thee, and . . . will bless thee." (Exod 20:24)

A name given to God that speaks of serviceability and durability also connotes monotheism. This is a deity whose self-declaration is that he rules above the other gods of men. His First Commandment advises men that they should have "no other gods before me." (Exod 20:3; Deut 5:7) In this sense, the name, then, might be rendered "I am above all others." This is the sense that the prophet Zephaniah sees: "I am, and there is none besides me . . . " (Zeph 2:15) Isaiah expresses God's self-revelation thusly: "I am the first, and I am the last; and besides me there is no God." (Isa 44:6) Yahweh's task is to diminish the other gods that men worship and replace them with the freedom doctrine that he brings and represents, which is desired by men everywhere: "He will famish all the gods of the earth; and men shall worship him . . . even all the isles of the heathen." (Zeph 2:11)

This God is the greatest, and is beyond the reach of all others, because he gives a continuous stream of prescient information to man. He reveals knowledge previously unknown to man, and leaves a record, by the mouth and the writing of prophets, of the things he reveals. Knowledge is power. Knowledge is liberating. God is liberating and makes laws which liberate society and nature. God is transcendent in the sense that his level of knowledge is difficult to attain, but immanent when he finds a one capable of reaching for it, understanding it, and publishing it.

At a time long after Moses, when the peoples' connection with God and with the land is brutally severed by the Babylonian conquest of Judah, Jeremiah sees that the exiles who went south into Egypt translated the name the way Abraham and Moses did, and the way we suggest here. God tells Jeremiah: "I have sworn by my great name . . . that my name shall no more be named in the mouth of any man of Judah that are in the land of Egypt, saying, The Lord God Liveth." (Jer 44:26) God forswears their use of the name because they no longer understand the meaning of it. A living God is a speaking God. The oracular God of Israel is effectively dead among the great majority of the exiles there who no longer believe in new prophecy, since the people do not hearken to Jeremiah's words, which are from God. Those few who do not shun the oracle of a prophet—the "remnant" who are presumably the followers of Jeremiah—"shall know whose words shall stand, mine, or others." (Jer 44:28) Ezekiel, for his part, is equally explicit about the meaning of the name "I am": "For I am the Lord; I will speak . . . " (Ezek 12:25) Perhaps the best rendition of the name of God, then, is "I speak to you here and now, and I will speak to you again in the future."

A SONG IS THE MIND'S FLOWER: PSALMIC REPRESENTATIONS OF PERPETUAL PROPHECY

The Psalms are songs celebrating God's presence in Israel, particularly as they reflect the intense spiritual experiences of the prophet-king David and the memories of those stirring days. They promise that individuals of a great variety of types can be recipients of God's revelation. If they believe God can speak, they must wait then until he does: "I wait for the Lord, my soul doth wait, and in his word do I hope." (Ps 130:5) Such revelation tends to come when people most need it, when sin and alienation overwhelm people and places.[9]

While associated with David, Psalms also likely provided hymns for worship in the wilderness period, during the settlement period of Judges, and both in the first and second temple periods. The greatest part of that worship was remembrance of the moments when God condescended through a prophet to inspire and lead the people at critical times. The songs of Moses (Ps 90), and Deborah (Judg 5) celebrate those times, as do many of the psalms of David and some attributed to Solomon. (Ps 72, 127)

Several passages in Psalms demonstrate fundamental support for new light revelation. One such passage is attributed to David. It is a prayer by the author for joyful embracing of the notion of a God who dispenses righteousness by means of a living prophet: "Let them shout

---

9. Childs, *Theology*, 103.

for joy, and be glad, that favour my righteous cause: yea, let them say continually, Let the Lord be magnified, which hath pleasure in the prosperity of his servant." (Ps 35:27) There is a kind of liturgical prayer for the future return of prophecy in a Psalm attributed to Moses: "Let thy work appear unto thy servants." (Ps 90:16) Another Psalm hints at a factor which can hasten the day of the return of understanding about the ancient revelation—immersion in the "law," "testimony," and "statutes," the sacred history and constitutional precepts written by the earlier prophets. It is said, "By them is thy servant warned . . . " (Ps 19:7–11) A true student of the subject matter pays heed to them and teaches others, once he apprehends the meaning of those difficult statutes.

Psalm 24 celebrates the entry of Yahweh into the city of David: "Lift up your heads, O ye gates . . . and the king of glory shall come in." (Ps 24:7) Here, in the city of David, God potentially rules through the dynasty of David forever: "Of the fruit of thy body will I set upon thy throne. If thy children will keep my covenant . . . their children shall also sit upon thy throne for evermore." (Ps 132:11–12) Unfortunately, the messiah-deliverer understands that even the most fruitful of the boughs of God's revelatory tree can be severed from the trunk. One of David's psalms, for example, contains the worried refrain: "Take not thy holy Spirit from me." (Ps 51:11)

In Psalm 104 God is depicted as using his Spirit as a device not only in creation, but in his constant renewal of creation in the lives of individuals and whole peoples: "When thou sendest forth thy Spirit, they are created; and thou renewest the face of the ground." (Ps 104:30) But sin silences the creative process of the work of the Spirit. God is forced to "Hide thy face from my sins . . . "[10] (Ps 51:9) However, when the people approach God sincerely, he changes their hearts and recovers them: "Turn us again, O God, and cause thy face to shine; and we shall be saved." (Ps 80:3) This turning process happens through the offices of a prophet: "Let thy hand be upon the man of thy right hand, upon the son of man whom thou madest strong for thyself. So will not we go back from thee: quicken us, and we will call upon thy name." (Ps 80:17–18) In those times when there is no comfort through a prophet, Israel sings, acknowledging her expectation of regular revelation: "Rouse thyself!

---

10. Compare Isa 30:1: "Woe to the rebellious children . . . that cover with a covering, but not of my spirit, that they may add sin to sin . . ."

Why sleepest thou, O Yahweh." (Ps 44:23) Also, "It is time for thee, Lord, to work..." (Ps 119:126)

New revelation provides "rest" for people and prophets. This is as much to say that Sabbath rest and acceptance of the Spirit are linked.[11] Return of the Spirit through a prophet leads to true rest, true security, true and ultimate Sabbath: "The Lord looseth the prisoners." (Ps 146:7) Without prophecy, the people are bound up mentally in insecurity, and often physically in chains.

Psalm 22 elaborates the entire cycle of presence, abandonment, and eventual return of security. The poem complains about the absence of rescue and rest in its first couple verses: "My God . . . why hast thou forsaken me? Why art thou so far from helping me?" (Ps 22:1) The next set of verses recall, however, that the ancestors "trusted, and thou didst deliver them." (Ps 22:4–5) In fact, the testimony of people of old is that God has not "hid his face from him [the afflicted], but when he cried unto him, he heard." Finally, the Psalmist recognizes that "the kingdom is the Lord's: and he is the governor among the nations." (Ps 22:28) This means that soon enough, somewhere, a "seed shall serve him." (Ps 22:30) The key to this happy ending is the nexus between God and prophet: "Be not thou far from me, O Lord." (Ps 22:19)

The so-called "Zion psalms" (Ps 46, 48, 76, 84, 87, 122) identify the temple mount at Jerusalem as the place of God's continuous revelatory presence.[12] The psalms which describe the enthronement of God as the political king or political inspiration of the polity of Israel (Ps 47, 93, 96–99) stress the necessity of on-going revelation, since God as governor must issue executive decrees from time to time. The psalms which praise "torah," or the instructional law, emphasize that the people are at liberty to approach God freely in Israel and to obtain a new place and a new following for him. God, in fact, is free to reciprocate and lead them in the direction of such renewal. (Ps 1, 19, 119)

---

11. If Israel repents, the "Spirit of the Lord" will cause the nation "to rest" and become "a glorious name." (Isa 63:14)

12. Anderson, *Old Testament*, 513.

WHAT DOES PUBLIC HEALTH HAVE TO DO WITH ANYTHING?: PROPHETS AND HEALTH

The God of free political and religious exercise, as we will explore below, is not a provincial, time- or place- or people-bound god. The spirit of freedom which he fosters is known the world over and is not the proprietary possession of any one religion or political tradition. In fact, it often happens that not long after a messenger has passed away, the people who revere both God and messenger slide into ignorance and even rebellion against the charter made with them. God, then, is forced to wander throughout the globe in search of another capable messenger and another forthright people. (2 Chr 16:9)

At about the time Israel began to assemble its own historical canon during the global Golden Age of the sixth century, the world outside Israel was aflame with a similar spiritual and intellectual understanding of God and man, and thus was able to provide independent attestation of the universal liberatory and exploratory ethic of the God of Israel. Many cultists and philosopher-scientists in Greece, in particular, saw God as one, and found unity in the cosmos and in humanity. This unity, for the Stoics, was expressed in the form of an ethical law, universally recognized by a single inter-related cosmopolitan world, all of whose people experienced similar trials and triumphs, and all of whom were generally amenable to moral instruction.[13] The Judaic political theory of the universal equality of man stems from the law given to Noah, which was subsequently binding upon all human beings living on the earth. (Gen 9.1–17) The Hebrew name given to the first man, "adam," meaning humanity, suggests that the special relationship which the first man had with God is open to all of his descendants. Even the uniformity of function of the human body seemed to suggest to the ancient physicians the essential unity of mankind, and the equality of their potential.

The Greek god Apollo, patron of the health sciences, and physicians like Alcmaeon and Hippocrates, matched Israel's tradition of the liberating and healing God Yahweh, who inspired prophet-physicians like Moses and Elijah, and later Jesus and Luke. Even the much earlier Abraham seemed to have been drawn to the sphere of medicine and public health, directed as he was by God to enforce the broad use of a surgical preventative procedure like circumcision. (Gen 17:9–14) It is

---

13. Taylor, "Unity," 747.

not surprising that ancient physician-prophets sought answers to questions about man's abilities and disabilities in the realm of both heaven and earth, where the indelible spirit of life and death was available for all to observe and catalogue.

In fact, in ancient Egypt, Mesopotamia, India and China, the tribal priest typically functioned as the tribal physician-scientist. Priests and priestesses promoted a variety of amulets and incantations designed to assist in the healing process. In many places the priest's temple served as the local hospital. The priestly shrine also served as the authorized establishment where butchery of animals for sacrifice could be carried out in a sanitary environment. (Lev 17:1-9; Exod 20:24-26; Deut 27:4-7) Ancient physician-priests used body parts to assist them in ascertaining the will of God (an early form of prophecy known as divination), and in the process learned a good deal about the anatomy and function of organs of the body.

There was a natural connection here between religion/ethics and public/personal health. If nature's God was the source of blessing and good feeling, he was also the source of cursing and disease. There was a clearly demonstrated connection between moral or ritual un-cleanliness, or impurity, and physical disease—for example, sexual licentiousness and sexually transmitted disease. (Gen 19) There was also a clearly demonstrated connection between ethically ignorant, foolish behavior and untoward physical or socio-economic consequences. (Prov 1:7, 14:9, 28:26)

It required advanced learning of the type undertaken in the priestly schools to discern these relationships. Israel understood this from the beginning and installed the Levite priests as the schoolmasters in the new nation. In their explorations of the function of both body and mind, early physicians discovered the uniformity of the body across all mankind and linked diseases of the body and discomforts of the mind to universal environmental, social, and political conditions experienced by everyone. These universal conditions were clearly associated with the realm of the natural, unseen, universal power known as Lord or God, and given many names by the people. It was not a grand leap for Israel's prophet-believers to see that all the people of the earth could come to know free exercise and free exploration of the world in the way Israel had come to know it. (1 Kgs 8:41-44; Isa 2:2-4, 25:6-8)

God is, therefore, in addition to being a king, also a scientist who promotes knowledge of the cosmos. Creation is the subject matter upon which wisdom operates. If God is creator of the cosmos, he is also the inventor and propagator of its "order" of creation, that is, its visible patterns and its natural laws of interaction. (Job 36:4) Thus revelation is also a process of scientific discovery in which the order of creation is revealed. This universal natural order was discernable in the cosmos and in the earth and thus was studied by early astronomers, engineers, agronomists and mathematicians.

God's continuing vocal presence is thus necessary and important among the communities of mankind because he is reasonable, and full of knowledge, and wishes to impart knowledge so people can progress in understanding nature and its laws. God wants to give human beings a rationale for his pronouncements, predictions and judgments. He knows that if it makes sense to people, it will be easier to convince them to do as he wills. In fact, there is a reason why providential events happen. Those events, while sometimes eclectic, incomprehensible, and apparently irrational, in the great majority of cases are rational, justifiable, discernible. Amos, as we saw above in chapter 6 (Amos 3:3–8), constructs an entire worldview around the concept of God's rationality as a causative agent in both human affairs and natural events. Most events of nature are ordered and predictable, damage is preventable, and the effects of nature are certainly ameliorable.

The great flood, for example, was easily predictable before it happened, because it was well known that the two rivers (Tigris and Euphrates) were prone to flooding heavily, especially during the spring, when the rain clouds of the heavens also opened frequently. In addition, the water table, the so-called "waters of the deep," sometimes rose precariously near to the surface of the land. Possibly climate change during the period 11,000 to 6,000 BCE caused the waters of the Persian Gulf to rise and to move the coastline inland and saturate the crust of the land.[14] It was believable and ascertainable that in a bad year, several acute water problems might come together like a confluence of stars in the sky, or a spate of bad luck. It is the job of the prophet, like a good insurance underwriter, to study these risks and insure against them. In the social realm God transmits to man only those things which are profitable to him in terms of social, political, and economic success. (Isa 48:17; Jer

14. Bauer, *History*, 4–5.

2:8; 1 Tim 4:8) It is man's job to use his faculties to study the natural and social sciences in order to learn what is available to him in the accumulated wisdom of mankind.

The book of Proverbs attempts to summarize this conventional wisdom as it was known to its writers. In spite of its assertion of man's own innate capacity to unlock many of the secrets of nature, Proverbs nevertheless is willing to define some of the most advanced of such learning as coming at the behest of God's own Spirit. It ultimately makes a plea for education of the type indispensible for the work of prophets: "How long, ye simple ones, will ye love simplicity? . . . Turn you at my reproof: behold, I will pour out my spirit unto you . . . " (Prov 1:22-23)

The book of Ecclesiastes likewise disputes the easiness and simplicity of wisdom's prevalent classifications and conclusions, while still ascribing a basic stability to its overall structure and concern. These books of wisdom are a part of the scripture because ancient Israel understood man's curiosity about the laws of nature and the skepticism that is part of man's innate nature and his learning experience, all of which provide fuel for enlightenment.

Profile—Hagar's Well (Muhammad)

The caravan trader Muhammad sat outside the cave where he frequently meditated and recited verses given to him by the angel Gabriel. Today he thought about the Jews and Christians with whom he had disputed so often on the matter of the oracular revelation.

He always took care to explain his thinking to them in terms they could understand. This meant using their own scriptures to make his point. Hagar, the Egyptian handmaid of Sarah, Abraham's wife, received a revelation indicating she would bear a son and name him Ishmael, meaning "God shall hear"—if only she would return to the mistress who had mistreated her and bear up under her glances. (Gen 16:9-11)

This, he would explain, is an admonition regarding submission to God's newly opened voice, the same principle of "islam" which now animated his own life and placed him in the tradition of the prophet. The problem was, Jews and Christians were adamant that heaven was evermore sealed against new oracles from God. But there is an antidote to this way of thinking, he would explain to them, found in the story of their own "book."

Hagar understood not only that God speaks to man and to woman in that day, but also that God speaks even to the lowliest if they are humble in affliction. Hagar named the God who spoke to her "Thou God Seest Me" and made a memorial of some sort by the well where the revelation occurred. She also "looked after" the revelation, that is, believed and acted upon it (Gen 16:13), just as Muhammad was now doing with respect to his own revelation.

In time, Hagar and Ishmael were sent into the southern wilderness of Beersheba, carrying with them the promise Abraham made to them that the mother and the son would together "make a nation." (Gen 21:13) After a period of days, their water was spent and the child Ishmael was near death. While weak and thirsty, he mouthed a few feeble words and "God heard the voice of the lad." (Gen 21:17) Hagar then heard the voice of God encouraging her to "Arise, lift up the lad." (Gen 21:18) Soon enough "She saw a well of water." (Gen 21:19) Furthermore, as the Jews' own Bible continues: "God was with the lad; and he grew, and dwelt in the wilderness . . ." (Gen 21:20)

By these events, Muhammad would suggest to his listeners, the God of the Hebrews meant to condition the people of Ishmael to understand that God would not deny his voice to them at any time, if they were modest and believing like Hagar and her son. Yet he was regularly rebuffed when he mentioned to Jews and Christians that God makes "no distinction among any . . ." (Quran 2:136) The "people of the book" denied that God could speak to whom he willed in the present day, because that day was so long after Moses and so long after Jesus Christ, and because the Arabs had such a history of idolatrous behavior. (Quran 2:285)

Also, it was not a problem, Muhammad would suggest to his theological tormentors, that the story in the Bible about the people of Ishmael stops at the point that Ishmael settled in the wilderness. God's intent was to later report the details of the story by means of a prophet-historian who works to uncover those details and give them life. God revealed to Muhammad many of those details both in his moments in the cave and in his studies of the religion and government of early Arabia.

Muhammad would then fill in some of that historical detail to his hearers. Abraham himself notified God, "Lord, I have settled some of my offspring in a barren valley near Mecca, so that they may observe true worship." (Quran 14:37) There Ishmael labored as a prophet all his days. Later, Abraham visited Mecca with Ishmael, and they made a shrine of worship there at the Ka'bah, and cleansed it for all who should resort there in the future. (Quran 2:124)

Muhammad would invite his Jewish and Christian hearers to understand that cleansing was needed again in the Arabian culture, precisely because of the return of idolatry among the offspring of Ishmael. Abraham had turned against the culture of child sacrifice in Canaan. Muhammad today led the people of Islam against the culture of female infanticide in Arabian culture. But would Jews and Christians ever recognize the extraordinary parallels between their own founders and the founder of Islam?

And then he had a sinking thought. Would the people of Islam one day mimic the behavior of Jews and Christians and announce that there is to be no more word from God after Muhammad? He resolved to make it clear in his recitation today that there will be others who bring warnings directly from the face of God after he himself passes from the earth: "Children of Adam, when apostles of your own come to proclaim to you my Revelations, those that take warning ... will have nothing to fear or regret ..." (Quran 7:35)

GOALKEEPER OF THE NATION: GOD AS KEEPER OF THE PEOPLE

In the view of the Bible writers, God exhibits a number of oracular attributes having to do with leadership. At times he speaks and acts in the role of a political ruler or king, and at times in the role of a parental or fatherly figure. As sovereign political leader of the realm, he is legislator or law-giver, he is government administrator or "keeper," and he is adjudicator of the law or "judge." As fatherly parental figure he is mentor/counselor and exemplar, he is instructor or teacher, and he is merciful redeemer. In all of these roles, some of which overlap, he exercises discretion, emotion, intellect, and considerable ethical dimension.

We have said that God asserts a paramount role in the affairs of mankind by virtue of his name, which commits him to action on behalf of the oppressed. But he acts in the world not merely because he is responsible and because man is not, but because his role is to lead. God is sovereign—wise, powerful—and will work what he wills, regardless that some of the culture say he is far away and committed to silence. The God of Isaiah, for example, announces: "I am the Lord, that is my name: and my glory will I not give to another." (Isa 42:8) This is tantamount to saying that God will not delegate his sovereign power to princes, priests and pastors so they can rule in his stead. Also, "I am God, and there is none else; I am God, and there is none like me." (Isa 46:9) Ezekiel re-iterates the great law of sovereign speech in these terms: "I am the Lord: I will speak and the word that I shall speak shall come to pass; it shall be no more prolonged: for in your days . . . will I say the word, and will perform it, saith the Lord God . . . " (Ezek 12:25) Because he is God, he will speak how and when he pleases. He will not abide a gag order imposed by mankind and its petulant priests. He speaks because it is time for action.

In fact, the method God typically chooses to assert his sovereignty, to "make (his) holy name known," (Ezek 39:7) is to act providentially in history after he has predicted its course by the mouth of prophets: "I have spoken it; I will also bring it to pass." (Isa 46:11) If a people forget that he is creator of the earth and its species and peoples, if they forget the covenants he made with their ancestors and instead go the way of their own adolescent will, then God is perfectly capable of acting to fulfill the consequences of those broken covenants, for good or for evil. We see evidence of this propensity in Isaiah: "I will do all my pleasure." (Isa 46:10) When he acts in history to fulfill prophecy, he has confidence that his action will encourage the people to recall their relationship with him, so that they will perhaps return to him. "And they shall know that I am the Lord, when I shall scatter them among the nations . . . " (Ezek 12:15) He acts in history so people will not forget that there is a supreme personality and ethic at large in the universe.

In sum, it seems that God asserts his sovereignty not only by announcing his authority and his message through prophets, but by periodically demonstrating it. He is not only sovereign, but he is trustworthy. He will perform his part of the bargain, whether the people do or not. "Hath he said, and shall he not do it? Or hath he spoken, and shall he not make it good?" (Num 23:19) He wishes to be known, to be remembered, to be recognized, to be trusted and to uphold his reputation. Also, he does not want to discredit his earlier prophets, who delivered messages from him. God says, "I am the Lord . . . that performeth the counsel of his messengers." (Isa 44:24, 26)

If God's sovereignty is to remain intact, his providential track record must remain intact as well. If one principle of sovereignty suggests that God can speak whenever he wills, another suggests he can act whenever he wills. As we shall see, the inherent and undiminished ability to speak and to act is linked inextricably to the necessity for new prophets to appear on the scene.

There are many biblical passages that suggest that God sends a new prophet precisely because he is preparing to intervene in history, and that the appearance of the new prophet is linked in a powerful way to his sovereignty and providence. For example, Malachi wrote, "I will send my messenger and he shall prepare the way before me." (Mal 3:1) In fact, God uses the new prophet to make sure the people make a connection between the impending events and the predictions the old prophets made about the present day. In effect, he sends the new prophet to announce, "Today the prophecies of the last prophet are fulfilled." They are fulfilled in the sense that the new prophet predicted by the old has finally arrived, and in the sense that the new events predicted by the old prophet have arrived as well. It is necessary to provide this link because without a new prophet linking events to God and to the old prophet, both might potentially go ignored or discredited during the course of the event and in the historical writing about the event. The people might simply say, "This was a very bad happening, but it had nothing to do with God or the commandments, or the covenant, or what the prior prophet said would happen. Bad things happened to us because of the evil of others or, because of the evil intent of the gods, or by accident, not because our own ways brought it upon us."

Thus, we hear the God of Isaiah relating, "Before it came to pass I showed it thee: lest thou shouldest say, Mine idol hath done them; and my graven image, and my molten image, hath commanded them." (Isa 48:5) No indeed, says the new prophet, this was done by the God of the prophet who predicted it. And it so happens that when the great event happens soon after the new prophet's announcement of it, some of the people make the connection and return to the God their ancestors knew. He demonstrates his currency in a world whose priests have written him off as impotent by providing new revelation that proves quickly fruitful. Hence, he will act providentially in the world when he sees an opportunity: "Behold, I will do a new thing.; now it shall spring forth . . . " (Isa 43:19) In sum, God sends prophets to summarize the latest dispensation of political history in terms he approves of. He also makes new benchmark prophesies which, in turn, require yet later voices to arise and summarize. "The former things are come to pass, and new things do I declare: before they spring forth I tell you of them." (Isa 42:9)

Both Christian and Jewish traditions see the delivery of the Ten Commandments to Moses on Sinai as representative of God's role as legislator in the affairs of mankind. Commandments are universally regarded in the scripture as public ordinances or statutes.[15] (Deut 10:13; Ps 89:30–32) God delivers these high ethical laws to a foundational prophet, who in turn emphasizes their undiminished importance by writing them in stone (Josh 8:32), and symbolizing them by means of accessories to clothing. (Deut 6:8)

The prophet also sets in place both political and liturgical means of memorializing the laws, including national holidays and pilgrimage rites which take place during the time of covenant renewal. Such a prophet also promotes education about the original intent of the laws by promoting legal education among the citizenry. (Deut 6:9)

God's commandments illuminate truth for man (Ps 119:142), bring peace (Ps 119:165) and happiness (Prov 29:18), make things right (Ps 119:172) and promote life. (Matt 19:17; Rev 14:12) When those laws are neglected, God sends reformationist prophets to resurrect them. (Hos 4:6, 12:13; Amos 1:2, 2:4; Isa 5:24, 6:1) These same laws also occupy a place of supreme importance in New Testament times. (Matt 5:17–19; Rom 3:20; Gal 3:24; Jas 2:10)

God is the head of the executive branch of government as well. He is "keeper" of his elect people, and indeed of all people on earth.[16] (Ps 121:4–5) In order to fulfill this role, he actively takes the initiative and inquires about man's doings. For example, he says, "Adam, where art thou?" (Gen. 3:9) He has a plan.[17] His purposes are carried out in different seasons. (Isa 28:23–29)

God's function with respect to the people is the same as man's function with respect to things of value in his domain. The word "keep" is used variously in the scripture to refer to man's responsibility to manage the land, the covenant, the commandments, the way, the Sabbath, the tradition, judgment, the city, vineyards, silence, storage, unity. As "keeper" or leader, God has a manifest interest in protecting/guarding, holding together/preserving, provisioning, housing, conforming, care-

---

15. Collins, "Commandment," 1097–1099.
16. Hamilton, *Pentateuch*, 59.
17. Childs, *Theology*, 39.

taking, observing/maintaining both the people and the tranquility of their civilizations. The particular method that he uses for accomplishing his purpose is his ongoing conversation, advice, information and his equitable decision-making—in short, his presence among them. God's goal in speaking is to reveal a plan for salvation, a political, social, economic and instructional apparatus which can be used as a platform for success, happiness, and profitability. In general that plan is codified into the constitutional laws of the nations he founds with the help of prophets. God's plan also reveals itself by means of the events of history.

God keeps his current word among the people because *He* is Israel's king, and not any man. As a king having a unified command and a variety of functions, God must promulgate not only foundational laws and executive orders, but also judicial opinions, or judgments. Like a good judge, God withholds judgment until all the evidence is in. Isaiah writes of God's temperament in this regard: "I have long time holden my peace; I have been still, and refrained myself." (Isa 42:14) But when the time for judgment comes, he will render the judgment in no uncertain terms: "Now will I cry like a travailing woman; I will destroy and devour at once ... They shall be turned back, they shall be greatly ashamed." (Isa 42:14-15, 17) "He put on the garments of vengeance for clothing, and was clad with zeal as a cloak. According to their deeds, accordingly he will repay, fury to his adversaries, recompense to his enemies; to the islands he will repay recompense ... When the enemy shall come in like a flood, the spirit of the Lord shall lift up a standard against him." (Isa 59:17-19)

But the most frequent way God renders judgment is by a tongue-lashing, and certainly not always by war and destruction. The prophet Hosea mentions God's long providential course of interim judgments in respect of his people: "I have hewed them by the prophets, slain them by the words of my mouth." (Hos 6:5) He sends prophets to pronounce preliminary judgments. If the people fail to repent, he may send armies against them as a final witness of his conviction.

God, like a good jurist, is fair, egalitarian, just. He does not discriminate: "O house of Israel, are not my ways equal?" (Ezek 18:29) If he sends one people a prophet, he is also willing to send such a leader to other peoples. Because God is a good judge, he is not a respecter of persons. He does not discriminate across time or across cultures. If he speaks to a people in one day, he will not leave another people in another day without the opportunity of hearing directly from him. He gives them that opportunity. If his own ways are equitable, the ways of man are not so: "But as for them, their way is not equal." (Ezek 33:17) The priests and pastors of partisan denominations want unequal distribution of God's word. They want to hold that privilege alone. The world is discriminatory: "Truth is fallen in the street, and equity cannot enter." (Isa 59:14)

Because God is just, he is also unchanging: "I am the Lord, I change not." (Mal 3:6) If he speaks on one day, he will also do so on another. God and doctrine do not change because the climate changes. God sends the same kind of messenger to teach the same kind of civic doctrine. He does not speak by the mouth of prophets in one case, and by the mouths of ordained ministers in another. Of those who claim to interpret God's word without God's direct help: "I am against them that prophesy false dreams." (Jer 23:32)

But God is also a protective, reliable servant of the family of nations—of priests, prophets, kings, and citizens of the realms. He serves them by mentoring, modeling, directing, teaching and motivating, and providing. God is Father to all. He knows how innocent and bereft of experience his children are and takes them under his wing to protect and raise them, as a parent does, until they are grown: "Like as a father pitieth his children, so the Lord pitieth them that fear him." (Ps 103:13)

God is a father in the sense of a mentor. He serves as a loudspeaker and guidance counselor throughout the life of a nation and its people: "Wilt thou not from this time cry unto me, My father, thou art the guide of my youth?" (Jer 3:4) If the ancestors and their traditions leave the children of Israel alone as an abandoned child, God at least will not do so: "Doubtless thou art our father, though Abraham be ignorant of us, and Israel acknowledge us not; thou, O Lord, art our father . . . " (Isa 63:16)

All living humans have but one father, and all his living children should listen for the voice of their parent and thus live honorably in the father's household: "Have we not all one father? Hath not one God created us? Why do we deal treacherously every man against his brother, by profaning the covenant of our fathers?" (Mal 2:10; Matt 5:16) This father provides welfare services in the community: "A father of the fatherless . . . God sitteth the solitary in families." (Ps 68:5–6)

God never stops parenting, and thus repeats his admonitions to children who are perpetually less able than he. Like a human parent,

God never stops being one. Because his experience is vaster than that of his children, he is always wiser than them. Because God loves his innocent creation, he calls to them by revelation and teaches them how to mature. But as adolescents often do, "The more I called to him, the more he turned away from me." (Hos 11:2 GNB) Also, "Sons have I raised and reared, but they have disowned me." (Isa 1:2 NAB)

As father, God is also Instructor: "Who teacheth like him?" (Job 36:22) He instructs by means of "torah." A teacher does not abandon his students or leave his classroom. He wants to maintain discipline and not let his students slip into ignorance. He repeats his message like a teacher, updates it with new editions to suit the language, the times, and the culture. The psalmist writes: "God gave the word, and great was the company of those who published it." (Ps 68:11) In fact, God publishes it so often, by means of so many voices, he is able to chide his students:

> For this commandment which I command thee this day, it is not hidden from thee, neither is it far off. It is not in heaven, that thou shouldest say, Who shall go up for us to heaven, and bring it unto us, that we may hear it, and do it? Neither is it beyond the sea, that thou shouldest say, Who shall go over the sea for us, and bring it unto us, that we may hear it, and do it? But the word is very nigh unto thee, in thy mouth, and in thy heart, that thou mayest do it." (Deut 30:11–14)

We learn that in the day of Moses God wants to teach individuals directly, but they fear to draw close enough for him to do so. The people ask that a prophet take on the task as an intermediary so that they will not be destroyed by the glory and searing judgment of his presence: "And they said unto Moses, Speak thou with us, and we will hear: but let not God speak with us, lest we die." (Exod 20:19) In one sense, then, the prophet is called by the people as much as by God. His job is to draw near God and in turn feed them with his knowledge. A prophet is an elected leader of the people.

A parent, as long as yet alive, will serve as redeemer of the child. He will rescue, as well as confide, like a devoted friend. Because God creates all living, he redeems all living as well in times of distress, contingent upon just judgment and righteous living. The law he gives to the people provides mechanisms for kinsmen to sustain persons and property on behalf of a troubled brother, and to deliver them back to the brother once he is on his feet again.[18] Hosea reminds us: "When Israel was a child, then I loved him, and called my son out of Egypt." (Hos 11:1) God provides a remnant of the faithful who follow the new prophets. (Hos 1:10, 2:18; Isa 28:16; Jer 31:31; Ezek 37:1–5)

God is Merciful, and thus sends helpers to guide the people and give one last warning before destruction. "As I live, saith the Lord god, I have no pleasure in the death of the wicked." (Ezek 33:11) God would rather turn away the coming destruction, because he remembers the lovely espousals of his beloved bride Israel and knows their potential if they mend their ways. Isaiah provides a text for this argument. God says, "I have set watchmen upon thy walls . . . which shall never hold their peace day nor night; ye that make mention of the Lord, keep not silence." (Isa 62:6) The watchmen are prophets. God calls men and women from time to time to deliver a timely message to the people. By means of the prophet and his final warning, God gives one last opportunity for the people to flee or rally. If they ignore the warning, God allows the disaster to come upon them as a natural consequence of their ignorance and selfishness. He is reconciled to the sorrow he will therefore suffer, as does any parent who watches a child make self-destructive decisions.

God provides "hesed," or loving kindness, to his children and desires them to provide the same to others. In fact, he desires "hesed" in place of sacrifice. (Hos 6:6) God enjoys providing for his children. (Jer 9:24; Mic 7:7) He is committed to providing liberation for them because he does not want to see his children taken captive and their capacities suppressed. It is this reason for prophecy that the book of Chronicles presents to us: "And the Lord god of their fathers sent them by his messengers, rising up betimes and sending, because he had compassion on his people . . . " (2 Chr 36:15)

Profile—Fortifying Babylon (Second Isaiah)

The one whom his followers called "The Servant"[19] animatedly knocked on the door of a small two-room cottage on the outskirts of Babylon. He and his scribe, who labored inside making copies of his prophesies, would continue today their discussion of the politics of Chaldean Babylon. Their main topic—their hope for the overthrow of Nabonidus, who had

---

18. See, for example, the law of Jubilee in Leviticus 25.

19. Scholars point out that the term "servant" is used a number of times apparently in self-reference to Second Isaiah himself in Isa. 40–55; see Clifford, "Isaiah," 499.

long luxuriated in the Arabian desert oasis of Tema to the south, while his son Belshazzar minded the affairs of state in Babylon.

Today he brought spectacular news for his scribe, who frequently insulated himself from the outside world, until updated by these visits. Nabonidus had just returned to the city and would be making haste to inspect the progress of the Median Wall currently in construction to the north. This project, a hot political topic in the city for the past many months, was a rampart which stretched across the land at the point of the smallest distance between the two great rivers, near the city of Sippur. Here Babylonian forces hoped to stall or turn back the Medes advancing on Babylon from Lydia in Asia Minor.[20] The Servant previously had explained to his student, "This is seemingly a good plan, but there is the prospect that either river could be diverted to undermine the defenses, depending upon who hold the strongest positions slightly up river of the wall."

In their almost palpable hope that Nabonidus would fall to Cyrus, the news of this day was exhilarating. They briefly recalled the series of events leading to their considerable hope in Cyrus for the cause of Jewish return to the holy land. Cyrus, exercising compassion for small religious groups who could also be of use to him, had overthrown the Median ruler Astyages in 550, thus incorporating Media into the Persian Empire. After having conquered Lydia in 546 and restoring minority rights there, he now had directed his armies toward the great Chaldean city with the goal of bringing relief to the worshippers of Marduk and Yahweh, long held captive of the state moon god cult of Sin.[21] Nabonidus, in fanatical devotion to Sin, had effectively abandoned his own culture for the tradition of the Arabians of Tema, long associated with moon worship there.

After pacing back and forth about the front room together as they discussed the news, the two finally sat down on benches opposite each other and turned to the work both were so diligently engaged in. "My son," said the Servant, "what do you think of the word I have obtained from God for our people?" The scribe expressed satisfaction with the notion of God as a political deity who favored liberation of any and all people from intellectual captivity. The universal God of all mankind

---

20. Pritchard, *Atlas*, 89.
21. Clifford, "Isaiah," 492, 494.

was now using Cyrus to restore political sentience among many of the peoples west of the Zagros Mountains.

"Good," judged the Servant. "Now we must carry the writings to the brethren in the settlements in the region of Nippur. We need to show the revelations in particular to the elders in charge of conscription, the carpenters' guilds, and the orchardists. We must even approach the commercial houses of the area, as many are favorable to our desire to return to our ancestral lands. They themselves cannot imagine the horror we have endured in having to leave our fields and fords to the vultures of Edom and Samaria."

LIKE FATHER, LIKE SON

A prophet is employed by God to do the work of God. A prophet is properly called "child of God," or "son of God," or "of God." All of these are titles that many of the kings of the earth claimed for themselves as well. In their protestations of kinship with God, both prophet and king functioned in the ancient world as exalted figures, somewhat like sons, who gathered around God in the council in heaven. (Ps 82)

The prophet, like any son, is much like his father. The love of God for a specially chosen son is passed along in the love of a prophet for the people. The prophet may rightly be called a manifestation of God on earth. The spirit that the prophet brings is like the Spirit of God: "The Lord of hosts hath sent in his spirit by the former prophets." (Zech 7:12)

But institutional religion seeks after something different than an equitable spirit. It seeks after a sign of its own superiority over other faiths, a witness of its own surpassing excellence. Ignorant people who follow institutional leaders forever seek a miracle, something convincing about God's power, his doctrine, his majesty, his creative power. They look for a sign outside themselves, and outside that of the spirit of a prophet. (Luke 11:29; Matt 16:1–4) They look for just-in-time rescue from predicaments by a super-hero or a super-institution. But the prophet knows that it is each mortal individual, emboldened and instructed by God, who is the finest and clearest example of God's creative power and perfection. The prophet knows that long and hard effort is necessary by each citizen to prevent or ameliorate errant conditions in the community. A prophet, too, is mere man, a frail and imperfect being who becomes "perfect" through constant efforts at righteousness. (Gen 6:9, 17:1; Deut 18:13; 2 Sam 22:23; 1 Kgs 15:14; 2 Chr 16:9; Prov 11:5; Matt 5:48, 19:21; 2 Cor 12:9; Col 1:28; Heb 12:23)

The problem is that, when a prophet comes, he nearly always brings something different from what most people are looking for. He brings a message criticizing them rather than praising them. He brings difficult instructions and directives, not justification and affirmation of their views. Rather than deferring to the political and religious power structures, he attacks and condemns them. Seeing real righteousness is painful for them, and reminds them of their own secret inadequacies. It makes them feel insecure and defensive.

Some are looking for the status quo, for the protection provided by the existing religious and political authorities, as inadequate as those efforts may be. Some are looking for a sensational religious experience, something wild, ostentatious, and supernatural—flying angels, lurking devils, dominating heroes, great voices in the sky, earthquakes, falling stars, a darkened sun, and glory surrounding the pious churchgoers. They are looking for cataclysmic signs and instead hear only the intense but humble teachings of a man "of God," who tells uncomfortable truths that reveal an erring past, describe a confused present, and make unsparing predictions about the future.

So it is that God has spoken again, and again, and again, through those who have attained relative moral perfection. The real miracle, the real vision, the first resurrection, the real sign, the real portent, is the prophet and his message. Beyond use of the spoken and written word, the prophet is free to use dramatic theater as well. God instructed Ezekiel to dramatize the captivity of Judah by carrying his belongings out of his own house into the street. As they marveled at his bizarre behavior, he warned: "Say thou unto them, Thus saith the Lord God; this burden concerneth the prince in Jerusalem, and all the house of Israel that are among them. Say, I am your sign; like as I have done, so shall it be done unto them: they shall remove and go into captivity." (Ezek 12:10-11) God announced: "Ezekiel is unto you a sign: according to all that he hath done shall ye do." (Ezek 24:24)

Isaiah's actions, words, and prophesies were a sign to the people in his day: "The Lord said, Like as my servant Isaiah hath walked naked and barefoot three years for a sign and wonder upon Egypt and upon Ethiopia, so shall the king of Assyria lead away the Egyptians prisoners, and the Ethiopians captives, young and old, naked and barefoot, even with their buttocks uncovered, to the shame of Egypt. (Isa 20:3-4)

The Psalmist wrote sensitively about what God considers to be the real sign and authentic vision from God: "We see not our signs, there is no more any prophet." (Ps 74:9) God wants his people to see a visible sign of his own moral perfection. He does this by providing them with a prophet, whose example and doctrine are truly divine. God is not known except by one who approximates his behavioral perfection. Thus, he sends prophets so he can be known, so he can be seen, in a sense, with the naked eye.

Epilogue

WE HAVE ASSERTED THAT the dominant theology of both the Hebrew Bible and New Testament is that God continues to live and speak to humankind throughout all ages of time and in all places on the globe. The ultimate "sign," or evidence of God's returning presence—a new prophet's work and word—is no more concluded or withdrawn than the perennial sign of the rainbow given to Noah. (Gen 9:12–17) God's ethical sovereignty, along with the human capacity to govern self and others in small political units according to the ethical instructions mediated by messengers, is as durable as the rainbow. While new prophets are disowned because old institutions see them as a threat, the advent of new revelation is eternal, in fact, like God.

The conversations with God recorded by prophets are testimonials of great power and sophistication in terms of promoting the rights and capacities of even the poorest classes of mankind. The conversational nature of the God of the Israelites inheres both in the names given him by the prophets and in his personal historical propensity, which is to arouse a prophet-leader in a time of grave political crisis. The argument God makes to the prophet and to the people is searingly rational, but undergirded by a deep and abiding emotional passion.

God searches throughout the entire earth to find a humble, yet learned servant who will carry a confrontational message to the political, economic, and religious powers that be. This encounter is frequently remembered in terms of an extraordinarily powerful calling which leaves an indelible mark on the prophet, and which motivates life-long, usually unsalaried effort.

Prophets are students of the histories of their own nations and also of the histories of neighboring nations which historically interact with their own. They speak almost as frequently to those neighbors as they do to their own native citizenries. They put great effort into arguing the fact of the re-emergence of the sacred presence of God among the people, and God's intent to enfranchise both the prophet and the people. They predict that others like themselves will be called in due course of time.

The Hebrew Bible and Christian Testament are replete with narratives relating to the struggle for political and religious liberty among dissidents and the people as a whole. The Exodus and Sinai experiences, as well as the patriarchal stories, provide the cornerstone of the Israelite version of the Mediterranean highland tradition of local home rule. The New Testament struggles of Jesus, Paul and the early martyrs provide the capstone of that tradition. The two books are replete with language which suggests the long and successful history of oracular revelation in the ancient Near East and its reception by the people at many times and in many places there. There is, moreover, considerable evidence of the intentional protection of political and religious liberty by means of ancient provisions of law.

Overall, the Bible suggests that the canon of sacred history of a given culture is never closed, unless it is by means of the total destruction of such a culture. If a tradition lives on, even in exile, its scripture must inevitably grow. Institutional interests may selectively choose an anthology of works to include in an authoritative scripture for a particular audience, and set themselves up as guardians of the only true tradition and faith. This it is their right to do. But invariably an authentic, new prophet comes along to point out obvious flaws in the institutional interpretation of the faith, and to point out innocent mistakes or deliberate distortions of the writings of the founders of the faith. This causes no small amount of friction between the two parties, and may lead to the institutional powers' rejection of their own tradition of tolerance and to persecution of the new prophet and his party.

Historical hindsight shows that the mainstream Judaic and Christian traditions often marginalized dissident voices in their far-flung cultures rather than welcomed them. Not surprisingly, some of the early marginalization stories are recorded in the Bible itself, while, not surprisingly, many are just now beginning to emerge 2,000 years later. The priests of the epic tradition of the Torah/Pentateuch marginalized the traditions of many of the classical prophets, to the point that their works were not accepted into a common canon for centuries after they were first delivered. The Samaritans were one faction we know about that pursued this course. The Sadducees were another. These two groups shunned Isaiah, Jeremiah, and Ezekiel, as well as the other nine classical prophets of the

Bible. The Pharisees of the New Testament, on the other hand, were hospitable to these twelve prophets and included them in their canon of scripture. But at some point, now teaming with the Sadducees, the Pharisees turned against new prophecy. That point seems to have been the advent of the apostles and prophets of the New Testament, and the person of Jesus of Nazareth himself. Paul, for example, at first heavily persecuted the Christians on behalf of the Pharisee leadership. (Acts 8:1–3, 9:1–2)

The Pharisees, together with the Sadducees, also seemed to have marginalized to the point of near extinction the new light Essenes, one of whose cult locations was uncovered at Qumran. The unearthings at Qumran reveal new scrolls which rivaled the older scrolls of the Pharisees and included such books as Enoch, the War Scroll, the Temple Scroll, and testaments of Levi and Naphtali.[1] The Pharisees, together with the Sadducees, seem to have marginalized to the point of extinction, almost, the many voices unearthed at Nag Hammadi and other places in the Judean desert as well. Many of these voices constitute what are called the Jewish "pseudepigrapha," written under assumed names in part due to popular literary convention, in part to give them greater authority, and in part (likely) because to give the author's actual name was to invite persecution by the dominant sects. The excluded pseudopigrapha include, among others, three books of Enoch, fourth Esdras (Ezra), Book of Noah, second and third Baruch, Sibylline Oracles, Assumption of Moses, Jubilees, Letter of Aristeas, Joseph and Asenath, third, fourth and fifth Maccabees, and the Testaments of the Twelve Patriarchs.[2]

Some of the voices that were more popular were harder to silence. The Hebrew Bible "apocrypha" are such books. Palestinian Judaism left out additional material about Esther. It also left out the book of Judith, written perhaps 150 years before the time of Christ (but purporting to describe events nearly 500 years earlier than that), a book containing a crazy quilt of interesting and instructive ancient Near Eastern historical motifs.[3]

The Pharisee collection also neglected to utilize several available additions to the book of Daniel, which deal with legal matters of Torah. The small book of Susanna, for example, is a narrative dealing with the

1. Alexander, et al., eds., *Handbook of Style*, 74–75.
2. Ibid., 74–75.
3. Coogan, *Old Testament*, 530.

importance of uncovering false witness (Ninth Commandment) and overturning the corrupt administration of justice by means of citizen oversight and activism. Bel and the Dragon is a narrative polemic against idol worship which provides insight into apparently common magical claims made by priesthood concerning the disappearance of food devoted to a god.

Wisdom of Solomon is a highly sophisticated book of theology and prophecy, and Ecclesiasticus, or Wisdom of Jesus Son of Sirach, is a collection of proverbial material which rivals that of the book of Proverbs. These two giant works, as well as two books of Esdras (Ezra), two books of Maccabees, Tobit, Baruch, and the Letter of Jeremiah, were also left out of the compendium. All the above books of "Jewish apocrypha"were accepted as scripture by many early Christians, since they used the Greek Septuagint translation of the Old Testament which contained them, rather than the Palestinian compendium which did not. The Catholic Christian tradition continues to use these books down to today, while the Protestant tradition jettisoned them. The Greek and Russian Orthodox churches added a third book of Maccabees to its canon, and placed a fourth book of Maccabees in an appendix, along with a third book of Enoch.

THE NEW TESTAMENT ADDITION TO THE ANCIENT SCRIPTURE

As we mentioned above, the Pharisees, after graciously accepting the works of twelve long dead classical prophets into their canon, then ignored John the Baptist, Jesus of Nazareth, Paul of Tarsus, John of Patmos and others, when those Jews voiced concern about the now staid and repressive institutional legal culture of the once open-minded sect. It seems that no part of the Jesus interpretive corpus, strongly related as it was to the Jewish tradition, was considered as material worthy of addition to the Judaic canon. Several specifically Pharisee-friendly interpretations of Christ—sayings, gospels, letters, acts, apocalypses—were apparently available to the Rabbis, and might have been used to assimilate a friendly, Judaic Jesus into the long and varied tradition of Abraham and Moses contained in the Hebrew Bible. Matthew's gospel, for example, makes great effort to provide a Christian perspective extremely hospitable to Judaism. Ultimately, Matthew and other New Testament sources failed even to achieve deutero-canonical status within the Jewish tradition. On the other hand, the early Christians recognized their political affinity with the ancient Hebrew political tradition of human rights and incorporated the whole of that earlier Hebrew Bible tradition essentially as the first chapter of their own scripture.

In this essay we have shown how the sayings of Jesus, and the fundamental events of his life story, demonstrate his continuity with the Hebrew Bible/Old Testament theological tradition regarding oracular revelation and the First Commandment legal tradition regarding political and religious liberty. For example, Jesus boldly predicted the continuation of canonical revelation, and gave it an extremely long shelf life with the terse statement, "There is nothing covered that shall not be revealed." (Matt 10:26) He also taught that whoever does not suffocate religious diversity is a supporter of the Kingdom of God. (Luke 9:50)

The New Testament gospel writers Matthew, Mark, Luke and John, Paul, and other contributors to the canon, have no qualms about promoting a doctrine of new light revelation, and much of their writing is devoted to doing just that. The Gospel of Luke, together with its companion piece the Book of Acts, is particularly careful to track the prophetic movement initiated by Jesus' sayings and actions. Acts, for example, mentions a number of Christian prophets like Agabus (Acts 11:27–30), Judas and Silas (Acts 15:32), and Phillip's four daughters. (Acts 21:9) Paul himself claims to be an oracular prophet (1 Cor:13:2, 14:6, 37) and receives revelations. (1 Cor 15:51–52; 1 Thess 4:15–17)

In addition, Jesus' parables are a veritable curriculum on political and religious freedom.[4] His life and passion are an indictment of those who refuse to grant it. The "new" commandment to love one another is, above all, an encouragement to allow and promote diversity in thought. The reports of Christ's appearances after the crucifixion lent themselves to a variety of early Christian interpretations, as archeology is now discovering. The First Commandment tradition of Israel and Judea, together with the assent of the Greco-Roman overlords, allowed followers of Christ to settle upon various points of view about these appearances suitable to their own personal beliefs and the teachings of their own church fathers and mothers. Without a degree of religious freedom granted by both Jewish and Roman society, Jesus' own immediate disciples might never have been able to pass along a word for us to ponder today. Of this,

---

4. See, for example, the stories of the Pharisee and the Publican, the Wicked Husbandman, and the Sower.

Jesus was aware, and likely grateful. While in the countryside, Jesus was able to teach with relative impunity and thus presented the bulk of his sayings there. That somewhat tolerant environment in the countryside, however, evaporated when he walked straight into Jerusalem and into the precincts of Hasmonean, Herodian, Sadducee, high priestly, Pharisee, and scribal central power and challenged those political institutions at their core. That he well understood the First Commandment tradition of tolerance had slipped under their leadership he was acutely aware. It led him to predict unequivocally that he would not be teaching in the flesh much longer. (Matt 16:21, 17:22–23, 20:17–19)

In spite of nominal respect for diversity during the time of Jesus' life and during the time of the development of dozens of new cult denominations in his name across the first- and second-century Mediterranean world (on the positive side of the instructional ledger), and in spite of persecution suffered by many Christian individuals and groups as the Roman monarchy slipped into and out of sullen dictatorship from time to time, which should have militated against similar treatment of minorities by later Christians (on the negative side of the instructional ledger), a large number of important testimonies of Jesus still were regularly withheld from the view of Christianity by its mainstream proponents— the factions which canonized the Christian Testament and ruled over its interpretation for two millenia. Those Christian traditions have long mimicked the behavior of the ancient institutional authorities Jesus so roundly condemned.

Many of the early testaments of Jesus thus dropped completely out of sight until discovered in the process of historical inquiry. For example, there is a gospel which claims to be written by Jesus' closest follower, Peter, and which was used by a group of Christians at Rhossus in early times. There is also a gospel attributed to the apostle Phillip, one attributed to Jesus' constant companion Mary Magdalene, and one attributed to his own (one tradition says) twin brother Didymus Judas Thomas. (Mark 6:4) Gospels named after Eve, Nicodemus, and Gemaliel are also now known, among many others.

The early church father Origen knew about some of these others: Gospel of the Egyptians, Gospel of the Twelve Apostles, Gospel of Basilides, Gospel of Thomas, and Gospel of Matthias.[5] Eusebius mentions the Gospel of the Hebrews, the Gospel of Peter, and the Gospel of

---

5. Ehrman, *Lost Christianities*, 13.

the Savior, this last not discovered until 1967, and published in 1999. At least seventeen different Acts are now known, including Acts of Paul and Thecla, Acts of Thomas (which undergirds the theory that Thomas became a missionary to India), Acts of Thaddeus, and Acts of Barnabas. There are at least five different apocalypses and seven epistles now known as well.[6] The spectacular new revelation Shepherd of Hermas was included in the canon by some early Christian groups and excluded by others. An important manual of early church organization and conduct called the Didache was discovered in a library in Constantinople in 1873, and dates as old as the four New Testament gospels. Finally, the sayings and writings of the prophets Montanus were excluded from the outset since they claimed not merely to remember or interpret Jesus, but to lay down a new direction for the church dictated by new revelation from Christ himself. Revelation, Montanus claimed, was not final with the apostles, but only with Montanus himself.[7]

If the Montanist revelation was unsettling and shunned by the institutional Christian church, how much more the Islamic revelation, which occurred, or began, about 610 CE. Muhammad challenged the comfortable notion that prophecy had ceased within the Abrahamic tradition, had permanently diminished to a lower level, or had simply and naturally morphed into new forms like clerical interpretive prophecy exercised by the Rabbis of Judaism and the Papal and Patriarchal authorities of Roman and Eastern Christianity. Muhammad claimed to hear the plenary, verbal, direct revelation of God's will, mediated by the mouth of the angel Gabriel. Muhammad's followers collected those revelations into a new book of canonical scripture, just as the Christians had done 300 years before.

Muhammad's Quran, or "recitation" (repeating) of the word from God, devotes, as with all high canonical prophets before him, a good deal of effort to asserting and arguing that God still speaks directly to humankind. In that literature, God delivers a scandalized protestation of the popular Christian view that God made an end of speaking to humankind with the Christian revelation. Unfortunately, the legal, social, economic and scientific tradition established by the new prophet ultimately succumbed to an institution-preserving ideology, not supportable in the Quran itself, which says that God ended his vocal profession with Islam, thus precluding any

---

6. Alexander, et al., eds., *Handbook of Style*, 83–84.
7. Hvidt, *Christian Prophecy*, 89.

more revelation after Muhammad. On the other hand, the history of the 2,000 years after the formation of the Judaic canon, the 1,600 years after the formation of the Christian canon, and the 1,300 years after the formation of the Islamic canon, suggests that Old Testament, New Testament and Quranic predictions about new prophets and new scripture to come in the future were not uttered in vain.

Of the Jewish diviners since the time of the canon closing, we have earlier suggested Philo and Josephus as candidates for evaluation as prophets. Shemaiah and Avtalyon, and after them Hillel and Shammai, and Rabbi Eleazar, among the early Rabbis, deserve mention, as do those who compiled the Mishna, Rabbis Yohannan, Akiva, and Ishmael. Medieval Jewish religious "mystics," such as Rabbi Samuel the Elder, Rabbi Judah the Pietist, and Rabbi Eliezer ben Judah of Worms, made important religious and political statements. Moses of Leon, who wrote the Zohar, claimed personal revelation from God. Abraham Abulafia claimed to be a Judaic prophet during the time of this twelfth and thirteenth century Kabbalah movement. The sixteenth and seventeenth century iteration of that earlier Kabbalah movement featured yet more prophetic voices, such as that of Isaac Luria, Shabbetai Zevi, and Nathan of Gaza. Following them, came Rabbi Israel Baal Shem Tov, the originator of Hasidism, and Rabbi Zalman.

A number of Jewish philosophers and reformers embody much of the essence of old time prophecy. During the high middle ages, Judah Halevi, Saadiah Gaon, Maimonides, Rashi, and Nissum Gerondi rate among the most sophisticated. These are followed chronologically by Isaac Abravanel, Judah Loew (Maharal of Prague), and Baruch Spinoza, all writing after the expulsion of Jews by Spain, and Joseph Karo, who sought to redeem God's presence once again for the people. In the premodern period we find the philosopher Moses Mendelssohn and historian Samuel Hirsch, among others. In the modern period philosophers, theologicans, academicians, and politicians like Yeshayahu Liebowitz, Hermann Cohen, Samuel Hugo Bergman, Martin Buber, Theodore Herzl, Abraham Isaac Kook, David Ben Gurion, Abraham Joshua Heschel, Moshe Weinfeld, and Michael Walzer mimic the prophetic function.[8]

8. For this section on Judaic figures, I am indebted to Karen Armstrong, *A History of God*, especially chapters 6–8; also Michael Walzer, et al., eds. *The Jewish Political Tradition*.

The earliest Christian prophets include John the Baptist, the canonical writers Matthew, Mark, Luke, and John, the author of the Q source, the authors of Hebrews and Revelation, Paul, Stephen, the author of Shepherd of Hermas, Valentinus, Marcion, Theodore, and the Montanists. This list might be expanded to include early church fathers, theologicans and Christian philosophers such as Tertullian, Arius, and the fourth and fifth century prophet-heretics Apollinarius, Nestorius, and Eutyches.

Medieval theologians and mystics like St. Basil, Pope Gregory the Great, Diodochus, and Symeon, monastics like Benedict and John of the Cross, and missionaries like Francis Xavier functioned like prophets. The female mystics Hildegard of Bingen and Birgitta of Vadstena (Bridget of Sweden) spoke out strongly like ancient prophets.[9] Other mystics surfaced before the Reformation as well: Meister Eckhart, Johannes Tauler, Gertrude the Great. A literary effort associated with one of these new formulations was a book titled *Imitation of Christ*, by Thomas a Kempis. Catherine of Siena and Teresa of Avila brought personal religious experiences to bear on charitable and political reform in the Catholic Church. Francis of Assisi set an extraordinary example of prophetic piety. Joan of Arc functioned like a classical Old Testament prophetess-deliverer like Deborah. Christian philosophers such as Denys the Areopagite, Duns Scotus Erigena, and Peter Abelard, and later Matthew Tindal, challenged the prevailing wisdom. Reformers like Nicholas of Cusa, John Wyclif, Erasmus, and Savonarola did as well. John Ball and Jan Hus encouraged Christian peasant revolts in England and central Europe. Renaissance religious scientists like Galileo, Descarte, Pascal and Newton rocked the religious establishment. Luther, Zwingli, Calvin, Beza, Servetus, Arminius, John Knox, Socinus, Menno Simons, George Fox and Francis David made reformationist statements, and the Anabaptist Hans Hut in Austria proclaimed himself a prophet.[10] Puritan leaders in England like Oliver Cromwell and John Milton and America theologians like Richard Hooker and revolutionary Protestants like Roger Williams made great impacts.

Historians such as Gottfried Arnold, von Mosheim, Samuel Reimarius, Voltaire and Edward Gibbon summarized the long travail of Christian religious society like the authors of Kings or Chronicals of old. The eighteenth and nineteenth centuries in Europe and America

9. Hvidt, *Christian Prophecy*, 98–105.
10. Noss, *Man's Religions*, 485.

saw dissident religious movements form around the leadership of George Tyrrell, Alfred Loisy, Hermann Schell, John and Charles Wesley, James O'Kelly, Alexander Campbell, William Miller, Ellen Harmon-White, Mary Baker Eddy, Joseph Smith, Charles Parham, and Walter Rauschenbusch, and political reform movements around the literary leadership of ethicists like Ralph Waldo Emerson and Mark Twain.

Some of these figures published guides to the correct interpretation of the Christian faith. Some even published new revelations. For example, Joseph Smith published a book of pre-Columbian American cultural history after a spirit-assisted translation of an archeological find. His followers also published a book of day-to-day revelations used to guide the development of the Latter Day Saint church. The Swedish philosopher Emanuel Swedenborg, a spiritual explorer and revelator, was elevated to the rank of prophet by his followers. Others lived lives, wrote critical tracts and influenced associates in the direction of the ancient democratic ways.

Twentieth century American prophet-divines can be drawn from the ranks of the historical Jesus movement and the anti-war, anti-domination, anti-colonial, anti-sexist, anti-Communist, and anti-exclusivist theological schools: authors like John Yoder, Walter Wink and Walter Brueggemann; liberation theologists such as Gustavo Guttierez; the premier feminist theologians; and concentration camp visionaries like Alexander Solzynitsyn and Sun Myung Moon. The lethargy of the religious, socio-economic, and political institutions which these dissidents critique is measured by the degree of opposition or persecution they have placed in the path of these thinkers and activists.

Islam, for its part, has contributed lives and writings which rise to prophetic stature as well. After the period of the first four so called "rightly guided" Imams, known as "rashidun," came the saintly sixth Imam, Jafar ibn Sadiq. Al-Bukhari and al-Qushayri are renown collectors of "hadith," remembrances about the life of the prophet. Theologians like al-Karabisi, Hanbal, al-Ashari and al-Baqillani followed. Philosopher religionists abounded as well, the most able of whom are al-Kindi, al-Farabi, al-Khusraw, Ibn Sina (Avicenna), and Ibn Rushd (Averroes), and in the pre-modern period Mulla Sadra.

Islamic prophet-mystics emerged particularly in the Sufi tradition: al-Basri, Bistami, al-Junayd, al-Hallaj, al-Ghazzali, Suhrawardi, al-Arabi, Rumi, and the martyred Shams ad-Din. Early political and cultural reformers dot the landscape as well: Ibn Taymuyah, al-Jawziyah, and Akbar. In the seventeenth and eighteenth centuries we find Shah Walli-Ullah of Delhi, and al-Wahabi, founder of the Wahabist movement. In the nineteenth century the reformers al-Afghani and Muhammad Abduh are notable, as are the twin prophets of modern day Bahai, "The Bab" and Baha'ullah. In the twentieth century the Pakastani theologian Abu al-Kalam Azad made a vigorous statement as well.[11]

Modern commentators on the history of prophecy since the days of ancient Judaic, Christian, and Islamic canon-making fall into roughly three categories: those who reject any continuation of the ancient prophetic gift in any form; those who see a place for secondary level prophecy in the form of the exercise of spiritual gifts which make a positive contribution to the "deposit of faith" of the mainstream institutional religion; and those, who like the author of this essay, point to the likelihood of entirely new directions and covenants mediated by new prophets between God and new elect peoples. There are positive indications of a greater willingness in the mainstream monotheist faiths to embrace the second of the above categories, and some spirit of openness, at least, within the ecumenical and peace movements which dot the twentieth- and twenty-first-century landscape, to entertain the third category.

We have obliquely suggested in this essay, along with the classical literary prophets of the Old Testament, that there are essentially two categories of prophets in any given period of time. There are those prophets who can be identified with a lower case "p," and those who can be identified with an upper case "P." The first are, in New Testament terms, "priests" (religious leaders), "lawyers" (ethics and legal specialists), "scribes" (academicians and philosophers), "magistrates" (political leaders) and traditionalist historians. All of these make an effort at inspiration, authenticity, election. The second are the class of very rare, legitimate, high Prophets whose works stand a good chance of canonization over time, and whose followers believe the Prophet attained a high degree of personal "perfection" as a human being.

In order to assist with the process of evaluating candidates for the canon who have surfaced over the past 2,000 years in the Judeo-Christian-Islamic tradition, and in conclusion, I list a few criteria which may be used to distinguish between the two categories of prophets. The

---

11. For this brief section on Islam I am indebted to Karen Armstrong, *History of God*, particularly chapters 5–8.

high apostles of the Hebrew and Christian bibles, and of Islam, all positively promote the concept of ongoing divine revelation, and so we make that our first criteria. Secondly, the prophets of the great faiths have an unwaveringly universalist view of the places and times where God may communicate with humankind and thus an openness to the authentic founders of the major theo-political traditions. Jesus, for example, glorified virtually all the diverse prophets of the Old Testament canon who lived all over the known world. Muhammad very respectfully mentions both the Jewish prophets and Jesus as well. Thirdly, an authentic prophet is concerned with secular happiness—political, social, and economic justice and progress, including, above all, human rights. Promoting such happiness entails teaching about or building a political platform based on broad and responsible citizenship. This political base ultimately leads to greater personal and corporate spirituality and salvation. Upon this base church leaders may add their own particular prognostications about happiness in the after-life.

Fourthly, a high Prophet is as friendly to reason, wisdom, rationality, empirical science (religion of the mind), as to the mysterious elements of emotion, epiphany, joy, and miracle (religion of the heart). Fifthly, and very significantly, a Prophet necessarily experiences a theophany, or hierophany, an ineffable close encounter with the "divine," which provides a direct calling and motivates life-long work. Sixthly, Prophets are wont to seriously study history in order to allow them to effectively comment on current affairs, and to predict future, usually political, events. This assumes, certainly, that much of the work a Prophet is asked to do after the calling is left for the Prophet to figure out, in occasional consultation with God. Our seventh and final criteria is that a Prophet works with a group, if such a school of disciples can be found, to cement his message in the minds of those who will carry forth both a literature and a religious, political, cultural, or scientific movement after he is gone.

Bibliography

Albertz, Rainer. *A History of Israelite Religion in the Old Testament Period: From the Exile to the Maccabees.* Translated by J. Bowden. Louisville: Westminster John Knox, 1994.
Albright, William F. *From the Stone Age to Christianity: Monotheism and the Historical Process.* Baltimore: The Johns Hopkins Press, 1946.
Alexander, Patrick H., John F. Kutsko, James D. Ernest, Shirley A. Decker-Lucke, and David L. Petersen, eds. *The Handbook of Style For Ancient Near Eastern, Biblical, and Early Christian Studies.* Peabody, MA: Hendrickson Publishers, 1999.
Anderson, Bernhard W. *Understanding the Old Testament.* 3d. ed. Englewood Cliffs, NJ: Prentice Hall, 1975.
Anderson, Robert T. "Samaritans." In *ABD* 5:940-47.
Armstrong, Karen. *A History of God: The 4,000 Year Quest of Judaism, Christianity, and Islam.* New York: Ballantine Books, 1993.
Barton, John. "Post-exilic Hebrew Prophecy." In *ABD* 5:489-95.
Bauer, Susan Wise. *The History of the Ancient World: From the Earliest Accounts to the Fall of Rome.* New York: W.W. Norton, 2007.
Bergen, Wesley J. *Elisha and the End of Prophetism.* Sheffield, UK: Sheffield Academic Press, 1988.
Bromiley, G.W. "The Bible Doctrine of Inspiration." *Christianity Today* 4 (November 23, 1959) 139.
Brueggemann, Walter. *Old Testament Theology: Essays on Structure, Theme, and Text.* Minneapolis: Fortress, 1992.
———. *Texts That Linger, Words That Explode: Listening to Prophetic Voices.* Edited by Patrick D. Miller. Minneapolis: Fortress, 2000.
———. *Theology of the Old Testament: Testimony, Dispute, Advocacy.* Minneapolis: Fortress, 1997.
Boring, M. Eugene. "Prophecy, Early Christian." In *ABD* 5:495-502.
Borgen, Peder. "Philo of Alexandria." In *ABD* 5:333-42.
Catechism of the Catholic Church. 2d ed. New York: Doubleday, 1994.
Childs, Brevard. *Old Testament Theology in a Canonical Context.* Philadelphia: Fortress, 1989.
Chilton, Bruce. "Transfiguration." In *ABD* 6:640-42.
Clifford, Richard J. "Book of Isaiah, Second Isaiah." In *ABD* 3:490-501.
Collins, Raymond F. "Commandment." In *ABD* 1:1097-1099.
Coogan, Michael D. *The Old Testament: A Historical and Literary Introduction to the Hebrew Scriptures.* New York: Oxford University Press, 2006.
Crenshaw, James L. "Book of Job." In *ABD* 3:858-68.
Curtis, Edward M. "Image of God." In *ABD* 3:389-91.
Dalgish, Edward R. "Bethel, Deity." In *ABD* 1:706-10.

Danker, Frederick W. "Apollo." In *ABD* 1:297–98.
Diamond, James A. "The Face of Ethical Encounter." In *The Ten Commandments for Jews, Christians and Others*, edited by Roger E. Van Harn, 3–15. Grand Rapids: Eerdmans, 2007.
Ehrman, Bart D. *Lost Christianities: The Battles for Scripture and the Faiths We Never Knew*. New York: Oxford University Press, 2003.
———. *The New Testament: A Historical Introduction to the Early Christian Writings*. 3d. ed. New York: Oxford University Press, 2004.
Fogarty, Gerald. "Scriptural Authority, Roman Catholicism." In *ABD* 5:1023–26.
Fuller, Reginald. "Biblical Theology." In *OCB*, 88.
Gamble, Harry Y. "Canon, New Testament." In *ABD* 1:852–61.
Gottwald, Norman K. *The Politics of Ancient Israel*. Louisville: Westminster John Knox Press, 2001.
Grayson, A. Kirk. "History of Mesopotamia, Babylonia." In *ABD* 4:755–77.
Greenspahn, Frederick E. "Why Prophecy Ceased." *Journal of Biblical Literature* 1 (1989) 108.
Halpern, Baruch. "Kingship and Monarchy." In *OCB*, 415.
Hamilton, Victor P. *Handbook on the Pentateuch*. 2d ed. Grand Rapids: Baker Academic, 2005.
Heine, Ronald E. "Montanus, Montanism." In *ABD* 4:898–902.
Hildebrandt, Wilfred. "The Cessation of Prophecy in the Old Testament." PhD diss., The University of South Africa, 2004.
Horn, F.W. "Holy Spirit." In *ABD* 3:260–80.
Horsley, Richard A., and John S. Hanson. *Bandits, Prophets and Messiahs: Popular Movements at the Time of Jesus*. Harrisburg, PA: Trinity Press International, 1999.
Huffmon, H. B. "Prophecy, Ancient Near East." In *ABD* 5:477–82.
Hvidt, Neils Christian. *Christian Prophecy: The Post-Biblical Tradition*. New York: Oxford University Press, 2007.
Jenks, Alan W. "Elohist." In *ABD* 2:478–82.
Jeremias, J., and W. Zimmerli. *The Servant of God*. London: SCM Press, 1957.
Koch, Klaus. *The Prophets*. Philadelphia: Fortress, 1984.
LaSor, Sanford. "Temple, Zerubbabel's." In *OCB*, 733.
Levinson, Bernard M. "You Must Not Add Anything to What I Command You: Paradoxes of Canon and Authorship in Ancient Israel." *Numen* 50 (2003) 6–7.
Metzger, Bruce M. *The Canon of the New Testament: Its Origin, Development, and Significance*. Oxford: Clarendon Press, 2009.
Milgrom, Jacob. *Leviticus: A Book of Ritual and Ethics*. Minneapolis: Fortress, 2004.
Miosi, Frank T. "Oracle, Ancient Egypt." In ABD 5:29–30.
Moran, William L. "The Ancient Near Eastern Background of the Love of God in Deuteronomy." In *Essential Papers on Israel and the Ancient Near East*, edited by Frederick E. Greenspahn, 103–15. New York: New York University Press, 1991.
Mowinckel, Sigmund. "'The Spirit' and 'The Word' in the Pre-Exilic Reforming Prophets." *Journal of Biblical Literature* 3 (1934) 199–227.
Nielsen, Eduard. *The Ten Commandments in New Perspective: A Traditio-historical Approach*. Translated by David J. Bourke. Naperville, IL: Allenson, 1968.
Noss, John B. *Man's Religions*. 5th ed. New York: Macmillan, 1974.
Peters, F. E. *The Voice, the Word, the Books: The Sacred Scripture of the Jews, Christians and Muslims*. Princeton: Princeton University Press, 2007.

Phillips, Anthony. *Ancient Israel's Criminal Law: A New Approach to the Decalogue.* New York: Schocken, 1970.
Pilgrim, Walter E. *Uneasy Neighbors: Church and State in the New Testament.* Minneapolis: Fortress, 1999.
Porton, Gary G. "Sadducees." In *ABD* 5:892–95.
Pritchard, James B., ed. *Ancient Near Eastern Texts Relating to the Old Testament.* 3d ed. Princeton: Princeton University Press, 1969.
———. *Harper Collins Concise Atlas of the Bible.* New York: Harper Collins, 2006.
Pury, Albert de. "Yahwist ("J") Source." In *ABD* 6:1012–20.
Robinson, Stephen E. *Are Mormons Christian?* Salt Lake City, Utah: Bookcraft, 1999.
Rose, Martin. "Names of God in the Old Testament." In *ABD* 4:1001–11.
Sanders, James. "The Exile and Canon Formation." In *Exile: Old Testament, Jewish and Christian Conceptions,* edited by J.M. Scott, 58–59. Leiden: Brill, 1997.
———. "Canon, Hebrew Bible." In *ABD* 1:837–52.
Schneidewind, William. *The Word of God in Transition: From Prophets to Inspired Messengers in the Second Temple Period and the Book of Chronicles.* Sheffield, UK: Sheffield Academic Press, (forthcoming).
Smith, Morton. *Palestinian Parties and Politics That Shaped the Old Testament.* New York: Columbia University Press, 1971.
Sommer, Benjamin D. "Did Prophecy Cease? Evaluating a Re-evaluation." *Journal of Biblical Literature* 1 (1996) 115.
Taylor, Walter F. "Unity/Unity of Humanity." In ABD 6:746–53.
Terrien, Samuel. *The Elusive Presence: Toward a New Biblical Theology.* Eugene, Oregon: Wipf and Stock Publishers, 2000.
Thompson, Henry O. "Chebar." In ABD 1:893.
Vaux, Roland de. *Ancient Israel: Its Life and Institutions.* Translated by John McHugh. Livonia, Michigan: Dove, 1997.
Walsh, Jerome T. "Elijah." In ABD 2:463–66.
Walzer, Michael, Menachem Lorberbaum, Noam L. Zohar, and Yair Lorberbaum, eds. *The Jewish Political Tradition,* vol. 1 Authority. New Haven: Yale University Press, 2000.
Weinfeld, Moshe. *Social Justice in Ancient Israel and in the Ancient Near East.* Jerusalem: The Hebrew University Magness Press, 1995.
Wilson, Lynne Hilton. "The Holy Spirit: Creating, Anointing, and Empowering." In *The Gospel of Jesus Christ in the Old Testament,* edited by D. Kelly Ogden, Jared W. Ludlow, and Kerry Muhlestein, 250–81. Salt Lake City: Religious Studies Center/ Deseret Book, 2009.
Zevit, Ziony. *The Religions of Ancient Israel: A Synthesis of Parallactic Approaches.* London: Continuum, 2001.
Zimmerli, W., and J. Jeremias. *The Servant of God.* London: SCM Press, 1957.

Subject/Name Index

A

Aaron, 19, 61, 89, 90, 94, 115
Abduh, Muhammad, 181
Abel, 60–61, 103, 129
Abelard, 179
Abimelech, 48
Abiram, 61
Abraham
   Canaan, Israel's claim to, 116
   captivity, efforts to escape from, 112
   covenant with, terms of, 103
   dissent, prophetic tradition of, xiv
   God's revelation to, 1, 16
   Lot, strife with, 61
   names of God in time of, 145–46, 150
   as physician-prophet, 153
   pseudepigraphic texts involving, 70
   in servant narrative, 127, 128
   as spiritual umpire, 13
   theology of continuing revelation in narrative of, 142–44
   universalism and, 47–48, 53
Abravanel, Isaac, 78, 178
Abulafia, Abraham, 78, 178
Achish, 137
Acts, alternative, 177
Acts of the Apostles, 11, 19, 175
Adam and Eve, 1, 16, 53, 65, 102–3, 141
"adam," meaning human being or humanity, 45, 153
"The Admonitions of Ipu-wer," 47
adultery, Seventh Commandment against, 85, 86
al-Afghani, 181
Agabus, 175
Agade, Curse of, 113
age at calling to prophecy, 28
Ahab, 63, 90
Ahaz, 32, 33, 34, 89
Ahijah, 18, 41, 129
Ahura Mazda, 46, 80
Ai, temple site at, 49
Akbar, 181
Akiva, Rabbi, 178
Akkad/Akkadia, 7, 47, 53
Akkenaton (Amen-hotep IV; pharaoh), 7, 10
Alcmaeon, 153
Alexander the Great, 63
aliens, rights of, 101
"altar law" statute, 87–88, 89, 105
Amalekites, 82
Amarna revolution, 7
Amaziah, 10, 36
Amen-hotep IV (Akhenaton; pharaoh), 7, 10
Ammonites, 82, 113, 128
Amorites, 64, 82
Amos, 121–23
   calling to prophecy, 30, 31
   on continuing revelation, xviii, 5, 41, 118–23, 144, 155
   dissent, prophetic call to, 28
   new prophets, distrust of, 61, 62
   on other nations, 50–51
   predecessors, establishing links to, 34
   "The Prophecy of Doom," 119–20
   rejection, experience of, 35
   in servant narrative, 129
   successors of, 37
Amun, 46, 61n2
angels, as prophetic messengers, 69, 137–39

Subject/Name Index

Apocalypse (Revelation), book of, 2, 4, 16, 19, 103, 179
apocalyptic writing, 71
apocrypha and deuterocanonical books, 4, 173–74. *See also specific texts*
Apollinarius, 179
Apollo (Greek god), 153
apostasy and backsliding, 57–59, 99–100
al-Arabi, 180
Arabs, pre-Islamic, 95, 157
Aristeas, Letter of, 173
Arius, 179
ark of the covenant, 37, 98, 113, 134, 135, 148
arm of God, 136
Arminius, Jacobus, 179
Arnold, Gottfried, 179
Asa, 63
Asap, 59
Asenath, 132–33, 173
al-Ashari, 180
Assumption of Moses (pseudepigraphical work), 173
Assyria
    closure of canon and cessation of prophecy, 1
    dissent, prophetic call to, 28
    God's plan for, 52
    idols or gods of conquered nations, treatment of, 113–14, 125
    Israelite fall to, xv, 113, 122
    Nineveh, 29, 32, 54
    prophetic tradition in, 19
Athaliah, 10
Aton, 7
Atrahasis, 48
Averroes (Ibn Rushd), 180
Avicenna (Ibn Sina), 180
Avtalyon, 178
Azad, Abu al-Kalam, 181
Azariah, 41

B

The Bab, 181
Babel, tower of, 21, 44

Babylon and Babylonian exile, xv, 113, 165–67
    closure of canon and cessation of prophecy, 1, 63–68
    Daniel's reception of revelation for Babylon, 46
    dissent, prophetic call to, 28
    God's plan for Babylon, 52
    high god traditions in Babylon, 46
    Israel spoken to by God in Babylon, 55–57
    lioness, parable of, 56
    name of God and, 150
    nature worship in Babylon, 125
    transitions in cult membership and, 87–88
backsliding and apostasy, 57–59, 99–100
Bahai, 181
Baha'ullah, 181
Balak, 82
Balaam, 16, 19–20, 46, 49, 82
Ball, John, 179
baptism of Jesus, 27, 129
Baptist movement in Jesus's time, 90
al-Baqillani, 180
Barak, 130
Barnabas, 78
Barnabas, Acts of, 177
Baruch, 70
Baruch, books of, 173, 174
Basil the Great, 179
Basilides, Gospel of, 176
al-Basri, 180
bat qol (daughter of the voice), 3
Bel and the Dragon, 174
belief, concept of, 14
Belshazzar, 166
Ben Gurion, David, 178
Benedict of Nursia, 179
Bergen, Wesley J., 62n4
Bergman, Samuel Hugo, 178
Bethel, 10, 28, 62, 116–17, 123, 137
Beza, Theodore, 179
Bible. *See also* Hebrew Bible; New Testament; *specific books*
    division of, 16
    God, canon as replacement for, 71

Subject/Name Index   189

theology of continuing revelation in narrative of, 140–45
biblical universalism. *See* universalism
Birgitt of Vadstena (Bridget of Sweden), 179
Bistami, 180
blasphemy laws, 107
blessing and cursing, 11, 21, 38–39, 44, 52–53, 57–58, 89, 100–103, 106, 113, 143, 154
Bochim, 17, 138
Bridget of Sweden (Birgitt of Vadstena), 179
Brueggemann, Walter, 180
Buber, Martin, 178
Buddha, 53, 78
al-Bukhari, 180

C

Caiaphas, 28, 36
Cain, 61
calling, prophetic. *See* theophany or epiphany
Calvin, Jean, 179
Campbell, Alexander, 180
Canaan (land of)
 conquest of, 116
 as destination for religious dissidents, 112
 prophecy in, 47–49
Canaan (son of Ham), 44
canons and canonicity, xvii, 1–7
 apocrypha and deuterocanonical books, 4, 173–74. *See also specific texts*
 Biblical narrative, closure of canon rejected by, 172
 cessation of prophecy doctrines as part of, 60, 73–80. *See also* cessation of prophecy
 external traditions, tendency to reject, 19–21
 finalization of canon, multiple steps in, 4–5
 God, canon as replacement for, 71

Job and Jesus on reopening of canon, 12–15
of New Testament, 174–77
potential additions to canon, 178–82
previous expansions of existing canon, 54–55
promotion of ongoing prophecy in books of Bible, 16–19
religious liberty as foundation of canon, 79
Samaritan and Sadducee rejection of classical prophets, 20, 172
universalism and, 43, 54–55
Caphtor (Crete), Philistines' exodus from, 50
Cappodocia, 113
captivity, release from, xiv, 111–14
Catherine of Siena, 179
Catholicism. *See* Roman Catholicism
cessation of prophecy, xviii, 60–80
 apocalyptic writing and, 71
 Babylonian exile and, 1, 63–68
 canon, closing of, 60, 73–80. *See also* canons and canonicity
 direct versus indirect encounters with God, 65, 69–70
 God's withdrawal of favor, confused with, 65–67
 in Judaism and Christianity, 1–7
 messianism, 2–3
 politicized nature of religion as institution and, 60
 post-exilic prophets and, 69–72
 pre-exilic examples of, 60–63
Chaldea and Chaldeans, 48, 63, 165–66, 110112
Chemosh, 45
child sacrifice, 85
China, 53, 111, 154
chosen people, Israel's election as
 apostasy and, 57–59
 theology of continuing revelation and, 142
 universalism, concept of, 46–47, 49–51, 57–59
Christ. *See* Jesus

Subject/Name Index

Christianity
closure of canon and cessation of prophecy in, 1–7, 60, 73–78. *See also* canons and canonicity; cessation of prophecy
early denominational movements within, 90
exclusion of certain prophetic traditions by, 76, 176–77
expansion of canon by, 54, 174–76
external traditions and non-canonical literature, attitude toward, 20
messianism in, 2–3
potential prophets of continuing revelation outside existing canons, 179–80
theology of continuing revelation in early Christianity, 145
Zion theology, break with, 25
Chronicles, books of
cessation of prophecy doctrine and, 63, 70
on continuing revelation, 41
face of God in, 135
Kings, as revision of, 4
promotion of ongoing prophecy in, 18
universalism in, 9–10, 42
Cicero, 53
circumcision, 91, 153
Clement of Alexandria, 78
closed canons. *See* canons and canonicity
clouds, 13, 133, 134
Cohen, Hermann, 178
coming "in the name," 11, 13
Commentary on the Book of Kings, 12
common prophetic experience, xvii–xviii, 25–42
citizen prophets, 25
continuing revelation, promise of, 39–41
dissent, association with, 27–28, 35–36
fitness for prophetic task, doubts of appointed prophet regarding, 30–31
general revelatory process, 7–12
Hebrew Bible and New Testament, continuity between, 27–28
initial calling, 26–34
kingly prophetism, 25–26
leadership, prophets called to, 24, 28
multiple encounters with God, 36
predecessors, establishing links to, 34–36
professional pundit-prophets, 26
of rejection, 20–21, 35–36, 173–74
successors to prophets, 8, 21, 36–40
Confucius, 53, 78
Constantine (Roman emperor), 74
constitutional nature of Decalogue, xvi, 81, 84–85, 86, 90
continuing revelation, xviii, 118–39. *See also* theology of continuing revelation
common prophetic promise of, 39–41, 118
Deuteronomy, reasons for marginalization of, 97
influence of Amos on, 118–23
in Islam, 78, 156–58
law in prophet-based society promoting, 99–104, 140
natural and anthropomorphic metaphors for, 133–39
potential candidates outside existing canons, 178–82
promotion of ongoing prophecy in books of Bible, 16–19
sentinel or watchman metaphor explaining, 123–25
servant narratives, 126–29
shepherd metaphor and, 129–31
council in heaven, 70
Covenant Code, 105–6
covenants, 5, 53, 55, 103, 143–44, 146
Crete (Caphtor), Philistines' exodus from, 50
Cromwell, Oliver, 179
crucifixion and resurrection of Jesus, 175–76
cursing and blessing, 11, 21, 38–39, 44, 52–53, 57–58, 89, 100–103, 106, 113, 143, 154
Cyrus Cylinder, 112

Cyrus the Persian, 10, 42, 72, 112, 128, 130, 166–67

D

Daniel
  additions to book of, 173
  cessation of prophecy doctrine and, 62, 63, 69
  Jesus's citation of, 35
  as last authorized addition to Jewish canon, 1
  law in prophet-based society and, 112
  promotion of ongoing prophecy in, 19
  "son of man" prediction, 38
  theology of continuing revelation and, 145
  universalism and, 46, 51, 54
Dathan, 61
daughter of the voice (bat qol), 3
David, 97–98
  attenuation of messianic movement following death of, 7
  calling to prophecy, 28
  dissent, prophetic tradition of, xiv
  God, natural and anthropomorphic metaphors for, 134, 135, 138–39
  God's revelation to, 1, 17, 18
  Jesus speaking of, 35
  new religious denominations arising under, 89
  priesthood's role in revelatory process following death of, 8
  Psalms, association with, 150, 151
  reforms, short-lived nature of, 10
  on religious liberty, 111, 112
  Samaritan rejection of, 20
  in servant narrative, 127, 128
  shepherd metaphor and, 130
  successors of, 36, 37, 39
  theology of continuing revelation and, 144
  universalism and, 53, 58, 59
David, Francis, 179
"the Day of the Lord," 40

death of prophecy. *See* canons and canonicity; cessation of prophecy
Deborah, 17, 28, 93, 95, 98, 112, 130, 144, 150, 179
Decalogue. *See* Ten Commandments
Deir Alla, 20, 49
Denys the Areopagite, 179
Descartes, René, 179
deuterocanonical and apocryphal books, 4, 173–74. *See also specific texts*
Deuteronomistic historian(s), 25, 39, 91, 105, 116
Deuteronomy
  as law code. *See* law in prophet-based society, promotion of religious tolerance by
  marginalization, reasons for, 97
  promotion of ongoing prophecy in, 16
  theology of continuing revelation in, 140
  universalism in, 55
Didache, 177
Didymus Judas Thomas, 176
dietary laws, 105
Diodochus, 179
direct versus indirect encounters with God, 65, 69–70
dissent and reform, xiv–xv
  cessation of prophecy doctrines and, 74
  as common prophetic experience, 35–36
  general revelatory process, as part of, 10–11
  historical marginalization of voices promoting, 172–73
  Josiah, reforms of, 12, 117
  law in prophet-based society and, 96
  as part of prophetic call, 27–28
  short-lived nature of prophetic reforms, 10
  theology of continuing revelation and, 167–68
distrust of new prophets, 11, 14, 60–63
dreams, prophecy via, 9, 19, 54, 70, 132, 163
Duns Scotus Erigena, 179

Subject/Name Index

E

E or Elohist source, 17, 54, 119
Ebal, temple site at, 49
Ecclesiastes, book of, 18, 35, 156
Ecclesiasticus (Wisdom of Jesus Son of Sirach), 174
Eckhart, Meister, 179
economic rights, 108–9
Eddy, Mary Baker, 78, 180
Edom and Edomites, 15, 51, 52, 108, 167
Egypt. *See also specific pharaohs*
   creator gods in, 45
   Exodus of Israelites from, xiv, xv, 56, 58, 81–82, 84, 111, 112, 130, 143, 172
   as "firstborn" nation, 57, 77
   God's plan for, 52
   images as idols in, 137
   Joseph's prophetic mission in, 54
   oracular process in, 7, 8
   physician-priests in, 154
   prophetic tradition in, 19
   shepherd metaphor in, 129
Egyptians, Gospel of, 176
Eighth Commandment, 86
El, 45, 146
El Berit, 146
El Roi, 146
El-Shaddai, 46, 132, 146
Elam and Elamites, 112, 113, 125
Eldad, 16
Eleazar, Rabbi, 178
Eli, 37
Eliezer, 41
Eliezer ben Judah of Worms, 178
Elijah
   continuing revelation and, 119, 129, 135, 137
   dissent, prophetic call to, xiv, 28, 96
   God's revelation to, 1, 17
   Jesus and, 35
   Moses and, 36–37, 39, 62
   new prophets, distrust of, 63
   as physician-prophet, 153
   reforms, short-lived nature of, 10
   on religious liberty, 112
   return of, 3, 71
   in servant narrative, 129
   successors of, 39
   theology of continuing revelation and, 144, 153
Elisha, 39, 62n4, 119, 144
Emerson, Ralph Waldo, 180
end-of-prophecy doctrines. *See* cessation of prophecy
Enlil, 129
Enlil, desecration of Temple of, 113
Enoch, xiv, 19, 44, 45, 57, 65, 70, 142, 145
Enoch, books of, 173, 174
Enos, 44
Enuma Elish, 48
Ephraim, 58
epiphany. *See* theophany or epiphany
Erasmus, Desiderius, 179
Esarhaddon, 64
Esau, 57, 61
eschatological writing, 71
Esdras, books of, 173, 174
Essenes, 90, 173
Esther, 18, 63, 112, 173
Ethiopia and Ethiopians, 51, 168
Eusebius of Caesarea, 176–77
Eutyches, 179
Exodus, book of, 16, 105–6
exodus experiences of other nations, 50
Exodus from Egypt, xiv, xv, 56, 58, 81–82, 84, 111, 112, 130, 143, 172
Ezekiel, 124–25
   calling to prophecy, 28, 29
   on continuing revelation, 41, 123–25, 128, 134–36
   on God's withdrawal of favor, 66
   law in prophet-based society and, 88, 109, 112
   new prophets, distrust of, 61
   predecessors, establishing links to, 35
   promotion of ongoing prophecy in, 19
   Samaritan and Sadducee rejection of, 20, 172
   successors of, 37, 38

theology of continuing revelation and, 145, 150, 159, 168
universalism of, 48–49, 55–57
winged creatures, theophanic nature of, 134
Ezra, 79–80
cessation of prophecy doctrine and, 63, 74, 79–80
on continuing revelation, 145
law in prophet-based society and, 109, 112
Pentateuch and, 1, 4, 56, 62, 74, 79–80
promotion of ongoing prophecy in, 18
temple, rebuilding of, 18

F

face of God, 135
faith, concept of, 14
false prophets, 27, 38, 70, 77, 95, 96
false witness, Ninth Commandment against, 86, 174
al-Farabi, 180
father, God as, 158–65
feminist theology, 180
Fifth Commandment, 86, 107–8
fire, 13, 133, 134
First Commandment
  continuing revelation, as directive for, 99–104
  name of God and, 149
  political aspects of, 87, 93–97
  purpose and aim of, xiii–xv, xvi, 16, 84
  religious liberty and prophecy, supporting, 85–91, 95, 175, 176
  tree of knowledge of good and evil and, 102–3
First Isaiah. *See* Isaiah
firstborn, concept of, 18, 57–58, 77
flood story, 133, 155–56
foreigners and foreign nations. *See also* universalism

God's relationship with and expectations of, 49–57
human rights protections for aliens, 101
prophecy in nations surrounding Israel, 47–49
on religious liberty, 112, 113
Fourth Commandment, 86
Fox, George, 179
Francis of Assisi, 179
Francis Xavier, 179
free speech and election, First Commandment supporting, 87
freedom laws in ancient Israel, 104–10
freedom, religious. *See* revelation and religious liberty in the Bible

G

Gabriel (archangel), 156
Galileo, Galilei, 179
Gaon, Saadiah, 81, 178
Genesis, book of, 16, 45, 48, 136
Gerondi, Nissum, 178
Gertrude the Great, 179
al-Ghazzali, 180
Gibbon, Edward, 179
Gibeonites, 109, 116
Gideon, xvii, 17, 29, 83, 87, 89, 91, 93, 95, 98, 112, 137–38, 144
gifts of the Spirit, 3
Gilgal, 138
Gilgamesh epic, 47–48
"the glory of the Lord," 134
God
  names of, 134, 145–50. *See also specific names*
  natural and anthropomorphic metaphors for, 133–39
  as physician-scientist, 155
  revealed. *See* theophany or epiphany
  sovereignty of, 158–65
goel or redeemer, 127
golden calf incident, 58, 99
Gomer, 72, 73

Subject/Name Index

Gospels. *See* John's Gospel; Luke's Gospel; Mark's Gospel; Matthew's Gospel
Gospels, alternative, 12, 20, 176–77
great commandment. *See* First Commandment
Greece
   angels in, 138
   Israelites under Seleucid Greece, xv, 113
   law codes of, 53, 108, 109
   unity, philosophical concept of, 153
Greek Orthodox church, canon of, 174
Greek Septuagint translation of Hebrew Bible, 174
Greenspahn, Frederick E., 74n15
Gregory the Great (pope), 179
Guttierez, Gustavo, 180

H

Habakkuk, 31, 35
Haddad, 45
hadith, 180
Hagar, 95, 142, 146, 156–57
Haggai, 1, 63, 112
Halevi, Judah, 178
al-Hallaj, 180
Ham, 44
Hamath, prophetic text from, 50
Hammurabi, 113, 129
Hanani, 41, 70
Hananiah, 36
Hanbal, 180
Hannah, 59
Hanum, 128
Haran, 48, 112
Harmon-White, Ellen G., 78, 180
Hazor, temple site at, 49
healing, health, and prophecy, 91–93, 153–56
heavenly council, 70
Hebrew Bible
   continuity of New Testament prophetic tradition with, 27–28, 172, 175
   division of, 4–5, 16. *See also* Pentateuch; Prophets; Writings
   earliest sources of, 17
   Greek Septuagint translation of, 174
   sequencing of books in Jewish versus Christian canon, 63n6
Hebrews, epistle to, 103, 179
Hebrews, Gospel of, 176
Herodotus, 50
Herzl, Theodore, 178
Heschel, Abraham Joshua, 178
hesed (loving kindness), 165
Hezekiah, xvii, 91, 96, 112, 128
high god tradition in Israel, 45–46
"high places," freedom to worship at, 91, 116–17
high Prophets, criteria for, 9, 15, 23, 26, 70, 93, 181–82
Hildegard of Bingen, 179
Hilkiah, 12
Hillel, 178
Hippo, council of (90 CE), 2
Hippocrates, 153
history
   Decalogue's consciousness of, 84
   Deuteronomistic historian(s), 25, 39, 91, 105, 116
   primordial. *See* primordial history of Bible
   prophecy geared to particular times, places, and circumstances of, 145
   prophetic interpretations of, 75–76, 171–72
   prophets, modern historians as, 179–80
Hooker, Richard, 179
Hosea, 72–73
   Amos's influence on, 118, 123
   calling to prophecy, 28, 32
   cessation of prophecy doctrines and, 62
   on chosen people, 57
   on continuing revelation, 41, 118, 123
   Jesus citing, 35
   law in prophet-based society and, 99, 109

Subject/Name Index 195

marriage of, 32, 72–73
on mediated communication with God, 9
new prophets, distrust of, 62
predecessors, establishing links to, 34, 35
successors of, 37, 38, 39
theology of continuing revelation and, 144, 162, 165
Hozai, 41
Huldah, 17, 41
human potential for prophecy, 9–10
human rights protections, 101–2
Hus, Jan, 78, 179
Hut, Hans, 179

I

Ibn Rushd (Averroes), 180
Ibn Sina (Avicenna), 180
Ibn Taymuyah, 181
Iddo, 41
idols and idolatry
   Bel and the Dragon as polemic against, 174
   conquered nations, treatment of idols or gods of, 113–14, 125
   images, idols as, 137
   Second Commandment forbidding, 84, 85, 115–16
Ignatius of Lyons, 78
image and likeness of God, 136–37
"in the name of the Lord," 11, 13
India, 53, 154, 177
institution, politicized nature of religion as, 60, 75–76, 167
Isaac, 1, 57, 61, 78, 132, 143–44, 145, 146
Isaiah, 32–34. *See also* Second Isaiah; Third Isaiah
   Amos's influence on, 118
   on apostasy, 57
   calling to prophecy, 29, 30, 32–34
   cessation of prophecy doctrine and, 62, 69–72
   on continuing revelation, 41, 123, 126, 128–29, 130, 134, 136, 138
   dissent, prophetic call to, 28
   on distrust of new prophets, 14
   God's revelation to, 17
   on God's withdrawal of favor, 66
   infant birth and maturation, use of metaphor of, 34
   Jesus and, 38
   Jesus speaking of, 35
   king, association with, 26
   new prophets, distrust of, 61
   predecessors, establishing links to, 34
   promotion of ongoing prophecy in, 19
   on religious liberty, 112
   Samaritan and Sadducee rejection of, 20, 172
   successors of, 37, 39
   suffering servant in, 126, 128–29
   theology of continuing revelation and, 144, 149, 158, 159, 160, 162, 165, 168
   on waxing and waning of prophetic message, 23
Ishmael, 61, 156–58
Ishmael, Rabbi, 178
Ishtar, 47
Islam
   Christian attitude toward Quran, 2, 177
   closure of canon by, 76–77, 177–78
   on continuing revelation, 78, 156–58, 177
   development of sacred literature by, 2, 54
   potential prophets of continuing revelation outside existing canons, 180–81
Israel (northern kingdom), 7, 25, 28, 32, 75, 113, 121–23, 144
Israel, Jacob's change of name to, 147

J

J or Yahwist source, 17, 54, 119
Jabin, 113, 116
Jacob
   cessation of prophecy doctrines and, 61, 70, 72

196 Subject/Name Index

Jacob—continued
  God's revelation to, 1
  theology of continuing revelation and, 134, 139, 142–44, 145, 147
  universalism and, 56, 57
Jafar ibn Sadiq, 180
Jahaziel, 41
Jamnia, council of (90 CE), 2
Japheth, 44
al-Jawziyah, 181
Jebusite Jerusalem, 82, 98
Jeduthun, 17, 41
Jehoahaz II, 56
Jehoiakim, 21, 56
Jehoida, 10
Jehu, 10, 91, 96, 112
Jephthah, 87
Jeremiah, 110–11
  calling to prophecy, 29, 30, 32
  cessation of prophecy doctrine and, 63, 67
  on continuing revelation, 40–41, 123, 125, 128
  dissent, prophetic call to, 28
  on God's withdrawal of favor, 66
  Jehoiakim's rejection of, 21
  king, association with, 26
  law in prophet-based society and, 109–10
  Mesopotamian stories used in, 48
  multiple encounters with God, 36
  new prophets, distrust of, 61, 62, 63
  predecessors, establishing links to, 35
  on priesthood, 8–9
  promotion of ongoing prophecy in, 19
  rejection, experience of, 35
  on religious liberty, 112
  Samaritan and Sadducee rejection of, 20, 172
  successors of, 37, 38, 39
  theology of continuing revelation and, 145, 150
Jeremiah, Letter of, 174
Jericho, 82, 121
Jeroboam, 10, 112, 119
Jerusalem. *See also* temple at Jerusalem
  destruction of, 54, 88
  Jebusite city of, 82, 98
  Jesus and, 96–97, 100, 136, 145, 176
  "New Jerusalem," concept of, 88–89
  Zion theology and, 25, 55
Jesus, 68–69
  on Abel as prophet, 61n1
  on angels, 139
  baptism of, 27, 129
  calling to prophecy, 28, 30, 31, 88
  cessation of prophecy doctrine and, 63, 68–69, 72
  on continuing revelation, 5, 12, 38, 40, 68–69, 78, 88, 145
  crucifixion and resurrection of, 175–76
  dissent, prophetic call to, 28
  Isaiah and, 38
  law in prophet-based society and, 85, 88, 96, 100, 102, 110
  as messiah, 3
  Pharisees and, 102, 104, 129, 173, 174, 176
  as physician-prophet, 20, 68–69, 153
  predecessors, establishing links to, 35
  rejection, experience of, 35
  on religious liberty, 88, 112, 114, 175–76
  on reopening of canon, 13, 14–15
  as rock, 134
  Samaritans and, 20
  servant narrative and, 128, 129
  shepherd metaphor and, 131
  "son of man" prediction, 38
  Ten Commandments and, 85, 100, 102
  Zechariah, interest in, xvi, 11
Jethro, 49
Joan of Arc, 179
Joash, 10–11, 12, 63
Job, xvii, 12–15, 18, 23, 35, 48, 51, 63n6, 129
Joel, 1, 3, 4, 9, 11, 35, 38, 43, 120, 145
John of the Cross, 179
John the Baptist, 23, 37, 112, 129, 145, 174, 179
John's Gospel

Subject/Name Index 197

on lost remembrances of Jesus, 12
promotion of ongoing prophecy in, 19
prophet, author of John as, 179
theophany of God's voice in, 136
Jonah, 29, 30, 32, 35, 46, 54
Joseph, xiv, 16, 17, 46, 54, 61, 112, 131–33
Joseph and Asenath (pseudepigraphical work), 173
Josephus, 15, 78, 178
Joshua
   calling to prophecy, 28, 29
   continuing revelation and, 129, 138, 144
   death of, situation of Israel following, 21, 58
   law in prophet-based society and, 72, 80, 82, 99, 104, 112, 116
   promotion of ongoing prophecy in, 17
   in servant narrative, 129
   theophany at Gilgal, 138
Josiah
   law in prophet-based society and, 87, 90, 91, 93, 96, 105, 106, 112, 115, 117
   lioness, parable of, 56
   "lost" revelation, rediscovery of, 12
   plurality, religious, xvii
   reforms of, 12, 117
   resistance to new prophecy under, 11
Jubilees, Book of, 78, 173
Judah (southern kingdom), 1, 7, 25, 32, 35, 62, 64, 75, 113, 121–23, 144, 150
Judah the Pietist, 178
Judaism. *See also* Pharisees; rabbinic Judaism
   closure of canon and cessation of prophecy in, 1–7, 60, 73–78. *See also* canons and canonicity; cessation of prophecy
   Essenes, 90, 173
   exclusion of Christian prophetic tradition by, 76, 173, 174
   expansion of canon after closure, 54

   Kabbalah movement, 178
   messianism in, 2–3
   potential prophets of continuing revelation outside existing canons, 178
   Qumran community, 12, 78, 173
   rabbinic, 3, 23, 45, 63, 74, 76, 78, 105, 145, 174, 177, 178
   Sadducees, 12, 13, 14–15, 69, 90, 129, 172–73, 176
   Samaritans, 20, 35, 79, 80, 90, 172–73
   Samaritans and, 20
Judas, in Acts, 90, 175
Judas Maccabee, 112
Jude, book of, 103
Judges
   captivity, Israelite experience of, xiv, 112–13
   cessation of prophecy doctrines following Moses under, 64–65
   dissent, prophetic tradition of, xiv
   law in prophet-based society and leadership of, 93–95
   promotion of ongoing prophecy in, 17
   in theology of continuing revelation, 144
Judith, 173
al-Junayd, 180

K

Kabbalah movement, 178
Kadesh, 61n2, 95, 115
al-Karabisi, 180
Karo, Joseph, 178
kenosis, concept of, 63–64
al-Khusraw, 180
killing, Sixth Commandment against, 85, 86
al-Kindi, 180
King James Version (KJV), use of, xiii*n*1
kings and kingship
   in Biblical history, xiv–xv
   prophets and, 25–26
   theology of continuing revelation and, 144

Kings, books of
　Chronicles as revision of, 4
　Commentary on the Book of Kings, 12
　promotion of ongoing prophecy in, 17–18
　in theology of continuing revelation, 144
Kir, exodus of Syrians from, 50
Knox, John, 179
Kock, Klaus, 63n5
Kook, Abraham Isaac, 178
Korah, 61, 99, 115

L

Lacish, temple site at, 49
Lahoi-Roi, well of, 95
land law, 109
Latter Day Saints (Mormons), 84, 180
law in prophet-based society,
　promotion of religious tolerance by, xviii, 81–117. *See also* First Commandment; Ten Commandments
　"altar law" statute, 87–88, 89, 105
　blasphemy laws, 107
　continuing revelation, directive for, 99–104, 140
　Covenant Code, 105–6
　dissent and reform, 96. *See also* dissent and reform
　economic rights, 108–9
　false prophets, dealing with, 95, 96
　freedom laws, 104–10
　Hammurabi, 113, 129
　human rights protections, 101–2
　limits on religious practice, 84, 115–16
　love commandment, 100–104
　negative evidence for religious liberty, 115–17
　places of judgment, 94–95
　political leadership and, 87, 93–97
　proclamations of religious freedom, 111–14
　sovereignty of God, 158–65

Sumer, law codes of, 53
　tribal government of early Israelites, xiv, 82, 94, 108, 143
　Ur-Nammu, 129
　vows and oaths, 107–8
leadership, prophets called to, 24, 28
Leontopolis, temple at, 88–89
Letter of Aristeas, 173
Letter of Jeremiah, 174
Levi, Testament of, 173
Levites, 82–83, 94, 95, 105, 154
Leviticus, book of, 16, 88, 101, 107
liberation theology, 180
liberty, religious. *See* revelation and religious liberty in the Bible
Liebowitz, Yeshayahu, 178
lion metaphor in Amos's "Prophecy of Doom," 120
lioness, parable of, 55–56
"living waters," concept of, 6
Loew, Judah (Maharal of Prague), 178
logical connection of God and prophetic voice, 120
Loisy, Alfred, 180
"lost" prophets (for whom no prophetic literature survives), 41
"lost" revelations, rediscovery of, 12
Lot, 61
love commandment, 100–104, 175
loving kindness (hesed), 165
Luke, as physician-prophet, 153
Luke's Gospel
　promotion of ongoing prophecy in, 19, 175
　prophet, author of Luke as, 179
　Q and, 4, 12
　relationship to other New Testament Gospels, 4
Luria, Isaac, 178
Luther, Martin, 179
lying, Ninth Commandment against, 86, 174

M

Maccabees, 112, 145, 173, 174

Subject/Name Index 199

Maharal of Prague (Judah Loew), 178
Mahavira, 53
Maimonides, 178
Malachi, 1, 4, 35, 37–38, 43, 55, 63, 145, 160
Manasseh, 58, 89, 90
Manoah and his wife, xv, 98, 138
Manu, Laws of, 53
Marcion, 179
Marduk, 10, 46, 114, 166
Mark's Gospel
   promotion of ongoing prophecy in, 19
   prophet, author of Mark as, 179
   relationship to other New Testament Gospels, 4
marriage, Hosea's calling to prophecy requiring, 32, 72–73
Mary Magdalene, Gospel attributed to, 176
Matthew's Gospel
   First Commandment stressed in, 88
   Jewish perspective of, 174
   promotion of ongoing prophecy in, 19
   prophet, author of Matthew as, 179
   Q and, 4, 12
   relationship to other New Testament Gospels, 4
Matthias, Gospel of, 176
Mazda, 16, 80
Medad, 16
medicine, healing, and prophecy, 91–93, 153–56
Megiddo, 48, 49
Meister Eckhart, 179
Melchizedek, 48
Mesha of Moab, 46
Mesopotamia
   captivity, Israelite experience of, 113
   creator gods and creation stories, 45, 48
   images as idols in, 137
   Israelite use of stories from, 47–48, 133
   oracular process in, 7
   physician-priests in, 154

prophetic tradition in, 19
messianism in Judaism and Christianity, 2–3
Micah, 34, 35, 61, 83, 108, 118, 145
Micah of Ephraim, 89
Micaiah, 36, 41
Michael (archangel), 103
Midian and Midianites, 112, 113
Miller, William, 180
Milton, John, 179
minorities, protection of, 101
Miriam, 61
Mishna, 178
Moab and Moabites, 20, 46, 52, 54, 82, 108, 113
monolatry, 45
monotheism, 45, 131–33, 145–50, 153
Montanus and Montanists, 74, 78, 177, 179
Mormons (Latter Day Saints), 84, 180
Moses, 91–93
   calling to prophecy, 30
   cessation of prophecy doctrines following, 64–65
   on continuing revelation, 77–78, 100
   dissent, prophetic call to, 28, 91–92
   distrust of new prophets and, 61–62
   Elijah and, 36–37, 39, 62
   Exodus from Egypt, xiv, xv, 56, 58, 81–82, 84, 111, 112, 130, 143, 172
   God, natural and anthropomorphic metaphors for, 13, 133, 134, 135
   God's revelation to, 1, 16
   golden calf incident, 58, 99
   on human potential for prophecy, 9
   multiple encounters with God, 36
   names of God in time of, 145, 146–48, 150
   Pentateuch, finalization of format of, 1–2
   as physician-prophet, 91–93, 153
   as political leader, 93, 94
   priesthood's role in revelatory process following death of, 8
   Psalms associated with, 150, 151
   rejection, experience of, 35, 36

Subject/Name Index

Moses—continued
  on religious liberty, xiv, 81–83, 88, 89, 103–4, 107, 115
  in servant narrative, 127, 128, 129
  sharing of prophetic spirit by, 39
  shepherd metaphor and, 130
  successors of, 36–37, 39
  theology of continuing revelation in narrative of, 142–44
  universalism and, 46, 49, 53
Moses, Assumption of (pseudepigraphical work), 173
Moses of Leon, 178
Mosheim, Johann Lorenz von, 179
mountain or rock, God as, 6, 133, 134
Muhammad, 76, 77–78, 156–58, 177–78, 182
Mulla Sadra, 180
multiple places of worship, 91, 105, 106–7
murder, Sixth Commandment against, 85, 86
Muslims. *See* Islam

N

Nabonidus, 165–66
Nabopolassar, 125
Nag Hammadi documents, 78, 173
Nahum, 32
names of God, 134, 145–50. *See also specific names*
Nanak, 78
Naphtali, Testament of, 173
Naram-Sin, 113
Nathan, 10, 37, 98
Nathan of Gaza, 178
Nathanael, 138–39
natural law, 103
Nazarites, 99
Nebuchadnezzar, 125
Neferti, Prophecy of, 47
Nehemiah, 18, 63, 80, 112, 145
Neith, 132
Nestorius, 179
"New Jerusalem," concept of, 88–89

new light revelation, 11, 20–21, 60, 61, 62, 74n15, 88, 96, 111, 151, 173, 175
new prophets, distrust of, 11, 14, 60–63
New Testament. *See also specific books*
  angels in, 138–39
  canon of, 174–77
  continuity with prophetic tradition of Hebrew Bible, 27–28, 172, 175
  divisions of, 16
  promotion of ongoing prophecy in, 19
Newton, Isaac, 179
Nicholas of Cusa, 179
Nineveh, 29, 32, 54
Ninth Commandment, 86, 174
Noah
  cessation of prophecy doctrines and, 61
  God's revelation to, 1, 5, 16
  theology of continuing revelation and, 133, 142, 153, 171
  universalism and, 44–45, 51, 53, 57
Noah, book of, 173
northern kingdom (Israel), 7, 25, 28, 32, 75, 113, 121–23, 144
Numbers, book of, 16, 49, 70

O

oaths and vows, 107–8
Obadiah, 35, 37
Oded, 41, 70
O'Kelly, James, 180
old light religion, 60
Old Testament. *See* Hebrew Bible
ongoing revelation. *See* continuing revelation
Onias IV (pharaoh), 54, 88–89
"oracles against the nations," 51
Origen, 176
Orthodox churches, canon of, 174

P

P or Priestly source, 17
Pahad, 132, 146

Subject/Name Index

papal infallibility, 3
parent, God as, 158–65
parents, Fifth Commandment to honor, 86, 107–8
Parham, Charles, 180
Pascal, Blaise, 179
Paul and Pauline letters
   initial persecution of Christians by Paul, 173
   lost/missing letters, 12
   promotion of ongoing prophecy in, 19
   prophet, Paul as, 175
   on religious liberty, 112
Paul and Thecla, Acts of, 177
Pentateuch. *See also specific books*
   cessation-of-prophecy doctrines and, 61–62
   defined, 4, 16
   finalization of, 1–2, 4
   primordial (pre-Abrahamic) history of. *See* primordial history of Bible
   promotion of ongoing prophecy in, 16–17
   sources and versions of, 17, 54, 119
Persia, God's plan for, 52
Peter (apostle), xiv, 3, 11–12, 112, 138
Peter Abelard, 179
Peter, epistles of, 9–10
Peter, Gospel of, 176
Pharisees. *See also* rabbinic Judaism
   on cessation of prophecy, 12, 13, 74, 76, 145, 173, 174
   classical prophets accepted by, 20, 173, 174
   on Covenant Code, 105
   as denominational movement, 90
   Jesus and, 102, 104, 129, 173, 174, 176
Philistines, 45, 50, 64, 82, 113, 134, 148
Phillip, 138, 176
Phillip, daughters of, 175
Philo of Alexandria, 78, 178
Phoenicia, 19, 45, 48–49, 51
physician-prophets, 20, 68–69, 91–93, 153–54

Plato, 108, 109
plurality of gods versus plurality of names for one God, 45–46
plurality, religious, xvi–xvii, 49
political aspects of First Commandment, 87, 93–97
political dissent. *See* dissent and reform
politicized nature of religion as institution, 60, 75–76, 167
politico-religious idolatry, 85
polytheism, 71, 85, 105, 117, 145–50
portents and signs, 167–69
prayer, as revelation, 5–6
predecessors, prophetic links to, 34–36
priesthood
   general revelatory process, role in, 8–9, 10
   Levites, 82–83, 94, 95, 105, 154
   modern professional priesthood and revelation, 6
   physician-priests, 154
   rejection of prophets by, 35–36, 118
primordial history of Bible
   cessation of prophecy predictions in, 60–61
   theology of continuing revelation in narrative of, 142
   universalism of, 43–45
"The Prophecy of Doom" (Amos), 119–20
Prophecy of Neferti, 47
Prophets (Jewish division of Hebrew Bible). *See also specific books and prophets*
   defined, 4, 16
   expansion of canon by, 54
   promotion of ongoing prophecy in, 17–19
prophets and prophecy. *See* revelation and religious liberty in the Bible
Protestantism
   potential prophets of continuing revelation outside existing canons, 179
   return of inspiration in, 3
   revision of canon by, 5
Proverbs, book of, 5, 16, 18, 156, 174

Psalms
   on God's relationship to other nations, 51, 52–53
   law in prophet-based society and, 103
   Mesopotamian stories used in, 48
   on multiple encounters with God, 36
   promotion of ongoing prophecy in, 18
   shepherd metaphor in, 130
   theology of continuing revelation in, 150–52
pseudepigrapha, 70, 173
public health and prophecy, 91–93, 153–56

Q

Q (Quelle), 4, 12, 179
Qohelet (Ecclesiastes), 18, 35, 156
Qumran/Dead Sea Scrolls, 12, 78, 173
Quran. See Islam
al-Qushayri, 180

R

rabbinic Judaism. See also Pharisees
   on bat qol (daughter of the voice), 3
   on cessation of prophecy, 45, 63, 74, 76, 78, 145, 177
   Christian texts available to, 174
   classical versus rabbinic Hebrew, 23
   on Covenant Code, 105
   potential new prophetic voices from, 178
rainbow, 171
Ramses II (pharaoh), 61n2, 112
Rashi, 178
rashidun, 180
Rauschenbusch, Walter, 180
redeemer or goel, 127
rediscovery of "lost" revelations, 12
reform, prophetic call to. See dissent and reform
Rehoboam, 113
Reimarius, Samuel, 179
rejection as common prophetic experience, 20–21, 35–36, 173–74
religious liberty. See revelation and religious liberty in the Bible
resurrection of Jesus, 175–76
revelation and religious liberty in the Bible, xiii–xviii, 1–24, 171–82
   canonical closure of revelation, xvii, 1–7. See also canons and canonicity
   cessation of prophecy, xviii, 60–80. See also cessation of prophecy
   common prophetic experience, xvii–xviii, 25–42. See also common prophetic experience
   continuation of, xviii, 118–69. See also continuing revelation; theology of continuing revelation
   dissent and reform, biblical tradition of, xiv–xv. see also dissent and reform
   First Commandment, purpose and aim of, xiii–xv, xvi, 16
   general revelatory process, 7–12
   high Prophets, criteria for, 9, 15, 23, 26, 70, 93, 181–82
   law and, xviii, 81–117. See also law in prophet-based society, promotion of religious tolerance by
   logical connection of God and prophetic voice, 120
   potential candidates outside existing canons, 178–82
   promotion of ongoing prophecy in books of Bible, 16–19
   prophets as primary beneficiaries of religious liberty, xv–xvi
   relationship between, xv–xvii
   types of prophets, 25–26, 181–82
   universalism, xviii, 42–59. See also universalism
   violence, religion-inspired, in Bible, xvii
   waxing and waning of prophetic message, 8, 21–24

Revelation, book of, 2, 4, 16, 19, 103, 179
Reynolds case (1878, U.S. Supreme
  Court), 84
Rimmon, 45
rock or mountain, God as, 6, 133, 134
Roman Catholicism
  on closure of canon and cessation of
    prophecy, 2
  "Jewish apocrypha," canonical status
    of, 174
  papal infallibility, 3
Roman society and government, xv, 53,
  113, 176
ruah elohim (Spirit of God), 3, 25, 149,
  167
Rumi, 180
Russian Orthodox church, canon of, 174
Ruth, 18, 54

S

Sabaoth, 146
sacrifice
  of children, 85
  dietary laws and, 105
  hesed or loving kindness in place
    of, 165
  revelation and, 6
Sadducees, 12, 13, 14–15, 69, 90, 129,
  172–73, 176
Sadra, Mulla, 180
Samaritans, 20, 35, 79, 80, 90, 172–73
Sampson, 99
Sampson, parents of, 17, 89
Samuel, xvii, 17, 30–31, 37, 39, 90, 97,
  99, 123, 144
Samuel the Elder, Rabbi, 178
Saul, 17, 83
Savior, Gospel of, 176–77
Savonarola, 179
Schell, Hermann, 180
Second Commandment, 84, 85, 115–16
Second Isaiah, 165–67
  Babylon, revelations in, 55
  calling to prophecy, 30
  on continuing revelation, 40, 123,
    127, 129
  monotheism and, 45n6
  predecessors, establishing links to, 35
  on religious liberty, 112
  servant narrative and, 127, 129,
    165n19
  theology of continuing revelation
    and, 145, 165–67
Second Zechariah, 35
Seleucid Greece, Israelites under, xv, 113
sentinel or watchman metaphor for
  continuing revelation, 123–25
separation of church and state in ancient
  Israel, 82–83
Septuagint, 174
Sermon on the Mount, 27, 88
servant narratives, 126–29
Servetus, Michael, 179
Seti I (pharaoh), 112
Seventh Commandment, 85, 86
Shaddai, 46, 132, 146
Shah Walli-Ullah of Delhi, 181
Shammai, 178
Shams ad-Din, 180
shekinah, 1
Shem, 44, 47
Shemaiah, 41, 61, 178
Shemiah, 41, 70
shepherd metaphor, 129–31
Shepherd of Hermas, 177, 179
Shiloh, 17, 64, 65, 109
Shishak (pharaoh), 113
Sibylline Oracles, 173
signs and portents, 167–69
Silas, in Acts, 175
Simeon and Anna, 23
Simons, Meno, 179
Sirach (Ecclesiasticus or Wisdom of
  Jesus Son of Sirach), 174
Sixth Commandment, 85, 86
slaves and slavery, xiv, 91, 93, 109, 111,
  113, 146
Smith, Joseph, 78, 180
Socinus, Faustus, 179
Solomon, 7, 18, 39, 89, 91, 113, 114, 119,
  144, 150

Subject/Name Index

Solzynitsyn, Alexander, 180
"Son of God" terminology, 139, 167
"son of man" predictions, in Daniel and New Testament, 38
southern kingdom (Judah), 1, 7, 25, 32, 35, 62, 64, 75, 113, 121–23, 144, 150
sovereignty of God, 158–65
Spinoza, Baruch, 178
Spirit of God (ruah elohim), 3, 25, 149, 167
stealing, Eighth Commandment against, 86
Stephen I (pope), 2
Stephen, in Acts, 11, 179
Stoics, 153
storm, theophanic nature of, 13, 45, 133, 134
successors to prophets, 8, 21, 36–40
suffering servant in Isaiah, 126, 128–29
Sufism, 180
Suhrawardi, 180
Sumer/Sumeria, 47, 48, 53, 64, 148
Sun Myung Moon, 180
Susanna and the Elders, 173–74
suzerainty treaties, Near Eastern, 100–101
Swedenborg, Emanuel, 78, 180
Symeon, 179
Syria, 16, 32, 44, 45, 46, 50, 145

T

Tauler, Johannes, 179
teacher, God as, 164
temple at Jerusalem
   destruction of, 1, 54, 88
   God's presence in, 1, 88, 148, 152
   Hellenistic corruption of, Onias IV on, 82, 88–89
   mainstream cult, as center of, 10, 106–7, 116, 117
   worship outside of, 49, 106–7, 116–17
temple prostitution, 85
Temple Scroll, 173

Ten Commandments, 85–90. *See also specific commandments, e.g.* First Commandment
   as civic and secular in nature, xiii, 81
   constitutional nature of, xvi, 81, 84–85, 86, 90
   history, consciousness of, 84
   Jesus and, 85, 100, 102
   leadership requirements of, 87, 93–97
   outline of, 85–86
   prophetic message and, 27
   purpose of, xiii
   religious liberty, promoting, xiii, xv, 81–85, 104
   sovereignty of God and, 161
   in theology of continuing revelation, 143–44, 161
   universalism of, 53
Tenth Commandment, 86
Terah, 112
Teresa of Avila, 179
Tertullian, 179
Testaments of the Twelve Patriarchs, 173
Thaddeus, Acts of, 177
Theodore, 179
theology of continuing revelation, xviii, 140–69, 171
   in Bible narrative, 140–45
   healing, health, and prophecy, 153–56
   in Islam, 156–58
   names of God and, 145–50
   prophet's role in, 167–69
   in Psalms, 150–52
   sovereignty of God asserted in, 158–65
theophany or epiphany
   cyclical nature of, 9
   initial calling, 26–32
   in John's Gospel, 136
   multiple encounters with God, prophetic experience of, 36
   natural and anthropomorphic metaphors for, 133–39
Theudas, 90
Third Commandment, 85–86
Third Isaiah, 35

Thomas a Kempis, 179
Thomas, Acts of, 177
Thomas, Gospel of, 12, 20, 176
Thucydides, 50
"Thus saith the Lord," 28, 53, 70, 109–10, 168
Thut-mose IV (pharaoh), 7
Tindal, Matthew, 179
Tobit, 174
Torah. *See* Pentateuch
tower of Babel, 21, 44
tree of knowledge of good and evil, 102–3
tribal government of early Israelites, xiv, 82, 94, 108, 143
Tukulti-Ninurta, 113–14
Twain, Mark, 180
Twelve Apostles, Gospel of, 176
types of prophets, 25–26, 181–82
Tyre, 48–49, 52, 68, 69
Tyrrell, George, 180

U

Ugarit, 7, 13, 51
universalism, xviii, 42–59
　apostasy and, 57–59
　canonicity and, 43, 54–55
　chosen people, Israel's election as, 46–47, 49–51, 57–59
　development of concepts behind, 153
　God's relationship with and expectations of other nations, 49–57
　high god tradition in Israel, 45–46
　of human potential for prophecy, 9–10
　nations surrounding Israel, prophecy in, 47–49
　primordial history of Bible, prophecy in, 43–45
Ur-Nammu, 129
Urijah, 63
Uruk, 7, 47
"Uruk Prophecy," 47
Utnapishtim, 133
Uzziah, 29, 83, 128

V

Valentinus, 179
vines, parables of, 56–57, 59
violence, religion-inspired, in Bible, xvii
visions
　calling to prophecy in, 29
　post-exilic prophecy manifesting as, 70
voice of God, 135–36
Voltaire, 179
von Mosheim, Johann Lorenz, 179
vows and oaths, 107–8

W

al-Wahabi, 181
Walz, Michael, 178
War Scroll, 173
watchman or sentinel metaphor for continuing revelation, 123–25
Weinfeld, Moshe, 178
Wesley, John and Charles, 180
White, Ellen G., née Harmon, 78, 180
Williams, Roger, 179
wind, 13
winged creatures, theophanic nature of, 133–34
Wink, Walter, 180
Wisdom of Jesus Son of Sirach (Ecclesiasticus), 174
Wisdom of Solomon, 62, 174
word of God, 136
Writings (Jewish division of Hebrew Bible). *See also specific books*
　cessation of prophecy doctrine and, 63
　defined, 5, 16
　expansion of canon by, 54
　promotion of ongoing prophecy in, 18
Wyclif, John, 179

Y

Yahweh
   El-Shaddai, identification with, 46
   freedom to worship, Decalogue
      establishing, 89–91
   meaning of name, 13, 127, 146–48
Yoder, John, 180
Yohannan, Rabbi, 178
Yom Kippur (Day of Atonement), 16

Z

Zadok, 10
Zechariah
   calling to prophecy, 31
   cessation of prophecy doctrine and,
      63, 69, 70
   on continuing revelation, 41
   Jesus's interest in, xvi, 11
   law in prophet-based society and,
      100, 112
   on lost revelations, 12
   new prophets, distrust of, 62
   post-exilic prophecy, characteristics
      of, 69, 70
   predecessors, establishing links to, 35
   Second Zechariah, 35
   in servant narrative, 129
   shepherd metaphor and, 131
   stoning of, 10–11
   successors of, 37
Zedekiah, 36, 63, 112
Zephaniah, 41, 149
Zevi, Shabbetai (Sabbatai Zvi), 78, 178
Zion psalms, 152
Zion theology, 25, 55
Zipporah, 92
Zohar, 178
Zoroaster, 78, 125
Zvi, Sabbatai (Shabbetai Zevi), 78, 178
Zwingli, Ulrich,

www.ingramcontent.com/pod-product-compliance
Lightning Source LLC
Chambersburg PA
CBHW060604230426
43670CB00011B/1962